PUGET SOUND

M000170063

Don Wilson / Port of Seattle Photo

SPECIAL THANKS to Our Sponsors & Contributors

THE DREAM DODGER by Randy's Boat Tops

Randy Wimer custom made and handcrafted *Dreamspeaker's* new dodger with diligence and respect for our practical and aesthetic needs, and he was a pleasure to work with. He brought to this project his 40 years of knowledge and experience. Randy services the Olympia and Tacoma areas and can be reached at 360-280-3923.

COVER IMAGE by Mike Martin

Mike Martin's image on the cover is of Gig Harbor, looking east from the Finholm District, and is the result of seven exposures shot from the Ruth M. Bogue Viewing Platform. Mike also specializes in Real Estate Photography and Virtual Tours (visit his website at *www.martinvirtualtours.com*).

DREAMSPEAKER GUIDES would like to thank the sponsors who came on board for the First Edition of
PUGET SOUND – A BOATER'S GUIDE

JOIN OUR SPONSORS
We would like to invite you, the Puget Sound communities represented in this guide, to become a sponsor for the Second Edition (2014) of *Puget Sound: A Boater's Guide*.

ELLIOTT BAY MARINA
www.elliottbaymarina.com

Marsh Andersen, llc
www.marshandersen.com

THE RESORT AT PORT LUDLOW
www.portludlowresort.com

PORT OF KINGSTON
www.portofkingston.org

Port of South Whidbey
www.portofsouthwhidbey.com

LANGLEY CHAMBER OF COMMERCE
www.visitlangley.com

Port of Seattle
www.portseattle.org

BELL HARBOR MARINA
A PORT OF SEATTLE PROPERTY
www.portseattle.org

SHILSHOLE BAY MARINA
A PORT OF SEATTLE PROPERTY
www.portseattle.org

FISHERMEN'S TERMINAL
A PORT OF SEATTLE PROPERTY
www.portseattle.org

CITY OF POULSBO VIKING CITY
www.cityofpoulsbo.com

PORT OF POULSBO
www.portofpoulsbo.com

HISTORIC DOWNTOWN POULSBO
www.historicdowntownpoulsbo.com

PORT OF BROWNSVILLE
www.portofbrownsville.com

Port of Silverdale
www.portofsilverdale.com

The Benefits of Being a Sponsor Are:
- Sponsors will be recognized for supporting their communities as key boating destinations.
- Sponsors' logos and websites will appear on their sponsored destination pages in both the print and digital formats of the guide.
- Sponsored destinations can be monitored and amended for updates and changes.
- Sponsors will have the personal support of the authors at boat shows, conferences and special presentations.

Contact us at info@dreamspeakerguides.com

PORT OF Bremerton Washington
www.portofbremerton.org

TRAVEL TACOMA+ PIERCE COUNTY, WA
www.traveltacoma.com

GIG HARBOR
www.cityofgigharbor.net

Gig Harbor CHAMBER of Commerce
www.gigharborchamber.net

DOWNTOWN WATERFRONT Alliance Gig Harbor
www.gigharborwaterfront.org

CITY OF BAINBRIDGE ISLAND
www.cityofbainbridgeisland.gov

NARROWS MARINA
www.narrowsmarina.com

ALDERBROOK RESORT & SPA
www.alderbrookresort.com

HOOD CANAL MARINA MOORAGE · FUEL · STORAGE
www.hood-canal-marina.com

Sound Experience
www.soundexp.org

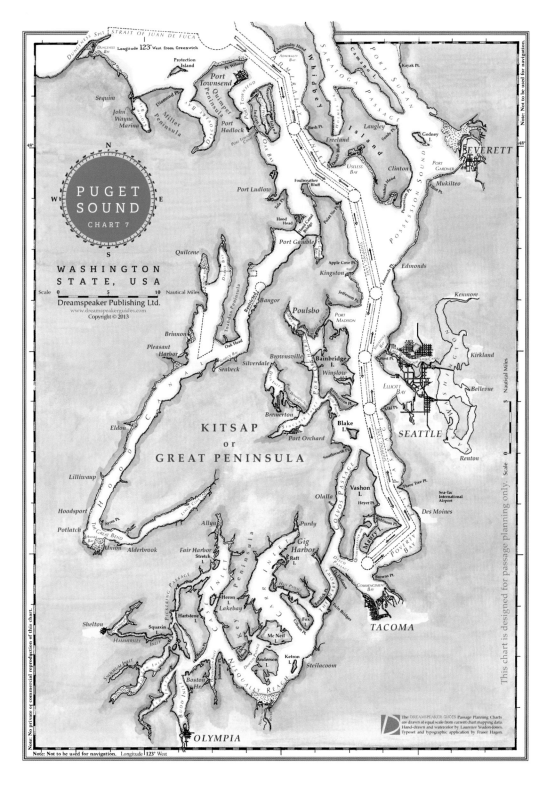

PUGET
SOUND
CHART 7

WASHINGTON
STATE, USA

Scale 0   5   10   Nautical Miles

Dreamspeaker Publishing Ltd.
www.dreamspeakerguides.com
Copyright © 2013

The DREAMSPEAKER GUIDES Passage Planning Charts
are drawn at equal scale from current chart mapping data.
Hand-drawn and watercolor by Laurence Yeadon-Jones.
Typeset and typographic application by Fraser Hagen.

PUGET
SOUND

A BOATER'S GUIDE

Anne & Laurence Yeadon-Jones

DREAMSPEAKER GUIDES

FEATURED DESTINATIONS

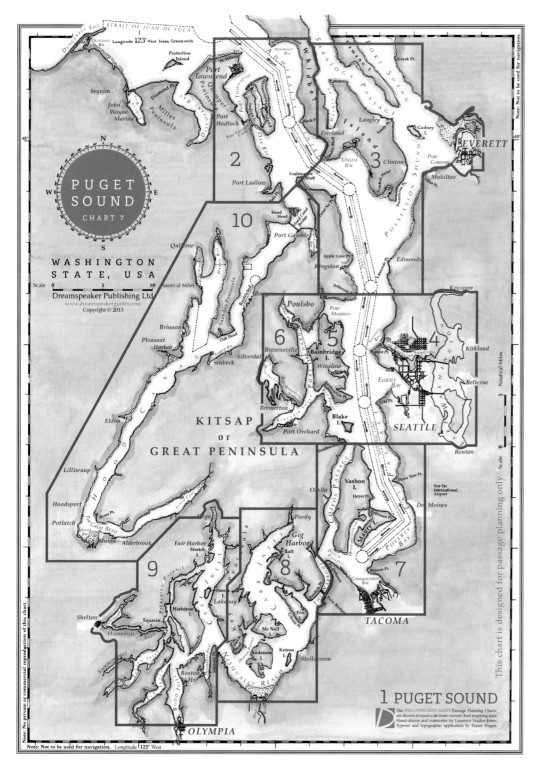

TABLE OF CONTENTS

1 2 3 4 5 6 7 8 9 10

Published by D R E A M S P E A K E R G U I D E S

an imprint of
Dreamspeaker Publishing Ltd
605-2075 Comox Street
Vancouver British Columbia
V6G 1S2 Canada

604.684.2189
info@dreamspeakerguides.com
www.dreamspeakerguides.com

Edited by Carol Watterson and Rachelle Kanefsky
Design by Fraser Hagen
Typeset by Yuriy Rzhemovskiy

Printed and bound in Canada by Friesens

LIBRARY AND ARCHIVES CANADA CATALOGUING IN PUBLICATION

Yeadon-Jones, Anne, author, illustrator
     Puget Sound : a boater's guide / Anne & Laurence Yeadon-Jones.

Includes bibliographical references and index.
ISBN 978-0-9739865-1-8 (pbk.)

     1. Boats and boating--Washington (State)--Puget Sound--Guidebooks.
2. Puget Sound (Wash.)--Guidebooks. I. Yeadon-Jones, Laurence, author, illustrator II. Title.

GV776.W2Y32 2013   797.12'50916432   C2013-903707-1

Caution: This book is meant to provide skilled boaters with boating information about the waters covered. The suggestions presented are not all-encompassing and, due to the chance of differences of understanding, omissions and factual errors, none of the information contained in this book is warranted to be precise or suitable for any purpose other than the quest for adventure and enjoyable voyages. *Puget Sound : A Boater's Guide* should be considered as a guide only and not as a substitute for official government charts, tide and current tables, United States Coast Pilots and/or local notices to boaters. Hand-illustrated charts are not to scale and are for passage planning only and are not meant to be used for navigation. The publisher and authors cannot accept any responsibility for mishaps resulting from the use of this guide nor accept any liability for damages incurred.

PREFACE

Our Dreamspeaker Guides began with Laurence's love of drawing, design and geography and my flair for descriptive and entertaining letters to family and friends. In 1987, we crossed the Atlantic Ocean aboard Dreamspeaker, and since then Laurence has kept a detailed series of logs filled with hand-drawn charts of our cruising destinations. Combining our talents, we were able to create a successful series of guides that promote a safe and fun boating lifestyle.

During the past 15 years, we have produced six comprehensive Dreamspeaker Guides that cover the coastal waters of the Pacific Northwest from Cape Caution, BC, to the San Jan Islands, WA. In this, our seventh guide, we detail our adventures below 48° North during the summer months of 2011 and 2012, when we sailed Dreamspeaker south to Puget Sound, the most populated boating area in Washington State.

We hope you enjoy our observations and portrayal of the sound as much as we enjoyed exploring its wonderful waters and communities, and we wish you safe voyaging on all of your forthcoming boating adventures.

– Anne and Laurence Yeadon-Jones

GRATEFUL APPRECIATION TO OUR COMMUNITY OF SUPPORT

We would like to extend our heartfelt gratitude to all of the following people who became sponsors for this first edition, or who went out of their way to help us in any way possible. We could not have done it without them!

Tami Allen - David & Maureen Baker - Bo Blakey - Bennish Brown - Rosie Courtney - Megan Deinas
Mary DesMarais - Becky Erickson - Marc Esterly - Edwin Field - Jan & Mic Fite - Kathy Gacia
Glenn Gaddis - Kathy & Chuck Gold - Dorene Gould & Jon Lopez - Ken & Kaye Greff
Jill Guernsey - Theresa Haaland - Jerry & Katherine Harbaugh - Guy Harper - Kori Henry
Dwight Jones - Kathryn Kamin - Agnes Mallet & Louis Carbonneau - Jeff Messmer - Jurgen Pichler
Hira Barbara Reid - Byron Richards and Sue Hunt - Jerry Rowland - The Team at San Juan Sailing
Stan Selden - Barry & Gill Sharp - Lita Dawn Stanton - Kirk Stickels - Gordon & Mary Stoll
Kip Summers - Cindy Sund - Debra & Ray Valpey - Scott Wagner - Kori Ward - Bob & Valerie Watson
Bob & Lisa Wise - Sherrye Wyatt - Wendy, Stevan & Bob - Warren Zimmerman

ACKNOWLEDGMENTS

We would also like to thank the Dreamspeaker Publishing team for their diligence and patience: Carol, Rachelle, Fraser, Yuriy, Matt and Jorge.

Our family and friends for their unyielding support. Dreamspeaker, Tink and the "motley crew" who helped to make this guide possible.

Dreamspeaker sailing to Seattle. George Maupin photo.

FOREWORD

For more than 15 years, boaters have relied on the Dreamspeaker Guides for their detailed charts and well-researched local information on the magnificent San Juan Islands and British Columbia coast. Even when weather, work and other commitments delay boating, these guides open our eyes to destinations we long to visit. At times, thumbing through the guides brings back memories of places and times that will always be the highlight of our lives.

Many boaters have asked Anne and Laurence to publish a guide to Puget Sound for those times when schedules keep us from traveling far from home, or when we want to explore our own backyard. We are fortunate that they have responded with an excellent boater's guide to the area, filled with meticulous hand-drawn charts and vital local information that, once again, guide us safely into busy harbors and marinas within Puget Sound and Hood Canal. And for those times when a quiet location is preferred, Anne and Laurence have used their two years researching this guide to select the best that the sound has to offer.

When using this guide, boaters may notice that cities and towns within Puget Sound have made significant progress in revitalizing their waterfront areas. They have made improvements for locals and visitors alike, and communities are laying out the welcome mat to boaters not simply because of the "boost" boaters bring to local economies, but because they are proud to share their maritime heritage.

Come visit our local festivals, markets, restaurants and shops, then walk along our waterfronts and experience our collective history.

We look forward to seeing you on the waterfront!

Jill Guernsey
Councilmember
City of Gig Harbor

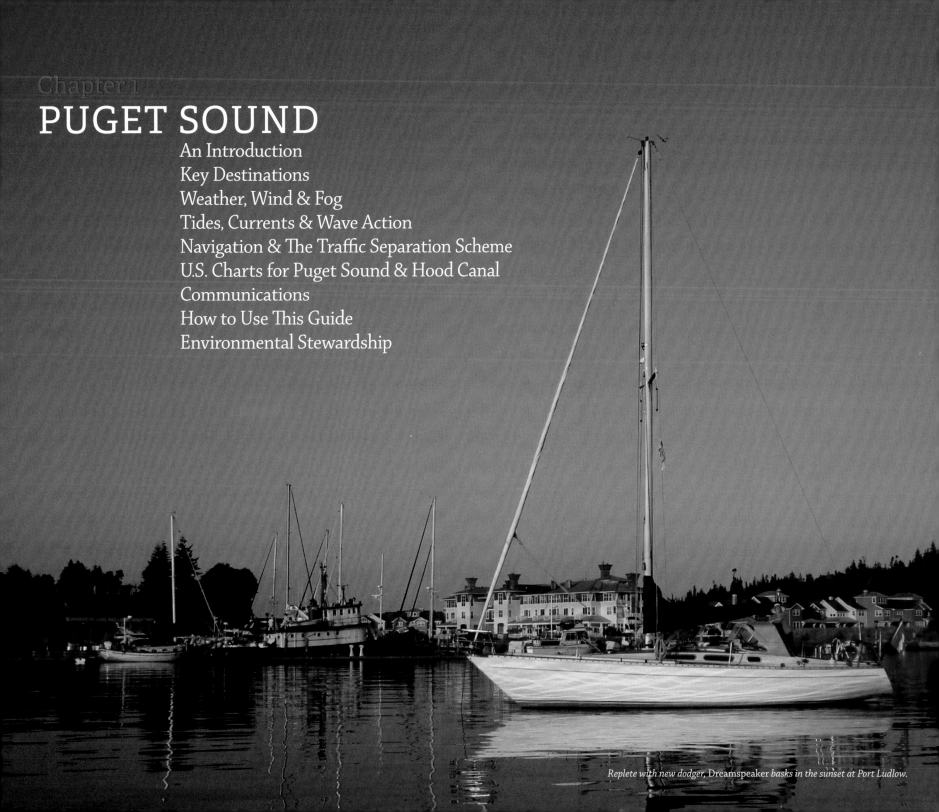

Replete with new dodger, Dreamspeaker basks in the sunset at Port Ludlow.

CHAPTER 1 PUGET SOUND – An Introduction

Mt. Rainier is Puget Sound's perennial landmark.

All vessels arriving in the United States from a foreign country must clear Customs. Listed below are the designated Ports of Entry that lie north of Puget Sound.

DESIGNATED PORTS OF ENTRY

Anacortes	360-293-2331
Friday Harbor	360-378-2080
Point Roberts	360-945-2314
Port Angeles	360-457-4311
Roche Harbor	360-378-2080

NOTE

U.S. Customs Port Townsend Office will clear private vessels if a scheduled appointment is made prior to arrival. Call 360-385-3777.

HISTORIC FACTS

Native Americans have lived in the Puget Sound region for over 10,000 years, and today, it is the ancestral home to 19 different Coastal Salish tribes, all of whom share the Lushootseed dialect, as well as many rich cultural traditions.These first inhabitants, whose tribes and villages were named for their surrounding waters, were intimately tied to the area's rivers, lakes and sea, which was rich with salmon, cod and shellfish, and they thrived on the hunting and gathering offered by the region's bountiful forests.

One of the last areas of the Americas to be explored by Europeans, Puget Sound was first discovered on May 19, 1792, by Captain George Vancouver, when he dropped anchor between Blake and Bainbridge islands. Ten days later, to commemorate Lieutenant Peter Puget's survey, Vancouver named the south extremity of the sound Puget's Sound.

In 1841, Lt. Charles Wilkes commanded six vessels of the United States Exploring Expedition, with the mission of charting the Puget Sound region. This opened up the Pacific Northwest, and within 100 years, land speculators, timber barons and homesteaders came to lay their claim to the sound.

CAUTIONARY NOTE

It is illegal to discharge untreated sewage within the 3-mile territorial limit, which includes all of Puget Sound and its freshwater tributaries. This guide lists pump-out facilities at the beginning of each chapter.

Pick up a Sound Information: Boater's Guide, published by Puget Soundkeeper Alliance and produced in partnership with Washington State Parks (available at most marinas and fuel docks). For more information on boating issues in Puget Sound, call the Information Center at 360-902-8555.

The Pacific Northwest is home to seven distinct boating regions sheltered by the natural breakwater of Vancouver Island. Puget Sound, the most southerly of these regions, has the added protection of the Olympic Peninsula as it dives south from 48° North, resembling a large octopus with numerous tentacles.

In the summer of 2011, Laurence and I headed south in *Dreamspeaker* to Puget Sound and Hood Canal and logged over 800 nautical miles, exploring and recording the labyrinth of inlets, passages, harbors and bays that make up the sound. We were pleasantly surprised to find a choice of quiet coves and beaches, and protected river estuaries teaming with wildlife. Returning in 2012, we retraced our route and reconnected with the welcoming communities we had met on our previous travels.

Although Puget Sound is the most densely populated area in Washington State, it offers a wealth of friendly, well-maintained marinas and landscaped downtown waterfronts, and you are never too far from a scenic state park or peaceful anchorage. We learned that it was wise to explore the popular anchorages midweek, when all was quiet, and to visit the cities on weekends.

Today, we feel at home in Puget Sound, and the sight of Mount Rainier, with its perpetual covering of snow, has become a familiar one. We enjoy visiting the lively waterfronts of Port Townsend, Seattle, Tacoma, Gig Harbor and Olympia, as well as the village-like towns of Langley, Kingston and Poulsbo. During the main months of the boating season expect mainly dry, sunny weather that allows for hiking, swimming, reading in the shade of a madrona tree or enjoying a watercolor sunset.

So, slip those dock lines from their cleats and set sail – the delightful waters, breathtaking scenery and welcoming communities of Puget Sound await!

1.1 PUGET SOUND

KEY DESTINATIONS

LEGEND

P   Provisions Within Walking Distance
M   Marina Visitor Facilities
MR Marine Repair Facilities
F   Fuel/Diesel & Gas
A   Adjacent Anchorage Nearby

1.2 WEATHER, WIND & FOG

WEATHER – Climatically, Puget Sound is the most southerly extension of the Pacific Northwest's temperate rain coast. Sheltered to the west from the Pacific Ocean, and in the rain shadow of the Olympic Mountains, Puget Sound is bordered to the east by the Cascade Mountains. In the summer months, the majority of weather originates in the northwest, producing northerly winds that funnel down the sound. In the fall, winter and spring, most of the weather originates from the southeast, producing southerly winds as it moves north.

In the summer months, the average temperatures range from 73° F in Puget Sound's upper protected reaches to 78° F in the vicinity of Olympia. Maximum winter temperatures average from 40° F to a 30° F minimum. Temperatures seldom drop lower than 10° F to 15° F. Annual precipitation ranges from 35 inches in Seattle, gradually increasing to 45 inches in Olympia.

In the summer of 2012, while cruising Puget Sound, Laurence and I experienced over 50 consecutive rainless days between mid-July and early September!

WIND – In the summer months, good weather is dependent on the arrival of the North Pacific High, which brings clear skies and afternoon winds that rarely exceed 20 knots and generally average 8 to 15 knots. The North Pacific High may arrive as early as April, but it seldom establishes itself until July. In the fall, winter and spring, the winds are predominantly from the south. Winds are strongest in winter and early spring, and storms that reach 40 knots, with 50-knot gusts, are almost always from the south, with periods of calm between fronts.

FOG – Fog in the Puget Sound area causes visibility problems on about 25 to 40 days each year, although poor visibility is more often encountered north and south of Puget Sound than in the sound itself. Fog can form in any month, but it is least likely during the months of May, June and July and is more probable in the fall, and again during the months of January and February.

WHEN TO GO – The boating season in Puget Sound is generally from late April until mid-October, although the major boating season seldom picks up before the Fourth of July weekend. At this time, many local boaters actually head north, leaving the area far less crowded than one would expect.

Fog! Relax and let it clear before moving on.

CAUTIONARY NOTE
Listening to or looking up the marine weather forecast should be every boater's number one priority before heading out on the water. Setting up a regular routine to do this is critical for a safe boating experience.

NOAA WEATHER WARNINGS
Small Craft Advisory – Winds 21 to 33 knots.
Gale Warning – Winds 34 to 47 knots.
Storm Warning – Winds 48 knots and above.
Hurricane Warning – Winds 64 knots and above.

WEATHER
Continuous information originates for the weather stations indicated and is broadcast by the National Oceanic and Atmospheric Administration (NOAA).
NOAA Weather Radio WX4: Puget Sound
NOAA VHF Weather Channel 1 or 3
www.nws.noaa.gov/nwr

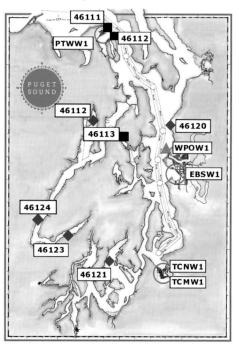

Weather monitoring stations.

NDBC	NATIONAL DATA BUOY CENTER
4611	Fort Warden Buoy
46112	Marrowstone Buoy
PTWW1	Port Townsend
46113	Poulsbo Buoy
46120	Point Wells
WPOW1	West Point
EBSW1	Seattle
TCNW1	Tacoma
TCNW2	Tacoma Met
46121	Carr Inlet
46122	Dabob Bay
46123	Twanoh – Hood Canal
46124	Hoodsport – Hood Canal

1.3 TIDES, CURRENTS & WAVE ACTION

TIDES – It is important to note the difference between tide height and tidal current. Tide is the vertical movement of water, which will rise (flood) or fall (ebb), and it is quite variable in Puget Sound. At the start of each chapter, we list the ● tide height station or stations that are referenced within the area covered.

It is important to note that the depth indicated on U.S. charts is based on a chart datum, which is calculated at mean low, low water (MLLW) and is commonly referred to as "zero tide." Tides that drop below this datum are called minus tides.

In Puget Sound, the tidal height range between high and low water is significant; typically, around 12 feet. On a large tide, however, this can reach 15 to 20 feet in Olympia. Knowing the height of water under your boat is especially important when anchoring or navigating in shallow water.

CURRENTS – Current, the horizontal movement of water, is directionally defined, and its speed is calculated in knots. At the start of each chapter, we list the ▲ tidal current station that is referenced within the area covered.

In Puget Sound, the current on an ebbing tide flows north, and on a flooding tide it flows south (there are a few directional anomalies). The current on the ebb is marginally stronger than on the flood.

The strongest currents are generated in the vicinity of the tidal current stations; north at Bush Point in Admiralty Inlet and south at Tacoma Narrows. Typically, current will run between 2 to 5 knots; on a large tide, it might exceed 6.5 knots. When planning a passage, knowledge of the current is of prime importance. Plan to travel with the current, as it will save you significant time and fuel consumption.

WAVE ACTION – Waves or wave action are generated in Puget Sound by wind interacting with an opposing current. In a summer, moderate northerly wind, a light chop may develop on an ebbing tide. A strong southerly wind over a flooding tide can create wave conditions that are potentially dangerous to small craft.

Depth and clearance datum from a modified NOAA diagram Chart 1 as referenced.

CAUTIONARY NOTE
A working knowledge of tides and currents and their interplay with winds is especially important in this region.

TIDES
● TIDE HEIGHT STATIONS

CURRENTS
▲ TIDAL CURRENT STATIONS

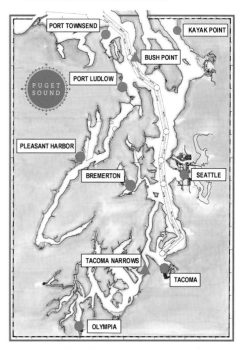

Locations of tide and current stations referenced.

TIDE AND CURRENT TABLES
Tide and current tables provide essential navigational information and must be acquired prior to venturing into these waters.

PUBLICATIONS
There are many tide and current tables for Puget Sound, and information can also be found online. We used *Capt'n Jack's Tide & Current Almanac*, which includes the Strait of Juan de Fuca, Hood Canal and the San Juan Islands (published annually by Coastwise Press, LLC).

Rule 10 applies to all vessels in the Traffic Separation Scheme (TSS). Puget Sound Pilots photo.

Puget Sound's aids to navigation, its buoys and its lighthouses are numerous, established and well maintained. Due to heavy vessel concentration, the waters of Puget Sound and all adjacent waters are a regulated navigation area.

The modern boater, with up-to-date charts and official publications, backed by the usual array of electronic aids, will have enough information to navigate safely.

SHIPPING - Boaters must be aware that these waters are shared with commercial shipping, which is controlled by the Vessel Traffic Service (VTS). This is monitored by the U.S. Coast Guard. All commercial vessels participate in the VTS system.

Commercial traffic must navigate within the Traffic Separation Scheme (TSS), a network of one-way shipping lanes marked with buoys and indicated on charts with purple dashes.

Seattle Traffic encourages recreational boaters to monitor VHF Channels 14 and 5A north of Marrowstone Point. The information on these channels is especially useful when you are in a busy harbor and crossing a traffic lane, or when you are near a ferry terminal.

Rules governing vessel movement inside a TSS apply to recreational as well as commercial vessels.

Boats under sail have no special privileges in a TSS, and recreational boaters should be knowledgeable about the rules before navigating these waters.

CAUTIONARY NOTE

Do not try to outrace a ship or a tug with the intent of crossing ahead of it. The speed of a large ship is difficult to judge accurately. Similarly, never cut between a tug and its tow. Make your intentions clear and, if necessary, contact the ship or tug. Commercial vessels monitor VHF Channel 13.

NOTE

Rule 10 applies to the TSS. For more information, visit the website of the U.S. Coast Guard Navigation Center (*www.navcen.uscg.gov*).

The TSS rules that most directly affect recreational boats are:

- Any vessel in a TSS, other than a crossing vessel, must move in the direction of the traffic flow.

- A vessel of less than 66 feet, or a sailboat of any size, must get out of the way of a power-driven vessel following a traffic lane.

- A vessel of less than 66 feet, or a sailboat of any size, must not navigate in such a way as to risk the development of a collision with another vessel.

- Any vessel crossing a traffic lane must do so at right angles to the direction of traffic flow, as far as practicable.

- All vessels are required to keep the precautionary areas to port. Precautionary areas are marked by yellow or yellow-and-black striped buoys, and they are charted with a circle of dashes (often referred to as "turning buoys").

- A vessel engaging in fishing must get out of the way of any vessel following a traffic lane.

- All vessels (other than crossing vessels) shall stay out of the separation zone.

VESSELS OUTSIDE OF THE TSS

In Puget Sound, recreational boaters will also encounter commercial vessels outside of the TSS, and they should not impede their progress; these include naval and fishing vessels, ferries and tugs and their tows. Ferries have designated routes, which are indicated on official charts by a single dotted line.

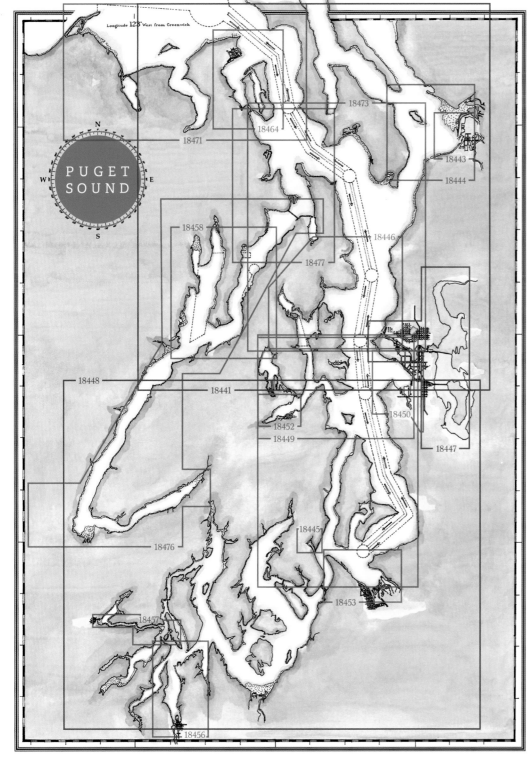

1.5 U.S. NOAA CHARTS FOR PUGET SOUND & HOOD CANAL

18441   Puget Sound – northern part

18471   Approaches to Admiralty Inlet, Dungeness to Oak Bay

18464   Port Townsend

18473   Puget Sound – Oak Bay to Shilshole Bay

18443   Approaches to Everett

18444   Everett Harbor

18446   Puget Sound – Apple Cove Point to Keyport and Agate Passage

18458   Hood Canal – South Point to Quatsap Point, including Dabob Bay

18477   Puget Sound – Entrance to Hood Canal

18449   Puget Sound – Seattle to Bremerton

18452   Sinclair Inlet

18450   Seattle Harbor, Elliott Bay and Duwamish Waterway

18448   Puget Sound – southern part

18447   Lake Washington Ship Canal and Lake Washington

18474   Puget Sound – Shilshole Bay to Commencement Bay

18453   Tacoma Harbor

18456   Olympia Harbor and Budd Inlet

18457   Puget Sound – Hammersley Inlet to Shelton

18476   Puget Sound – Hood Canal and Dabob Bay

OFFICIAL PUBLICATIONS

NOAA and the U.S. Coast Guard have free downloads of the following:

Coast Pilot 7. 45th Edition, 2013.
Chapter 13. Puget Sound, Washington.
www.nauticalcharts.noaa.gov

U.S. Chart No 1.
Symbols, Abbreviations & Terms Used on Paper & Electronic Charts.
www.nauticalcharts.noaa.gov

U.S. Aids to Navigation System.
www.uscgboating.org

1.6 COMMUNICATIONS

A stroll along the beach helps connect with the locals.

MAYDAY: For *immediate danger* to life or vessel.
PAN-PAN: For *urgency* but no immediate danger to life or vessel.
For MAYDAY or PAN-PAN, transmit the following on VHF Channel 16 or 2182 kHz.
1. MAYDAY, MAYDAY, MAYDAY (or PAN-PAN, PAN-PAN, PAN-PAN), this is [vessel name and radio call sign].
2. State your position and the nature of the distress.
3. State the number of people on board and describe the vessel [length, make/type, color, sail/power and registration number].

NOTE

If the distress is not life-threatening, the coast guard will put out a general call to boaters in your area for assistance. You can expect a commercial operator to respond.

Landline – if you can find one that works!

CAUTIONARY NOTE
Do not rely on a live Wi-Fi connection for navigation.

Not that long ago, the key attractions of a good boating destination were an anchorage with good holding and a marina with friendly people. Today, the number one priority is being connected.

VHF – VHF Radio is still the primary onboard communication tool, because it is a safety aid in emergencies, and rescue services can be guided in by its signal. VHF Radio is also regulated, and boaters must use proper operation procedures. All boaters should obtain a Restricted Radio Operator Permit, should know the VHF channels in the U.S. and should be familiar with the non-commercial VHF channels that recreational vessels might use.

LANDLINE – The good old pay phone, if you can find one that works, is rapidly becoming history in Puget Sound.

CELLULAR TELEPHONE – As visitors to the United States, roaming charges on our cell phone were prohibitively expensive. As a result, we purchased a reasonably priced cellular package for our trips, which suited our needs perfectly. The cellular coverage is excellent throughout Puget Sound.

WIRELESS INTERNET (Wi-Fi) – Wi-Fi is just about everywhere in Puget Sound, but logging on at anchor can be a challenge. Most marinas either offer free Wi-Fi with moorage, or for a small fee. Some local coffee shops provide free Wi-Fi with an order of espresso! We found that local libraries also offer excellent wireless service.

1.7 HOW TO USE THIS GUIDE

THE DESIGN OF A DREAMSPEAKER GUIDE

The Dreamspeaker Guides have been carefully designed and formatted to work in conjunction with the National Oceanic and Atmospheric Administration (NOAA) charts and publications, and the technical information provided at the beginning of each chapter references the appropriate NOAA charts.

NOAA nautical charts are a recreational boater's primary tool for safe navigation, while the hand-drawn charts and information in this guide endeavor to assist boaters by further clarifying each destination and by giving detailed information on marine facilities, anchorages, shoreside amenities and local events.

Dreamspeaker is a 36-foot SHE, a fibreglass sloop designed by Sparkman and Stephens and built by South Hants Engineering, UK, in 1979. She has a fin keel, draws 6.5 feet and sails like a dream.

Tink, our faithful dinghy, is a Tinker RIB, designed and built by Henshaw Inflatables, UK.

APPROACH WAYPOINT
The approach waypoints are positioned in deep water. The approach note guides the boater from the waypoint into the harbor, marina or anchorage.

DREAMSPEAKER type SHE 36
THE BENCHMARK

Length overall	37'
Length on water	27'
Beam	10.6'
Draft	6.6'
Height above water	50.0'

CAUTIONARY NOTE
These charts are not to be used for navigation. Depth contours are approximate and in fathoms.

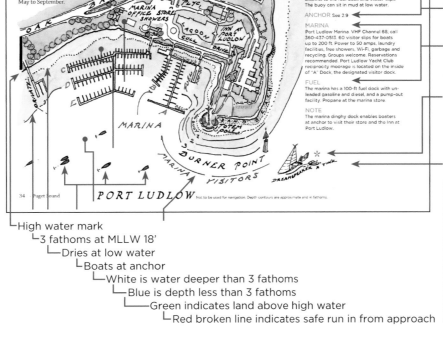

- Chapter and featured destination reference
- Chapter legend
- Destinations Locator
- Approach waypoint
- Chart referenced
- Tips on best approach and anchorage with depth and holding condition
- Marina and facilities, fuel, pump-out, etc. Note or cautionary note. Shore, access, shallow, etc.
- Approximate position of approach waypoint
- Graphic of boat commencing run in

High water mark
3 fathoms at MLLW 18'
Dries at low water
Boats at anchor
White is water deeper than 3 fathoms
Blue is depth less than 3 fathoms
Green indicates land above high water
Red broken line indicates safe run in from approach

Anne and Tink spend some quiet time together.

Adventuress, *the historic schooner with a mission. Zachary Simonson-Bond photo.*

ENVIRONMENTAL STEWARDSHIP

The mission of our Dreamspeaker Guides is to make it possible for recreational boaters to enjoy safe and fun boating by providing accurate and in-depth information through our on-site documentation and hand-illustrated charts. We feel strongly that boaters who sail in Puget Sound must value the future of the sound's marine environment and act as stewards of its fragile waters. Sound Experience is a nonprofit organization that operates its historic schooner *Adventuress* as an on-the-water teaching platform for the environmental stewardship and protection of Puget Sound. Youth and adults of all ages climb aboard the environmental tall ship, take the helm and sail as they did 100 years ago, thus inspiring future boaters to keep the sound's precious waters intact. We support their mission and hope that through our guides, we, too, can pass on this crucial message of conservation to other boaters.

SOUND EXPERIENCE ABOARD THE SCHOONER *ADVENTURESS*

VISION - We envision a future where everyone values Puget Sound and chooses to act as stewards of its treasured waters.

MISSION - Sound Experience sails the historic schooner *Adventuress* to educate, inspire and empower an inclusive community to make a difference for the future of our marine environment.

VALUES

- Deliver powerful shipboard youth and adult programs that emphasize environmental stewardship, leadership, community and historic preservation.
- Model low-impact, sustainable living practices aboard *Adventuress* that contribute to a healthy Puget Sound and planet.
- Steward the maintenance and restoration of the historic schooner *Adventuress* so that she will sail in perpetuity.
- Create nonprofit, private and public sector partnerships that contribute to environmental stewardship, youth engagement and historic preservation.

To learn more about Sound Experience's adult and youth education programs, call 360-379-0438, or visit their website.

Sound Experience is a nonprofit 501(c)(3) organization that operates its historic schooner *Adventuress* – Puget Sound's environmental tall ship – as a powerful platform for youth, adult and public education programs.

www.soundexp.org

Chapter 2

NORTHWEST PUGET SOUND – ADMIRALTY INLET

Port Townsend & Port Hadlock to Port Ludlow

Two classics at anchor off Port Townsend.

Port Townsend waterfront.

TIDES
Tide Height Station: Port Townsend and Port Ludlow

CURRENTS
Tidal Current Station: Bush Point
Strong currents run in Admiralty Inlet; up to 4.2 knots north on the ebb and 4 knots south on the flood (tabulated at Bush Point Tidal Current Station).

WEATHER
NOAA Weather Radio WX4: Puget Sound
NOAA VHF Weather Channel 1 or 3
www.nws.noaa.gov/nwr

HISTORIC FACTS
A natural, protected port at the entrance to Puget Sound, Port Townsend was a major West Coast shipping port during the Age of Sail. In the late 19th century, Washington State's western railroad expansion stopped at Tacoma, and Port Townsend's ambitions to become the largest commercial harbor on the West Coast were abandoned.

Today, with Victorian waterfront buildings and elegant homes on the bluff, charming Port Townsend is one of three Victorian seaports on the National Register of Historic Places. With its rich maritime history and its world-renowned, highly skilled marine trades industry, it is recognized as a key tourist destination by both sea and land visitors.

Port Townsend, a picturesque harbor and city of the same name, lies to the west of Point Hudson. Visiting boaters are attracted to the architecture of this preserved Victorian seaport and to the friendly locals who are mad about boating and boats, especially wooden classics. To the north of Point Hudson, Fort Worden State Park has it all – from the fort's campus and museum to the marine science center, with its interpretive displays.

When we visit Port Townsend, Laurence and I like to divide our time between Point Hudson Marina and the downtown anchorage, with its cool breezes and colorful sailing craft. We then secure day moorage at the Port Townsend Boat Haven to fuel up and provision before moving on.

After transiting the entrance channel to Kilisut Harbor, we never miss a chance to explore Fort Flagler State Park, with its sandy spit and historic fort buildings. Protected Mystery Bay State Park offers a picnic area, pocket beach and warm-water swimming. On the eastern shore of Quimper Peninsula, Port Hadlock Marina provides sheltered moorage and is only a dinghy ride away from Port Hadlock Public Dock and the upbeat Ajax Cafe.

Transiting Port Townsend Canal south to Port Ludlow, the flooding tide was with us as we enjoyed a blissful sail into Oak Bay. Further south lies the hidden anchorage of Mats Mats Bay. The first time we explored the anchorage, it was shrouded in mist, but our subsequent visit was in warmth and sunshine.

Rounding Burner Point, we were delighted with the New-England-style architecture of the Port Ludlow Resort and the sheltered anchorage located southwest of Port Ludlow Marina. The marina is rendezvous-friendly, with numerous gathering areas for potluck dinners. We enjoyed a picture-postcard sunset while sipping cocktails on the shaded veranda of the Inn at Port Ludow.

CAUTIONARY NOTES
Rounding Point Wilson from the Strait of Juan de Fuca is best transited on a flooding tide. The shoal N of Point Wilson creates tide rips on an ebbing tide when the current opposes a westerly wind, and steep and potentially dangerous seas may occur. This is known locally as the "Point Wilson Rip." Rounding on the ebb is best done at least a quarter mile offshore.

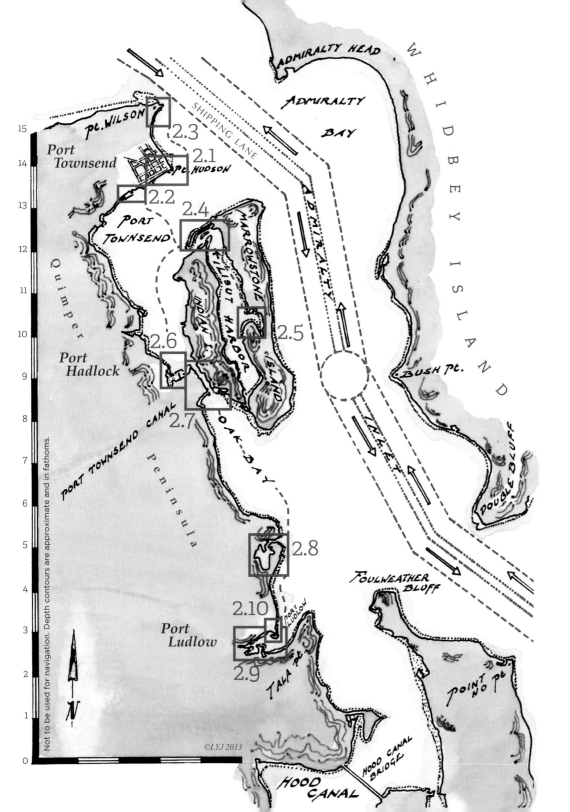

FEATURED DESTINATIONS

FUEL
2.2 Port Townsend Boat Haven; 2.10 Port Ludlow Marina

PUMP-OUT FACILITIES
2.1 Point Hudson Marina; 2.2 Port Townsend Boat Haven;
2.5 Mystery Bay State Park; 2.6. Port Hadlock; 2.10 Port
Ludlow Marina

2.1 PORT TOWNSEND Downtown Waterfront

Dreamspeaker off the Union Wharf.

Anne shops for boat treats.

Our first visit to Port Townsend by boat was during the internationally renowned Wooden Boat Festival in early September. With both the Point Hudson Marina (which hosts the festival) and the Port Townsend Boat Haven jam-packed with boats, we were happy to anchor off the downtown waterfront, which is backed by historic brick buildings and elegant uptown homes. The city was in a festive mood, as beautifully restored square-rigged schooners, traditional two-masted yawls and an array of classic, wooden craft crisscrossed the bay with colors flying and crews at the ready.

Charmed by the waterfront patios and vibrant shopping streets, with their choice of cafes, pubs and restaurants serving international and Pacific Northwest dishes, we roamed the downtown bookstores, art galleries and antique shops before climbing the flight of stairs at Haller Fountain to Uptown Port Townsend. The lively farmers' market at Tyler and Clay streets was in full swing, with tables displaying local fruit and vegetables, artisan cheese and breads, as well as an excellent selection of arts and crafts.

Uptown Port Townsend has a distinct local personality, with Sweet Laurette Cafe & Bistro serving tasty breakfasts, French-style bakery Pane d'Amore, the cosy Uptown Pub, Lanza's Ristorante, with its delicious Italian fare, and the historic Aldrich's Market, a Port Townsend icon selling quality groceries and produce since 1895 (ask about their "nearly free delivery").

Point Hudson Marina accommodates a selection of marine trades businesses, including world-renowned sailmakers Hasse and Company, and three good restaurants. Adjacent to the marina is the contemporary Northwest Maritime Center, home to the Wooden Boat Foundation. The center's Boat Shop offers first-rate boat-building classes, and the well-stocked chandlery carries marine supplies, clothing, books and boating guides.

LOCAL FACTS

The Port Townsend Farmers' Market happens twice a week. On Wednesdays, it runs from 3 to 6 p.m. on Polk and Lawrence streets (April to September). On Saturdays, it runs from 9 a.m. to 2 p.m. on Tyler and Clay streets (April to December).

The visitor information center is located on 12th Street near the Port Townsend Boat Haven. If you are downtown, pick up local maps, brochures and free magazines at one of the many hotels.

Ride the bus! Jefferson Transit; call 360-385-4777. Every bus goes downtown and uptown and also visits Fort Worden State Park, twice each hour.

FUN FACTS

Walk or pedal! Port Townsend is a pedestrian and bike-friendly city. Pick up a self-guided *Port Townsend Walking Map* and a *Quimper Peninsula Bicycle Map*. Bike rentals available at The Broken Spoke on Water Street.

Discover the beach at Point Hudson (fronting the marina), where Captain George Vancouver came ashore in 1792.

Indulge in a night out at the movies with fresh-popped popcorn. Two excellent and historic neighborhood cinemas include the Rose Theater on Taylor Street and the Uptown Theater on Lawrence Street.

FOOD FACTS

Try Sirens on Water Street for authentic hamburgers and margaritas and a funky, local atmosphere. Also on Water Street, The Belmont serves delicious Pacific Northwest seafood on the shaded hotel patio, overlooking the harbor and mountains. Point Hudson Cafe, at the marina, dishes up hearty breakfasts.

PORT TOWNSEND Downtown Waterfront

Not to be used for navigation. Depth contours are approximate and in fathoms.

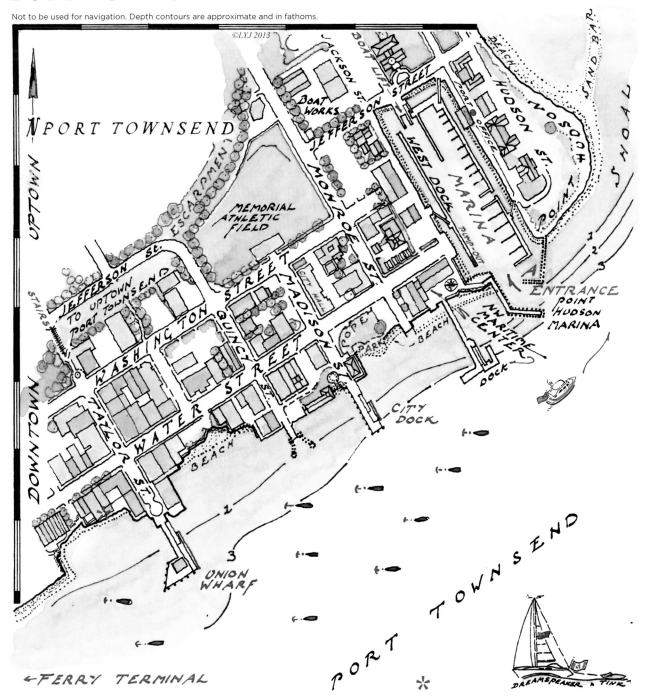

©LYJ 2013

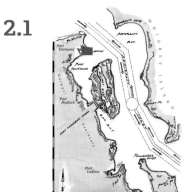

✳ 40° 06.67' N   122° 45.23' W

CHART 18464

APPROACH

From the approach waypoint, the run in to the anchorage, city dock facilities and marina is clear. No wake when entering the marina.

ANCHOR

As indicated, off the buoyed Voluntary Eelgrass Protection Zone. Moderate holding in sand and mud, in 3+ ftm (18+ ft). Ensure that the anchor is well set. A convenient anchorage in summer; offshore winds but unprotected from the S. Downtown dinghy tie up is possible at the City Dock and Union Wharf.

MARINA

Point Hudson Marina. VHF Channel 9; call 360-385-2828. Managed by the Port of Port Townsend. Reservations for boats up to 70 ft, and 4-hour temporary moorage, if slips available. Rafting permitted on West Dock. Power to 50 amps, free Wi-Fi and shower and laundry facilities. Check in at the moorage office for slip assignment.

Sea Marine is a full-service boatyard adjacent to the marina; call 360-385-4000. They also sell propane, ice and provisions.

FUEL

For fuel and boat launch, see 2.2 Port Townsend Boat Haven.

CAUTIONARY NOTE

If you are at anchor and strong southerlies are predicted, head for the anchorage in Mystery Bay (see 2.5), which offers good protection from the S.

PORT TOWNSEND BOAT HAVEN

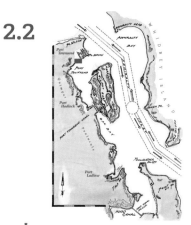

Although Port Townsend Boat Haven is located a mile west of downtown Port Townsend, provisioning and the city center bus route are conveniently close by. A left on Washington Street takes you to the visitor center, the Key City Fish Company (a seafood, meat and poultry market) and the Port Townsend Brewing Company, which offers 10 microbrew ales on tap that can be enjoyed in the cosy tasting room or the shady beer garden. Safeway is a short walk from here.

On a stroll to the junction of Washington and Kearney streets, I discovered a small village-like area, with marine stores, a vibrant shop filled with new and used clothing and home decor, and the local Dos Okies Barbeque, with its delicious sandwiches. Provisioning at the airy Port Townsend Food Co-op was a treat, as it stocks local and organic produce and has great customer service.

NOTE
Port Townsend Shipyard (360-385-6211), located at Port Townsend Boat Haven, is a modern, full-service yard that is home to more than 60 marine trades businesses and services, including a heavy-boat haulout facility, boat-building, repair and restoration, rigging and custom-canvas fabrication.

✴ 48° 06.67' N   122° 46.06' W

CHART 18464

APPROACH
From seaward, enter by rounding the end of the breakwater at the SE corner of the marina. No wake or sailing.

MARINA
Port Townsend Boat Haven. VHF Channel 66A; call 360-385-2355. Managed by the Port of Port Townsend, this is a large commercial and recreational facility with visitor moorage on a first-come basis. 4-hour temporary moorage, if slips available. Slips up to 50 ft; can accommodate boats up to 100 ft. Power to 50 amps and shower and laundry facilities. On arrival, tie up at the N end of the fuel/registration dock and check in at the moorage office for slip assignment.

Port Townsend Yacht Club offers reciprocal moorage.

✴

FUEL
The Fishin' Hole dock and store at the marina; call 360-385-7031. Gasoline, diesel, diesel stove oil and pump-out facility. Ice, snacks and bait available.

LAUNCH
At the marina.

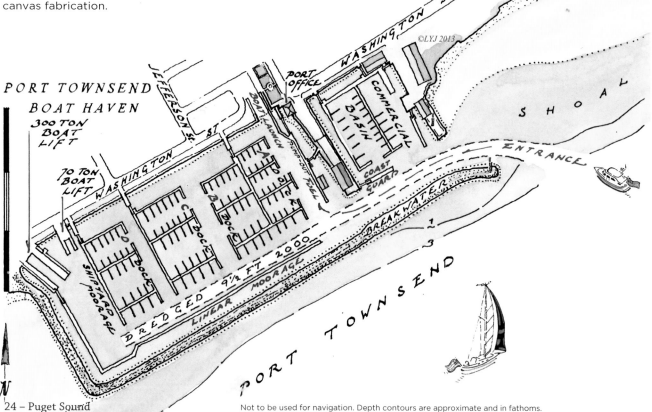

©LYJ 2013

Not to be used for navigation. Depth contours are approximate and in fathoms.

The Adventuress sports new sails off Point Hudson. Elizabeth T. Becker photo. Seaport Photography.

A family of otters take a keen interest in what's going on at the Northwest Maritime Center.

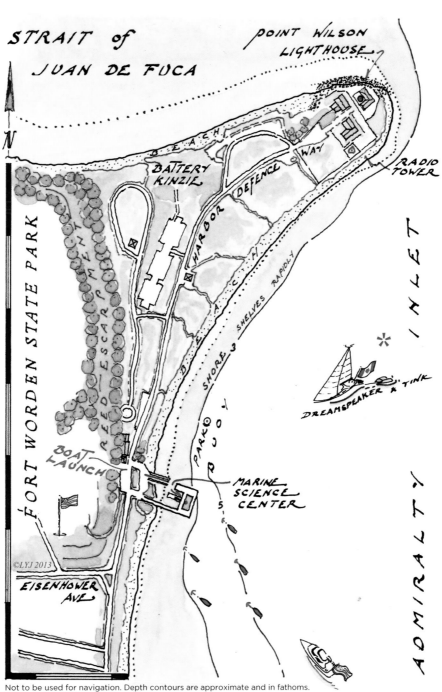

Impressive Fort Worden State Park and Conference Center has it all when it comes to things to see and do – from the fort's campus and maintained gardens, historic buildings, museum, chapel and theaters to the inspiring marine science center, with its interpretive displays.

Dropping anchor east of the maritime pier, Laurence and I rowed to the park dock and dropped in at the visitor center. Armed with maps and guides, we took ourselves on a historic hike around the fort's wealth of buildings and housing units to Battery Kinzie, where we were rewarded with a stunning view of Admiralty Inlet and the Strait of Juan de Fuca. This unique park also offers two very different beaches; you can enjoy an invigorating, windswept walk on the north-facing beach, before relaxing on the soft sand of the east beach to enjoy a delicious picnic.

✳ 48° 08.20' N 122° 45.24' W

CHART 18464

APPROACH
The run in from the waypoint is clear.

ANCHOR
Pick up a park buoy or anchor in 5+ ftm (30+ ft). Good holding in sand and mud. Good protection from summer offshore winds. Not protected from the S.

PARK DOCK
The Port Townsend Marine Science Center pier, a fishing pier and a 120-ft visitor dock designated for small boat and dinghy tie-up, is maintained by Fort Worden State Park.

LAUNCH
A 2-lane boat launch is located N of the wharf.

NOTE
The waves that break on the beach from the wake of commercial vessels rounding Point Wilson are alarming in size. It is recommended that you take your dinghy to the park dock or land it at the adjacent boat launch.

Not to be used for navigation. Depth contours are approximate and in fathoms.

FORT FLAGLER STATE PARK, Kilisut Harbor

Navigating the entrance to Kilisut Harbor is not as intimidating as it first appears, and the channel is well marked. Once moorage or a buoy has been found, days could be spent exploring Fort Flagler State Park, with its beaches, miles of interconnecting hiking and nature trails through woodlands, the historic fort buildings and interpretive museum and the imposing gun batteries standing on guard above the rocky bluff-tops of Marrowstone Island. A full circuit of the park is approximately five miles, and you may come upon local deer, raccoons and squirrels en route.

At low water, the inviting sand spit appears in all its glory. Armed with beach bags and spades, Laurence and I spent a glorious few hours digging for clams and walking barefoot along the beaches, watching boaters navigating the narrow entrance.

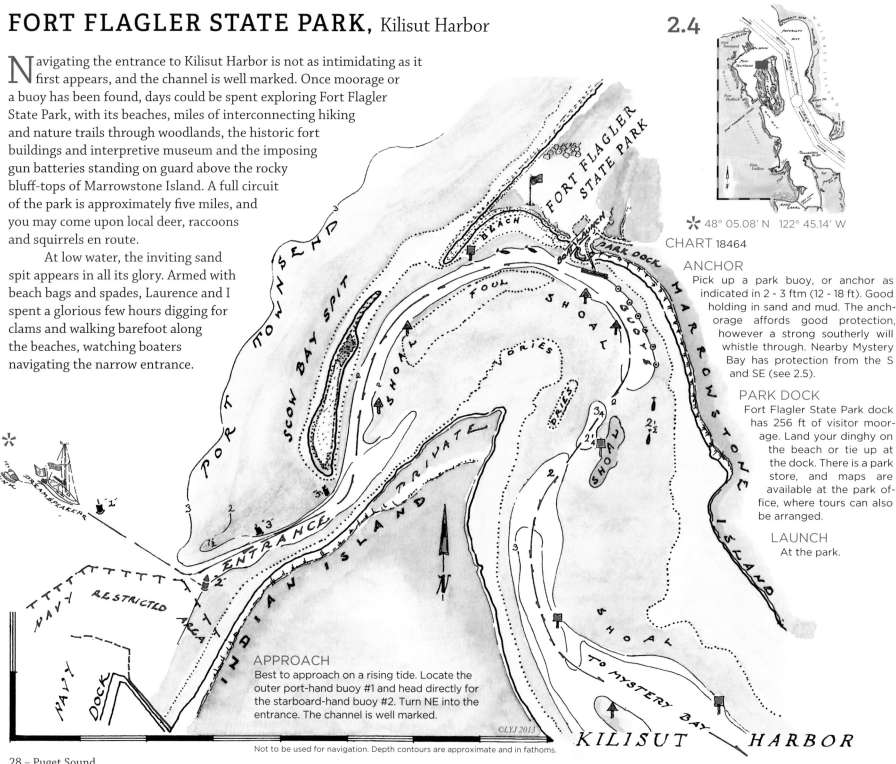

✵ 48° 05.08' N 122° 45.14' W

CHART 18464

ANCHOR
Pick up a park buoy, or anchor as indicated in 2 - 3 ftm (12 - 18 ft). Good holding in sand and mud. The anchorage affords good protection, however a strong southerly will whistle through. Nearby Mystery Bay has protection from the S and SE (see 2.5).

PARK DOCK
Fort Flagler State Park dock has 256 ft of visitor moorage. Land your dinghy on the beach or tie up at the dock. There is a park store, and maps are available at the park office, where tours can also be arranged.

LAUNCH
At the park.

APPROACH
Best to approach on a rising tide. Locate the outer port-hand buoy #1 and head directly for the starboard-hand buoy #2. Turn NE into the entrance. The channel is well marked.

©LYJ 2013

Not to be used for navigation. Depth contours are approximate and in fathoms.

Not to be used for navigation. Depth contours are approximate and in fathoms.

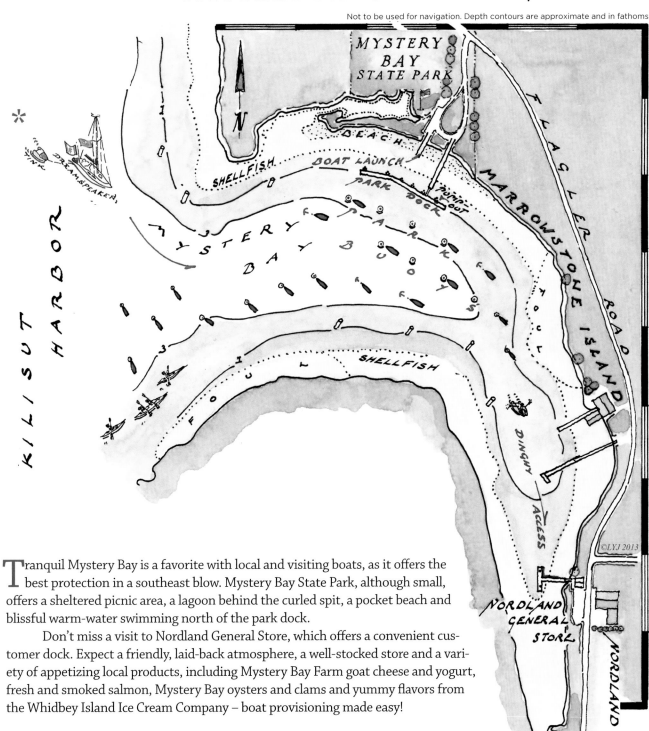

✳ 48° 03.54' N   122° 42.28' W

CHART 18464

APPROACH
The run in is clear.

ANCHOR
Pick up a park buoy, or anchor, although finding room between the local boats on private buoys and at anchor is a challenge. Good holding in mud, in 3+ ftm (18+ ft).

PARK DOCK
The well-maintained park dock has 683 ft of moorage and a pump-out facility. It has been reported that 2 concrete blocks lie 20 - 30 ft off the E end of the dock. Land your dinghy on the beach, or tie up at the dock.

LAUNCH
At the park.

NOTE
Shellfish leases occupy the shoreline at the entrance to Mystery Bay and S of the park. Do not anchor inside the buoyed areas.

Tranquil Mystery Bay is a favorite with local and visiting boats, as it offers the best protection in a southeast blow. Mystery Bay State Park, although small, offers a sheltered picnic area, a lagoon behind the curled spit, a pocket beach and blissful warm-water swimming north of the park dock.

Don't miss a visit to Nordland General Store, which offers a convenient customer dock. Expect a friendly, laid-back atmosphere, a well-stocked store and a variety of appetizing local products, including Mystery Bay Farm goat cheese and yogurt, fresh and smoked salmon, Mystery Bay oysters and clams and yummy flavors from the Whidbey Island Ice Cream Company – boat provisioning made easy!

Those mad about wooden boats will find all the action in Port Townsend Bay.

PORT HADLOCK

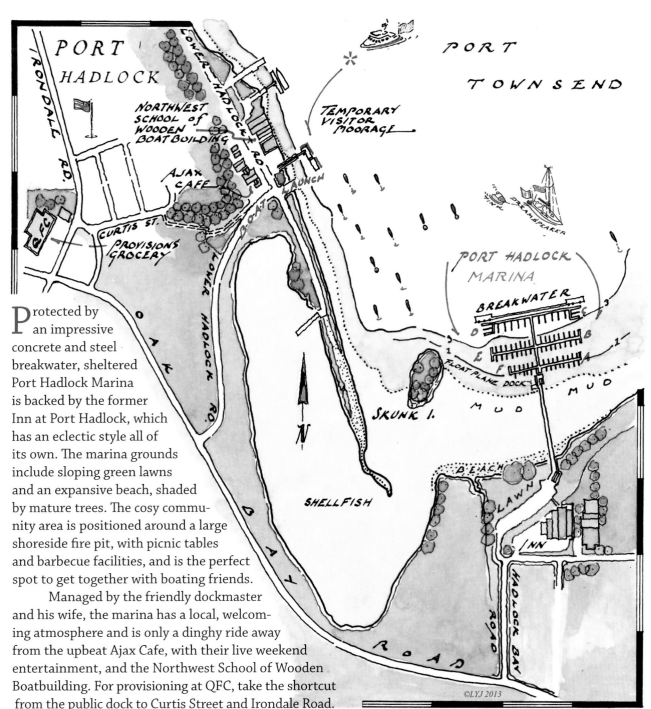

P rotected by an impressive concrete and steel breakwater, sheltered Port Hadlock Marina is backed by the former Inn at Port Hadlock, which has an eclectic style all of its own. The marina grounds include sloping green lawns and an expansive beach, shaded by mature trees. The cosy community area is positioned around a large shoreside fire pit, with picnic tables and barbecue facilities, and is the perfect spot to get together with boating friends.

Managed by the friendly dockmaster and his wife, the marina has a local, welcoming atmosphere and is only a dinghy ride away from the upbeat Ajax Cafe, with their live weekend entertainment, and the Northwest School of Wooden Boatbuilding. For provisioning at QFC, take the shortcut from the public dock to Curtis Street and Irondale Road.

✳ 48° 02.14' N 122° 44.99' W

CHART 18464

APPROACH
The run in to the public dock and marina is clear.

ANCHOR
As indicated, between the local boats on private buoys and at anchor. Good protection from the SE. Good holding in sand and mud, in 3+ ftm (18+ ft).

PUBLIC DOCK
Temporary visitor moorage at the dock. Managed by the Port of Port Townsend.

MARINA
Port Hadlock Marina. VHF Channel 16, switch to 66A; call 360-385-6368. Can accommodate boats up to 66 ft. Power to 50 amps and portable pump-out facility on the docks. Free Wi-Fi, garbage and recycling. Renovated shower and laundry facilities. Designated floatplane dock. Call ahead for visitor moorage availability.

LAUNCH
The public boat launch is heavily used by local boats. It's possible to land your dinghy here.

Marsh Andersen, llc

www.marshandersen.com

Not to be used for navigation. Depth contours are approximate and in fathoms.

PORT TOWNSEND CANAL 2.7

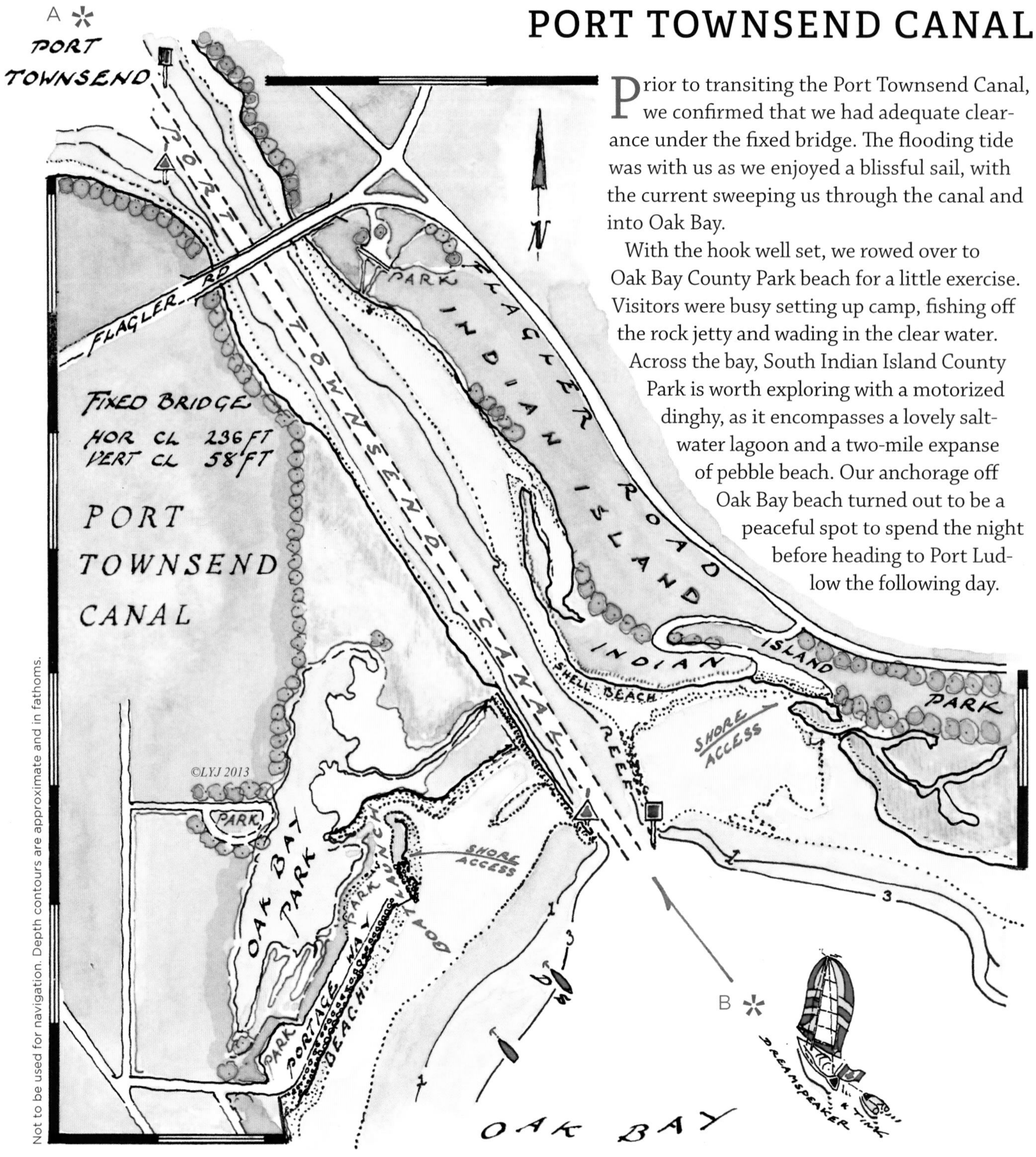
A
PORT TOWNSEND
PORT TOWNSEND CANAL
FLAGLER RD
FLAGLER ROAD
PARK
INDIAN ISLAND
FIXED BRIDGE
HOR CL 236 FT
VERT CL 58 FT
PORT TOWNSEND CANAL
INDIAN ISLAND PARK
SHELL BEACH
REEF
SHORE ACCESS
©LYJ 2013
PARK
OAK BAY PARK
PARK
PORTAGE WAY
BEACH
LAUNCH
SHORE ACCESS
B
DREAMSPEAKER & TINK
OAK BAY

Prior to transiting the Port Townsend Canal, we confirmed that we had adequate clearance under the fixed bridge. The flooding tide was with us as we enjoyed a blissful sail, with the current sweeping us through the canal and into Oak Bay.

With the hook well set, we rowed over to Oak Bay County Park beach for a little exercise. Visitors were busy setting up camp, fishing off the rock jetty and wading in the clear water. Across the bay, South Indian Island County Park is worth exploring with a motorized dinghy, as it encompasses a lovely saltwater lagoon and a two-mile expanse of pebble beach. Our anchorage off Oak Bay beach turned out to be a peaceful spot to spend the night before heading to Port Ludlow the following day.

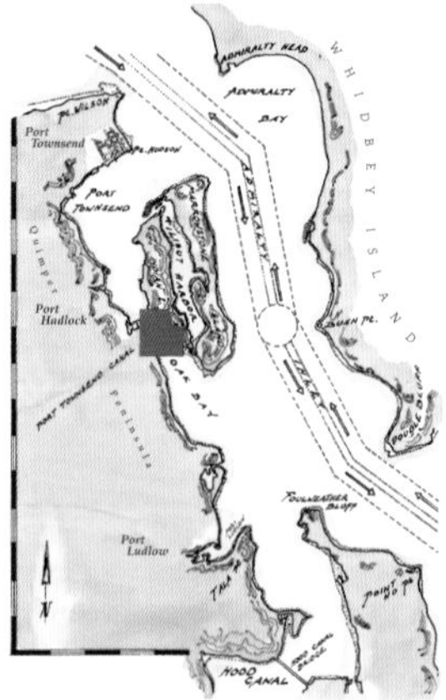

(A) 48° 02.22' N 122° 44.30' W
(B) 48° 01.30' N 122° 43.34' W

CHART 18464

APPROACH
From the N or S, the run in to the entrance between the markers is clear. Once within the canal, the bridge is the only obstruction – an important factor for sailboats with tall masts.

CANAL DEPTHS
A minimum depth of 13.5 ft (1995), but silting over the years may have reduced that figure.

BRIDGE
The fixed bridge has a horizontal clearance of 236 ft and a vertical clearance of 58 ft.

CURRENT
Current runs to 3 knots in the canal on both the ebb and flood tides.

ANCHOR
In Oak Bay, off Oak Bay County Park, as indicated. Good protection from afternoon northerlies in Port Townsend Bay. Open to the S. Good holding in mud and sand, in 2 - 3 ftm (12 - 18 ft).

LAUNCH
At Oak Bay County Park.

Not to be used for navigation. Depth contours are approximate and in fathoms.

MATS MATS BAY

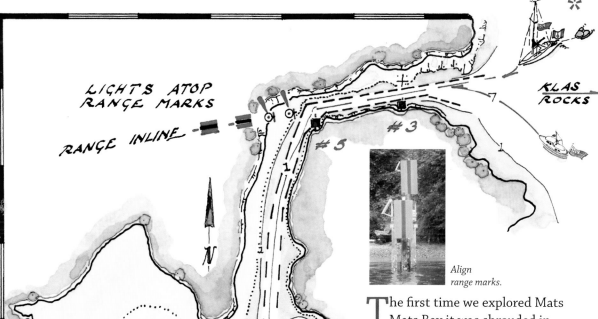

LIGHTS ATOP RANGE MARKS

RANGE INLINE

KLAS ROCKS

#5

#3

#7

N

MATS MATS BAY

#8

#7

RESIDENT BOATS

SHORE ACCESS

MATS MATS BAY

SMALL PARK

BOAT LAUNCH

©LYJ 2013

Align range marks.

The first time we explored Mats Mats Bay it was shrouded in mist, and the mood was one of an eerie backwater. The ambience a year later was very different. We were on our way home from Port Ludlow, and it was a warm, blue-sky sunny day as we anchored north of the resident boats. With intermittent cool-off dives from *Dreamspeaker's* bow, the day was spent relaxing in the cockpit under the shade of the canopy, reading and catching up on boating notes.

Anchored in a tranquil setting.

✳ 47° 57.85' N 122° 40.57' W

CHART 18477

APPROACH
The entrance to the bay lies directly E of Klas Rocks. The run in is dependent on the height of the tide (1 ftm [6 ft] is charted at mean low water) and is best transited on a rising tide.

RANGE
The initial run in W is marked by a range. Keep the range marks aligned until turning to curve S, abeam of the green port-hand daymark #5. Run S, favoring the E shore, and enter the bay between daymarks #7 and #8.

ANCHOR
To the E of resident boats. Protection from all quarters in depths of 2 ftm (12 ft), with good holding in mud. A short scope is adequate.

LAUNCH
At the S end of the bay. Operated by the Port of Port Townsend.

CAUTIONARY NOTE
Boats (mainly keelboats) do run aground in the channel, especially on a zero or minus tide. Because the mud is soft, just relax and wait for the tide to lift you.

Not to be used for navigation. Depth contours are approximate and in fathoms.

A spiritual awakening at Port Ludlow, with the fog burning off by midday.

PORT LUDLOW

Rounding Burner Point with *Dreamspeaker* under sail and *Tink* in tow, Laurence and I were delighted with the pastel, New-England-style architecture of the Port Ludlow Resort, which also includes a spacious marina located behind the point. The generous anchorage to the southwest is surrounded by a forested foreshore, with hiking trails and elegant homes tucked behind mature trees.

With the hook down, it was time to stretch our legs with a good walk. Stopping in at the marina office, we picked up a trail map and headed for the Village Center. A hike through pristine forest, with quiet "sit and listen" benches, took us to Ludlow Creek and up two stairways to the overlook at cooling Ludlow Falls. The trail past the Bay Club ends at a gazebo, with a clear view of the "Inner Harbor" (local name) and peaceful anchorage.

Two good eateries in walking distance from the marina are Cucina Pizza on Village Way and the Snug Harbor Cafe on Oak Bay Road.

THE RESORT AT PORT LUDLOW
www.portludlowresort.com

✳ 47° 55.24' N 122°

CHART 18477

APPRAOCH
The run in SE of Burner Point is clear.

ANCHOR
The main anchorage in the bay lies to the W of the marina, as indicated. Good all-round protection in 4+ ftm (24+ ft), with good holding in mud. Note that the anchorage in the "Inner Harbor" (local name), just S of The Twins islands, is subject to tide, with a depth of less than 1 ftm (6 ft) at the entrance. Enter or depart on sufficient tide. Room for 2 or 3 boats only.

✳ MARINA
Port Ludlow Marina & Resort (see 2.10).

Not to be used for navigation. Depth contours are approximate and in fathoms.

Puget Sound – 35

PORT LUDLOW Marina & Resort

Welcoming Port Ludlow Marina is both rendezvous and dog friendly. There are numerous gathering areas for barbecue and potluck dinners, and a large, social fire pit. The marina store carries gifts, guides, ice, beer and wine. The resort offers a free shuttle to their 18-hole golf course and Niblicks Cafe.

A short walk from the marina is the contemporary-style Inn at Port Ludlow. The Fireside Restaurant serves excellent Pacific Northwest dishes, and the shaded veranda is a relaxing spot to enjoy a picture-postcard sunset. Alternatively, picnic on the sandy beach adjacent to the hand-carved totem pole.

The vibrant Port Ludlow Farmers' Market sets up at the marina every Friday from 1 to 5 p.m., May to September.

THE RESORT AT
PORT LUDLOW
www.portludlowresort.com

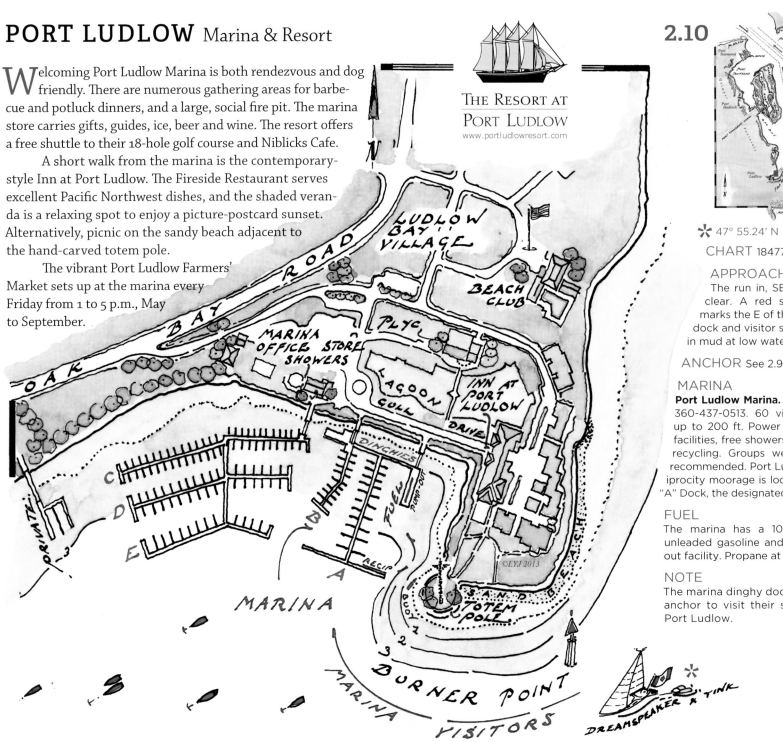

✳ 47° 55.24' N 122° 40.77'

CHART 18477

APPROACH

The run in, SE of Burners Point, is clear. A red starboard-hand buoy marks the E of the channel to the fuel dock and visitor slips. The buoy can sit in mud at low water.

ANCHOR See 2.9

MARINA

Port Ludlow Marina. VHF Channel 68; call 360-437-0513. 60 visitor slips for boats up to 200 ft. Power to 50 amps, laundry facilities, free showers, Wi-Fi, garbage and recycling. Groups welcome. Reservations recommended. Port Ludlow Yacht Club reciprocity moorage is located on the inside of "A" Dock, the designated visitor dock.

FUEL

The marina has a 100-ft fuel dock with unleaded gasoline and diesel, and a pump-out facility. Propane at the marina store.

NOTE

The marina dinghy dock enables boaters at anchor to visit their store and the Inn at Port Ludlow.

PORT LUDLOW

Not to be used for navigation. Depth contours are approximate and in fathoms.

NORTH &
NORTHEAST
PUGET SOUND
Langley, Everett & Kingston to Edmonds

The South Whidbey Harbor at Langley lies in a protected bight in Saratoga Passage.

Langley, Everett & Kingston to Edmonds

Dreamspeaker anchored off The Center for Wooden Boats, Cama Beach State Park.

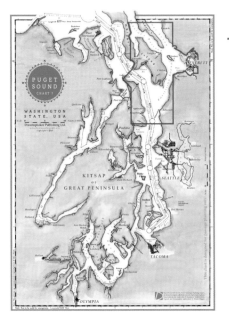

CAUTIONARY NOTE

There are two Washington State ferry routes in this chapter, with very frequent sailings every day: Mukilto to Clinton and Edmonds to Kingston. If a ferry is maneuvering, stay a minimum of 100 yds away.

Admiralty Inlet is the primary entrance to Puget Sound. Beyond Possession Point, Puget Sound extends northeast via Possession Sound, then north via Saratoga Passage to a second entrance at Deception Pass. Thirty nautical miles of sheltered water parallel Whidbey Island's eastern shoreline and become a popular boating highway in the summer months.

Our voyage into Holmes Harbor revealed that it extends so far inland that it seems to divide Whidbey Island in two, providing boaters with good overnight anchorage in Honeymoon Bay, as well as a chance to visit the friendly town of Freeland. Situated north of Sandy Point on South Whidbey Island, the charming town of Langley sits high on a bluff overlooking Saratoga Passage.

While enjoying a gentle sail along the southwest shoreline of Camano Island, Laurence and I were pleasantly surprised to find Cama Beach State Park. A mile-long trail connects this park to nearby Camano Island State Park, with its forested trails and long stretch of sandy beach.

The Port of Everett, on the mainland shore at the mouth of the Snohomish River, is the largest marina facility in Puget Sound, with 5,000 linear feet of visitor moorage at the South, Central and North docks. A sandy beach and warm-water swimming make nearby Jetty Island a fun day trip.

The Port of Kingston, below Apple Cove Point on the Kitsap Peninsula, is a favorite stopping-off point for boaters. They offer extensive visitor moorage, and downtown Kingston has a laid-back ambience.

We tied up at the Port of Edmonds marina on a glorious Friday afternoon and explored its inviting waterfront, which includes sandy beaches and landscaped parks. Nearby Marina Beach Park is an urban gem, while downtown Edmonds has an appealing small-town personality and a summer market that is not to be missed.

TIDES
Tide Height Station: Everett

CURRENTS
Tidal Current Station: Bush Point

WEATHER
NOAA Weather Radio WX4: Puget Sound
NOAA VHF Weather Channel 1 or 3
www.nws.noaa.gov/nwr

NOTE
Travel N with the ebb and S with the flood. When the current is with you, travel time can be cut down considerably.

HISTORIC FACTS
Whidbey Island was once inhabited by members of the Lower Skagit, Swinomish, Suquamish, Snohomish and other Native American tribes. The island was fully explored in 1792 by Captain George Vancouver. In May of that year, officers Joseph Whidbey and Peter Puget began to map and explore the areas of what would later be named Puget Sound. After Whidbey circumnavigated the island in June 1792, Vancouver named the island in his honor. Today, Whidbey Island is often referred to as Puget Sound's largest artists' colony and is home to numerous working artists, writers and performers.

LOCAL EVENTS
The Langley Art Walk takes place on the first Saturday of each month.

The two-day Choochokam Arts Festival, featuring art, jewelry and music, is celebrated on the first weekend in July.

Djangofest Northwest is a five-day festival in September celebrating the gypsy-jazz style of Django Reinhardt, and it features workshops, concerts and impromptu jam sessions.

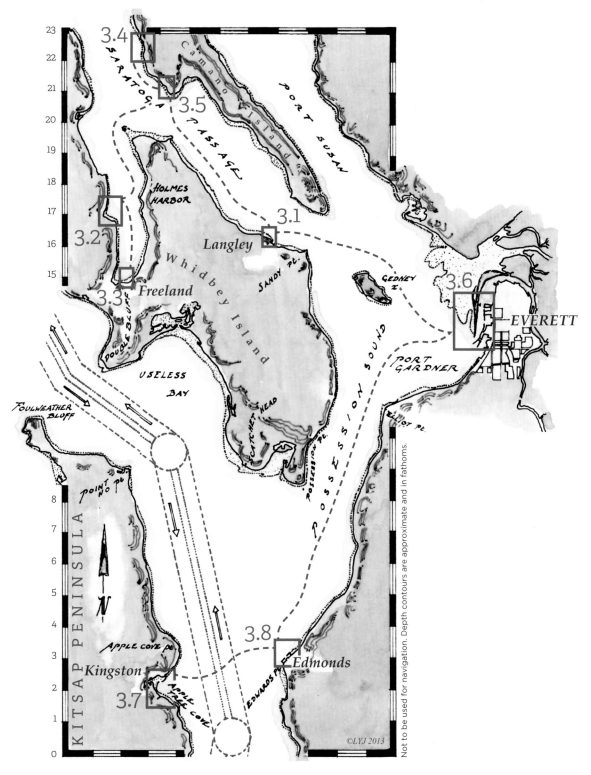

3 NORTH & NORTHEAST PUGET SOUND

FEATURED DESTINATIONS

FUEL
3.6 Port of Everett Marina; 3.7 Port of Kingston; 3.8 Port of Edmonds

PUMP-OUT FACILITIES
3.1 South Whidbey Harbor at Langley; 3.6 Port of Everett Marina; 3.7 Port of Kingston; 3.8 Port of Edmonds

3.1 LANGLEY – Whidbey Island

A morning spent exploring the historic "Village by the Sea."

Anne tucks into the delicious Penn Cove oysters at Prima Bistro.

Penguins enjoy the peace of a Langley resort.

Situated north of Sandy Point in a small bight on South Whidbey Island's eastern shoreline, the town of Langley sits high on a bluff overlooking Saratoga Passage, Mount Baker and the snow-topped Cascade Mountains. Sheltered by a substantial breakwater, the marina nestles comfortably below the town.

With the assistance of the friendly harbormaster, Laurence and I maneuvered *Dreamspeaker* into her allotted berth, secured all lines and walked up Wharf Street into historic downtown Langley, where eating, drinking and shopping on First and Second streets is a pleasure. Pick up a walking map at the Langley Chamber of Commerce and Visitor Information Center and enjoy a relaxing day exploring this historic "Village by the Sea," which offers an excellent selection of coffee houses, cafes and restaurants, as well as a great pizzeria.

The village of Langley has a true island ambience, and its flower-filled streets and colorful storefronts offer enticing clothing shops, gift, specialty and antiques stores, art galleries, independent bookstores and wine shops with tasting rooms (we also found an excellent thrift store). Don't miss the opportunity to blow your own glass at Callahan's Firehouse Studio and Gallery.

Provisioning is a delight at the stylish Star Store on First Street. Their full-service market and deli is stocked with an irresistible array of produce, food to go and wine, while their vibrant mercantile section offers an eclectic collection of contemporary fashion and island-lifestyle homewares.

Before treating ourselves to a special evening at the lively Prima Bistro, with its patio overlooking the sunset views, we visited the locally named "Boy and Dog Park." Stairs from this pocket-park lead down to the restful Seawall Park, which has a shady seawalk and sandy beach, where in season, gray whales can be seen up close, feeding on the abundant supply of ghost shrimp.

LOCAL FACTS

The Langley Chamber of Commerce and Visitor Information Center are located on Anthes Avenue and Second Street.

Island Transit provides free bus service on Whidbey Island; buses are equipped with bike racks. Pick up a *Riders Schedule* at the Visitor Information Center.

The Langley Second Street Market (close to the Useless Bay Coffee Company) takes place on Fridays from 2 to 6 p.m. (June to September).

Ring the brass whale bell at Hladky Park (off Anthes Avenue and 1st Street) if you spot an orca or gray whale in Saratoga Passage. And, every April, celebrate the return of the whales with Langley's Welcome the Whales festival.

Take in a good movie at the refurbished and friendly 1930s Clyde Theater on First Street.

The South Whidbey Historical Society Museum, located on the corner of Second Street and Melsen Alley, is well worth a visit. They collect information and preserve artifacts that reflect the history of South Whidbey Island.

FOOD FACTS

Try these favorites: Prima Bistro, above the Star Store, for seasonal and delicious French-inspired Pacific Northwest cuisine and live music; Braeburn Restaurant for great breakfasts and lunches made with fresh local ingredients; Mo's Pub and Eatery, on Second Street, for a relaxed local beer on tap.

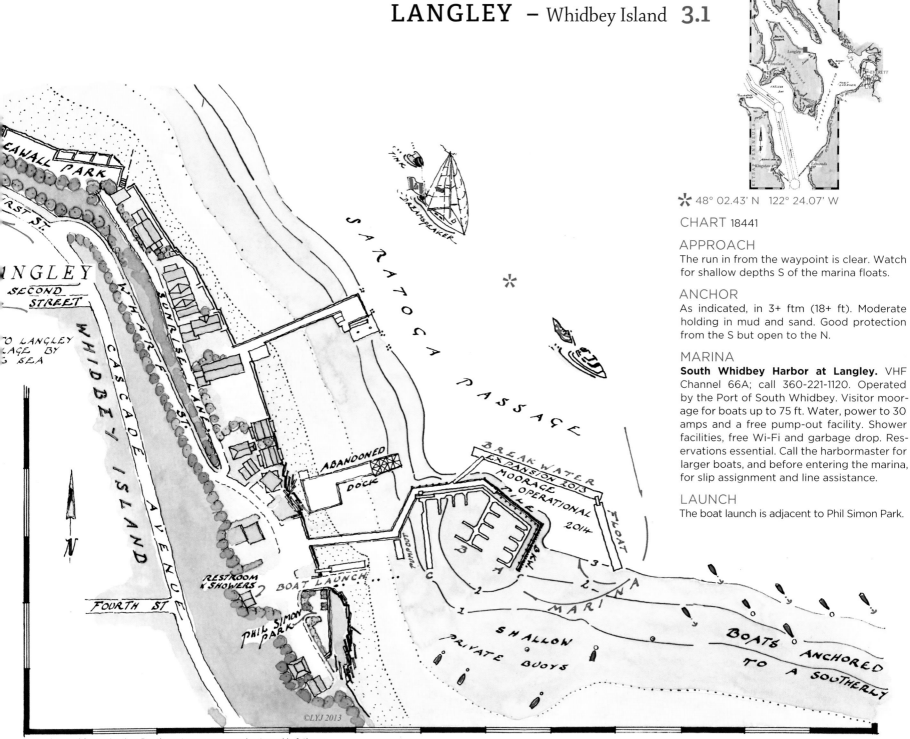

✳ 48° 02.43' N 122° 24.07' W

CHART 18441

APPROACH
The run in from the waypoint is clear. Watch for shallow depths S of the marina floats.

ANCHOR
As indicated, in 3+ ftm (18+ ft). Moderate holding in mud and sand. Good protection from the S but open to the N.

MARINA
South Whidbey Harbor at Langley. VHF Channel 66A; call 360-221-1120. Operated by the Port of South Whidbey. Visitor moorage for boats up to 75 ft. Water, power to 30 amps and a free pump-out facility. Shower facilities, free Wi-Fi and garbage drop. Reservations essential. Call the harbormaster for larger boats, and before entering the marina, for slip assignment and line assistance.

LAUNCH
The boat launch is adjacent to Phil Simon Park.

Not to be used for navigation. Depth contours are approximate and in fathoms.

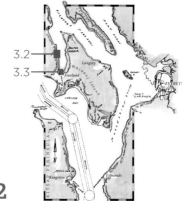

3.2 HONEYMOON BAY –
Whidbey Island

Deep Holmes Harbor almost divides Whidbey Island in two, and it provides boaters with a good overnight anchorage in Honeymoon Bay, as well as a chance to visit the small, friendly town of Freeland. The peaceful bay is a favorite local anchorage on sunny evenings and on weekends. All mooring buoys and tidelands are private.

3.2

48° 03.43' N 122° 32.38' W

CHART 18441

APPROACH
Honeymoon Bay lies in a triangular bight approximately halfway down the W shore of Holmes Harbor, S of Dines Point. The run in from the waypoint is clear.

ANCHOR
As indicated, in 3+ ftm (18+ ft). Good holding in mud and sand. This is the preferred Holmes Harbor anchorage, as it is protected from the SW. Open to the N and summer afternoon breezes.

CAUTIONARY NOTE
Keep a look out for the rock and spit between Rocky Point and Baby Island, on the E side of the entrance to Holmes Bay.

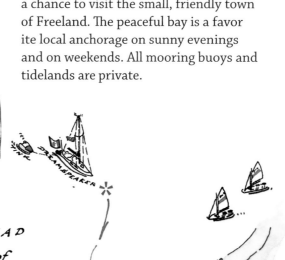

3.3 FREELAND –
Whidbey Island

Anchoring in Holmes Harbor, we walked up Shoreview Drive to the charming town of Freeland to discover a friendly community and a number of interesting local establishments, including a choice of great antique and thrift stores, the inviting WiFire Coffee Bar and the Roaming Radish, which features tasty organic fare. After provisioning at Payless Foods, we returned via Myrtle Avenue to relax on the green lawns of Freeland Park.

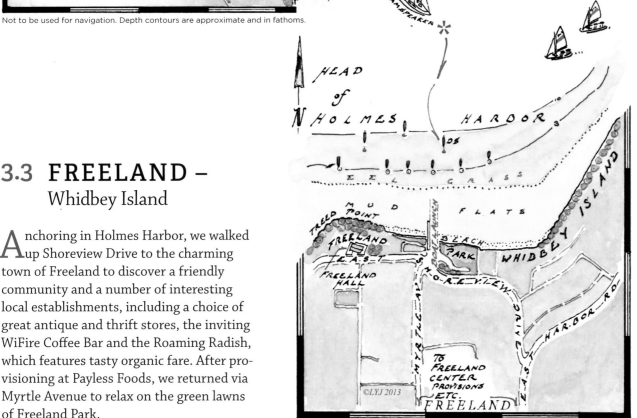

Not to be used for navigation. Depth contours are approximate and in fathoms.

3.3

48° 01.24' N 122° 31.75' W

CHART 18441

APPROACH
Freeland lies at the head of Holmes Harbor. The run in from the waypoint is clear.

ANCHOR
As indicated, N of the boats on buoys in 3+ ftm (18+ ft). Good holding in mud. Protected from the S but open to the N.

LAUNCH
The boat launch is off the park and beach.

A schooner, with clipper bow, sails with grace.

Kiteboarding off Jetty Island, Port of Everett.

3.4

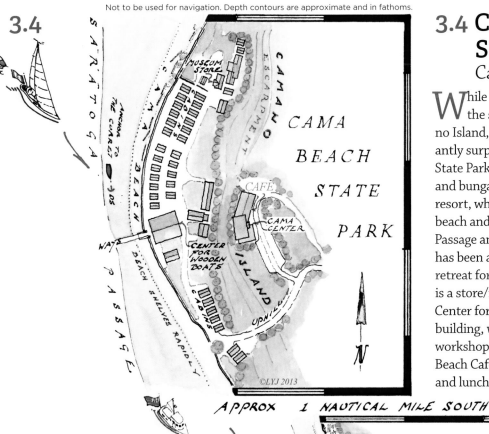

©LYJ 2013

APPROX 1 NAUTICAL MILE SOUTH

3.4 CAMA BEACH STATE PARK –
Camano Island

While enjoying a gentle sail along the southwest shoreline of Camano Island, Laurence and I were pleasantly surprised to find Cama Beach State Park. With its refurbished cabins and bungalows, this 1930s-era fishing resort, which has a beautiful sandy beach and sweeping views of Saratoga Passage and the Olympic Mountains, has been a favorite summer family retreat for more than 50 years. There is a store/museum on-site, and The Center for Wooden Boats offers boat-building, woodworking and restoration workshops, as well as rentals. The Cama Beach Cafe on the hill serves breakfast and lunch from 9 a.m. to 2 p.m.

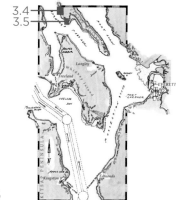

3.4

✳ 48° 08.75' N   122° 31.15' W

CHART 18441

APPROACH
The run in is parallel to the shore. Watch your depth sounder carefully, as the beach shelves rapidly.

ANCHOR
As indicated, making sure to set the anchor well and seaward of the eelgrass in 4+ ftm (24+ ft). Moderate holding in mud and sand. 4 park buoys are planned for 2014.

NOTE
This is a temporary day stop and not recommended for an overnight stay.

3.5

✳ 48° 07.49' N   122° 30.01' W

CHART 18441

APPROACH
Approximately 1 nautical mile S of Cama Beach State Park and just N of Lowell Point.

ANCHOR
As indicated, parallel to the shore in 4+ ftm (24+ ft). Moderate holding in mud and sand.

LAUNCH
This is the main Camano Island boat launch and is very busy in the summer months

NOTE
This is a temporary day stop and not recommended for an overnight stay.

3.5 CAMANO ISLAND STATE PARK

Camano Island State Park is a 134-acre camping park, with rustic cabins, forested trails and a long stretch of sandy beach for digging clams. The park is connected by a mile-long trail to Cama Beach State Park and its 15 miles of hiking and biking trails.

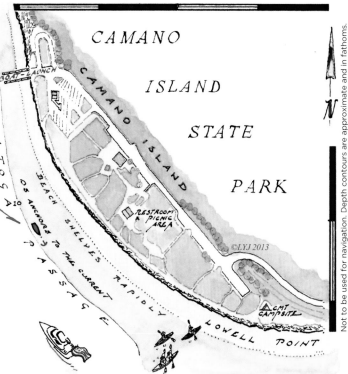

©LYJ 2013

Visitors to Everett Marina's South Dock enjoy a backdrop of the faux lighthouse at Anthony's HomePort Restaurant.

The Port of Everett is the largest marina facility in Puget Sound, with 5,000 linear feet of visitor moorage at the South, Central and North docks. The South Dock is home to Everett Marina Village, which has three restaurants, including Anthony's HomePort. Port Gardner Landing hosts the Sunday Farmers' Market (2 to 4 p.m.) and features Meyers Cafe for great breakfasts, Lombardi's Italian Restaurant and a West Marine store.

Waterfront walkways lead to the Central and North docks, where you will find the Craftsman District and the Waterfront Center, which houses the port office and the popular Scuttlebutt Brewing Company. For a fun day out, take the free ferry to Jetty Island and watch the colorful kiteboarders in action, hike the nature trails and swim in the warm, shallow waters off the beach.

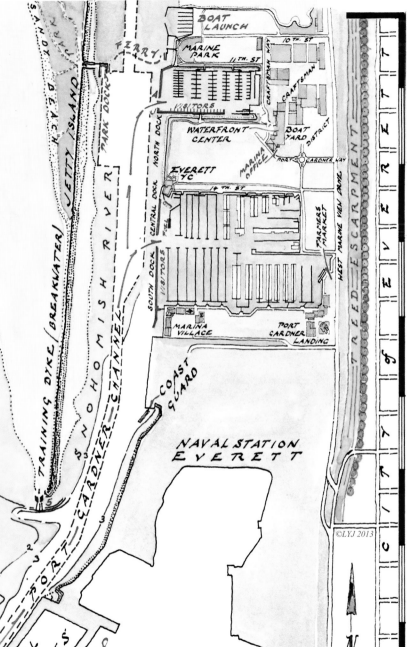

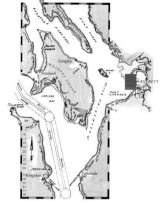

✳ 47° 59.19' N   122° 15.13' W

CHARTS 18443, 18444

APPROACH
The portside buoy # 3 (green) lies W of the naval wharves. Round the buoy into Port Gardner Channel, heading N into the Snohomish River.

MARINA
Port of Everett Marina. VHF Channel 16, switch to 69; call 425-259-6001. Operated by the Port of Everett. Ample handicap-accessible visitor moorage for boats up to 120 ft at the S, Central and N docks. Water, power to 50 amps and free pump-out facilities. 24-hour security. Showers, laundry facilities, free Wi-Fi, garbage drop and waste oil dump. Haulout to 75 tons, and full-service boat repair, maintenance and marine supplies at the Craftsman District. Reservations recommended. Groups and clubs welcome.

FUEL
At the Central Dock; operated by the port. Gasoline and diesel are available, and a free pump-out facility is just N of the fuel dock.

LAUNCH
There is a 13-lane boat launch N of the marina in Everett Marine Park.

CAUTIONARY NOTE
Be aware of strong currents when mooring at the visitors' docks.

NOTE
Warning signs for boaters in Port Gardner Channel specify "No Visible Wake."

Not to be used for navigation. Depth contours are approximate and in fathoms.

3.7 KINGSTON – Marina & Downtown

The anchorage in Apple Tree Cove is scenic, but the marina is more comfortable.

The electric pickup made light work of the provisioning.

Enjoying a shaded lunch at J'aime Les Crêpes.

The Port of Kingston, below Apple Cove Point on the Kitsap Peninsula, is conveniently situated and a favorite stopping-off point for boaters. It offers extensive visitor moorage, backed by the immaculately maintained Mike Wallace Park. Any activity from the Edmonds-Kingston ferry terminal is unobtrusive, as you savor the delights of Kingston's very walkable downtown.

Driving the port's courtesy electric car to the small shopping center about a mile from the marina, we found a well-stocked IGA, post office, second-hand bookstore and Henery Do It Best Hardware, which is difficult to pass by without stopping in. Boat provisioning completed, we indulged in a delicious strawberry, chocolate and toasted almond-filled crepe from J'aime Les Crêpes, just north of the marina. Turning east on Washington Avenue, we passed the Mirracole Morsels bakery (known for their yummy homemade granola) and followed the public trail signs to the soft sands of North Beach Park. Backed by silvered driftwood and a forested cliff, the beach is a tranquil spot to walk the pooch or just lean back and take in the view across Puget Sound.

Downtown Kingston has a relaxed ambience and is fun to visit on a weekend. Saturday begins with the farmers' market at Mike Wallace Park. Tables display baskets of freshly picked fruit and vegetables, baked goods, preserves and honey, handmade arts and crafts and delicious goodies to be enjoyed at the park picnic tables.

Kingston's main shopping street has a fabulous selection of unique gift and specialty stores, and cafes, coffee shops, pubs and restaurants abound. Sip a glass of local estate wine at Savage Vines, or sample a lavender-and-blackberry cone under the shaded awning of Mora Iced Creamery, then simply people-watch.

LOCAL FACTS

The Kingston Farmers' Market takes place at Mike Wallace Park on Saturdays from 9 a.m. to 2 p.m. (May to mid-October).

The free Concerts on the Cove take place at Mike Wallace Park on Saturdays in July and August. The Rotary Beer Garden opens at 5 p.m., and the concert begins at 7 p.m. They invite you to bring a blanket, your kids and the dog!

Take in a movie at the Firehouse Theater on Highway 104, just four blocks north of the marina. The atmosphere is intimate and friendly, and they serve real butter popcorn.

LOCAL EVENTS

On the Fourth of July, enjoy Kingston's special parade, farmers' market and fireworks show.

Take in the three-day Kitsap Arts and Crafts Festival that takes place at the end of August at Mike Wallace Park.

In August, don't miss the popular and fun annual Kingston Slug Hunt. Explore the hidden haunts of Kingston to uncover one of the 150 hidden slugs that have been decorated by artists at the Front Street Gallery.

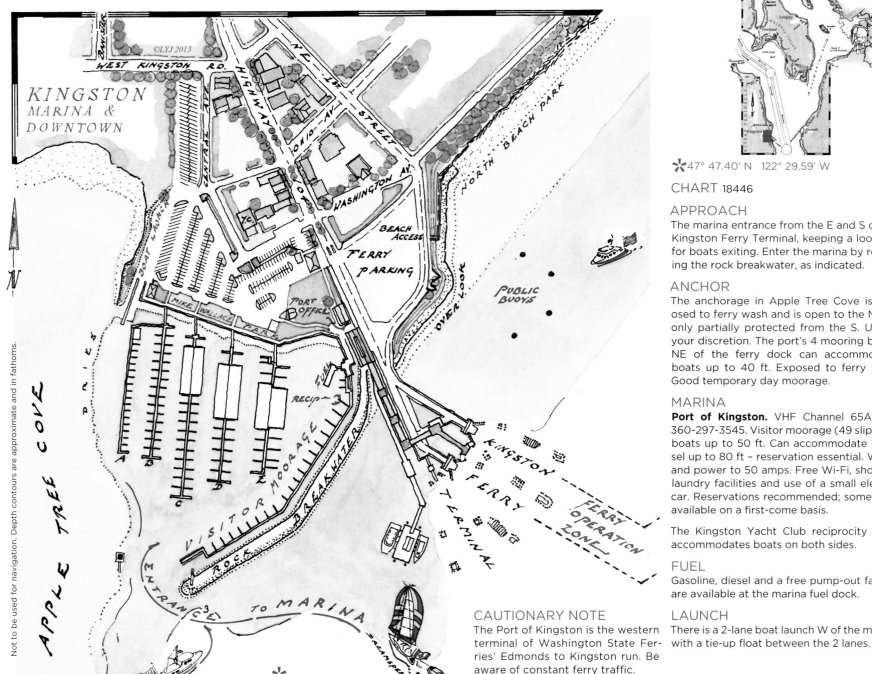

✳ 47° 47.40' N   122° 29.59' W

CHART 18446

APPROACH
The marina entrance from the E and S of the Kingston Ferry Terminal, keeping a look out for boats exiting. Enter the marina by rounding the rock breakwater, as indicated.

ANCHOR
The anchorage in Apple Tree Cove is exposed to ferry wash and is open to the N and only partially protected from the S. Use at your discretion. The port's 4 mooring buoys NE of the ferry dock can accommodate boats up to 40 ft. Exposed to ferry wash. Good temporary day moorage.

MARINA
Port of Kingston. VHF Channel 65A; call 360-297-3545. Visitor moorage (49 slips) for boats up to 50 ft. Can accommodate 1 vessel up to 80 ft – reservation essential. Water and power to 50 amps. Free Wi-Fi, showers, laundry facilities and use of a small electric car. Reservations recommended; some slips available on a first-come basis.

The Kingston Yacht Club reciprocity dock accommodates boats on both sides.

FUEL
Gasoline, diesel and a free pump-out facility are available at the marina fuel dock.

LAUNCH
There is a 2-lane boat launch W of the marina, with a tie-up float between the 2 lanes.

CAUTIONARY NOTE
The Port of Kingston is the western terminal of Washington State Ferries' Edmonds to Kingston run. Be aware of constant ferry traffic.

Map labels: KINGSTON MARINA & DOWNTOWN; ©LYJ 2013; WEST KINGSTON RD.; NE HIGHWAY 104; STREET; UNION AV.; WASHINGTON AV.; CENTRAL AV.; NORTH BEACH PARK; BEACH ACCESS; FERRY PARKING; BOAT LAUNCH; YC; MIKE WALLACE PARK; PORT OFFICE; PUBLIC BUOYS; OVERLOOK; VISITOR MOORAGE; RECIP; ROCK BREAKWATER; A B C D; APPLE TREE COVE; DRIES; ENTRANCE TO MARINA; KINGSTON FERRY TERMINAL; FERRY OPERATION ZONE; DREAMSPEAKER & TINK

Not to be used for navigation. Depth contours are approximate and in fathoms.

EDMONDS – Marina & Downtown

3.8

CHART 18446   ✳ 47° 48.59' N   122° 23.82' W

APPROACH
From the E. The run in is clear. The fuel dock and visitor moorage at the marina are arranged as indicated. Keep a sharp look out for boat traffic entering and exiting, as this is a busy marina.

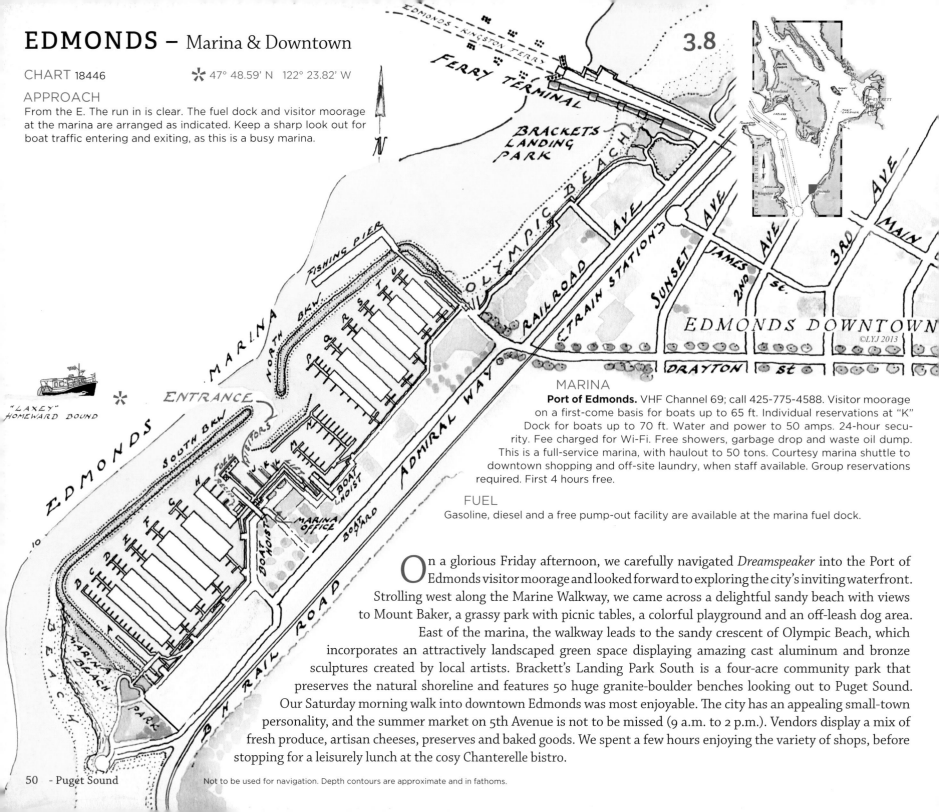

MARINA
Port of Edmonds. VHF Channel 69; call 425-775-4588. Visitor moorage on a first-come basis for boats up to 65 ft. Individual reservations at "K" Dock for boats up to 70 ft. Water and power to 50 amps. 24-hour security. Fee charged for Wi-Fi. Free showers, garbage drop and waste oil dump. This is a full-service marina, with haulout to 50 tons. Courtesy marina shuttle to downtown shopping and off-site laundry, when staff available. Group reservations required. First 4 hours free.

FUEL
Gasoline, diesel and a free pump-out facility are available at the marina fuel dock.

On a glorious Friday afternoon, we carefully navigated *Dreamspeaker* into the Port of Edmonds visitor moorage and looked forward to exploring the city's inviting waterfront. Strolling west along the Marine Walkway, we came across a delightful sandy beach with views to Mount Baker, a grassy park with picnic tables, a colorful playground and an off-leash dog area. East of the marina, the walkway leads to the sandy crescent of Olympic Beach, which incorporates an attractively landscaped green space displaying amazing cast aluminum and bronze sculptures created by local artists. Brackett's Landing Park South is a four-acre community park that preserves the natural shoreline and features 50 huge granite-boulder benches looking out to Puget Sound. Our Saturday morning walk into downtown Edmonds was most enjoyable. The city has an appealing small-town personality, and the summer market on 5th Avenue is not to be missed (9 a.m. to 2 p.m.). Vendors display a mix of fresh produce, artisan cheeses, preserves and baked goods. We spent a few hours enjoying the variety of shops, before stopping for a leisurely lunch at the cosy Chanterelle bistro.

    Not to be used for navigation. Depth contours are approximate and in fathoms.

Chapter 4
SEATTLE, LAKE UNION & LAKE WASHINGTON
Elliot Bay, Shilshole Bay & Lake Washington Ship Canal

Bell Harbor Marina is about as close to downtown Seattle as you can get in a boat. Don Wilson/ Port of Seattle photo.

CHAPTER 4 SEATTLE, Lake Union & Lake Washington
Elliott Bay, Shilshole Bay & Lake Washington Ship Canal

www.portseattle.org

A sleek cruise ship departs Elliott Bay.

CAUTIONARY NOTE
Boaters need to be aware of the proximity rules regarding large commercial and passenger vessels. Large vessel movement is a frequent event, as they transit Elliott Bay to the Port of Seattle docks. Monitor vessel movement on VHF Channel 14, Vessel Traffic Service Seattle.

From the sleek modern skyscrapers of the downtown core to the distinct profile of the Space Needle, Seattle's spectacular skyline looms large over Elliott Bay. In recent years the city's downtown waterfront has undergone an extensive revitalization and is now a lively, family-friendly destination, offering visitors a fun, multicultural urban experience.

Laurence and I enjoyed an exhilarating reach across Puget Sound to Elliott Bay before slipping into our assigned berth at Bell Harbor Marina, Seattle's only downtown public marina and just a short walk from Pike Place Market and the delights of the city.

For an alternative Seattle experience, private Elliott Bay Marina is tucked below the dramatic 200-foot expanse of Magnolia Bluff in Smith Cove. North of West Point, popular Shilshole Bay Marina has undergone major upgrades and also offers first-rate moorage facilities and a pleasantly landscaped foreshore. Conveniently close to the lively neighborhood of Ballard, we were able to view the boats locking through the historic Chittenden Locks before attempting it the following day.

Excited to begin our freshwater cruise through the Lake Washington Ship Canal, we made an early morning start and had *Dreamspeaker* tied up in the small lock, ready to lock through before the busy weekend boat-jam. Once through the gates, we headed to the marina at Fishermen's Terminal, the home port of the North Pacific fishing fleet.

For the next five days we put tide tables to one side, swam in blissful fresh water and explored Lake Washington's fun mix of destinations. We enjoyed Kirkland's Thursday evening summer concert at Marina Park from the dock, lazing in *Dreamspeaker's* cockpit surrounded by lavish homes in Meydenbauer Bay, hiking the trails in beautiful Luther Burbank Park and digging our toes into the sand on the beaches of Andrews Bay, surrounded by the lush greenery of Seward Park.

TIDES
Tide Height Station: Seattle

CURRENTS
Tidal Current Station: Bush Point

WEATHER
NOAA Weather Radio WX4: Puget Sound
NOAA VHF Weather Chanel 1 or 3
www.nws.noaa.gov/nwr

FACTS
Seattle is the largest city in the northwestern United States, with approximately 600,000 residents and 3.4 million inhabitants in the greater Seattle metropolitan area. The city is a major seaport, which is owned and managed by the Port of Seattle. The waterfront from Duwamish Head to Smith Cove is a commercial landscape of storage elevators, working cranes, warehouses, piers and wharves.

The port operates four public marinas, three of which are featured in this guide. The fourth, Harbor Island Marina, is located near west Seattle and primarily offers permanent moorage; call 206-787-3006.

LOCAL FACTS
Take in the panoramic view of Puget Sound, the Olympic Mountains and Seattle's dramatic skyline from the roof terrace of the Bell Harbor Conference Center (closed when cruise ships are docked at Pier 66). Cross the skybridge to the unique restaurants, art galleries and shops of Belltown.

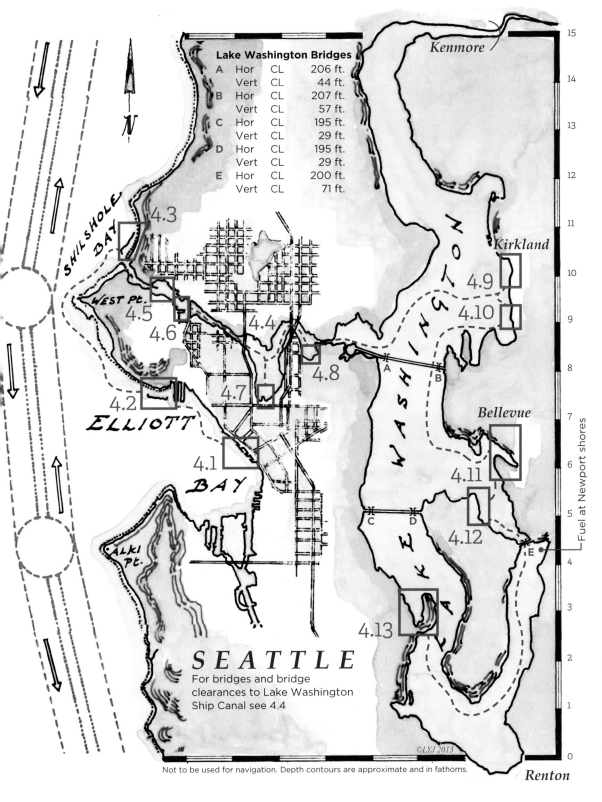

Lake Washington Bridges

A	Hor	CL	206 ft.
	Vert	CL	44 ft.
B	Hor	CL	207 ft.
	Vert	CL	57 ft.
C	Hor	CL	195 ft.
	Vert	CL	29 ft.
D	Hor	CL	195 ft.
	Vert	CL	29 ft.
E	Hor	CL	200 ft.
	Vert	CL	71 ft.

SEATTLE

For bridges and bridge clearances to Lake Washington Ship Canal see 4.4

©LYJ 2013

Not to be used for navigation. Depth contours are approximate and in fathoms.

Renton

4 SEATTLE,
Lake Union & Lake Washington

FEATURED DESTINATIONS

FUEL
4.2 Elliott Bay Marina; 4.3 Shilshole Bay Marina; 4.4 Lake Washington Ship Canal; 4.10 Yarrow Bay Marina. Fuel also available at Newport Shores SE of East Channel Bridge.

PUMP-OUT FACILITIES
4.1 Bell Harbor Marina; 4.2 Elliott Bay Marina; 4.3 Shilshole Bay Marina; 4.4 Lake Washington Ship Canal; 4.6 Fishermen's Terminal; 4.10 Yarrow Bay Marina

4.1 BELL HARBOR MARINA, Downtown Seattle

Pike Place Market is lively and eclectic.

Bell Harbor Marina.

Anne enjoys shopping for fresh fruit.

Well maintained by the Port of Seattle, the public marina, located at Pier 66, is backed by Seattle's dramatic skyline and provides the city's only downtown recreational moorage. We tucked *Dreamspeaker* into her assigned berth and immediately felt the city's energy right there in the cockpit. Armed with maps and hats, Laurence and I strolled along Alaskan Way to the Lenora Street Elevator and spiral staircase. Turning right onto 1st Avenue, we were overwhelmed by the choice of inviting espresso bars, teahouses and cafes.

Our next stop was the historic (and renovated) Pike Place Market. The market is patronized by locals and visitors alike, and the atmosphere is lively, eclectic and international. The colorful stalls are a feast for the eyes and offer freshly harvested seafood and farm-fresh fruit and vegetables from across Washington State. Specialty shops carry handcrafted cheese and freshly baked bread and pastries.

The Pike Place Stair Climb will take you to the Seattle Aquarium and its magnificent underwater exhibits, offering a chance to "take a dive" and observe the watery world below our keels. Alternatively, ride the Seattle Great Wheel, picnic with the locals and breathe in the salt air on the terraced deck of Waterfront Park, or dip your toes into the cool water of cascading Fitzgerald Fountain. If you have a day or two to spare, walk or cycle west along Alaskan Way to Pier 70 and the promenade of Myrtle Edwards Park and beach, which connects with the Seattle Art Museum's Olympic Sculpture Park – free and fun every day of the year!

The perfect end to our eventful day was to flop into a cozy chair on the shaded terrace of Anthony's Pier 66, just across from the public marina, and indulge in a choice of "Fun Food and Drinks" from their popular happy hour menu.

LOCAL FACTS

Seattle's waterfront has undergone an extensive revitalization – it is now a lively, boater-friendly destination that offers visitors walking and biking lanes, pocket parks and beaches, and a fun urban experience.

The Metro Transit Free Bus provides a handy downtown bus service. Hours of operation are 6 a.m. to 7 p.m. daily; call 206-553-3000.

For a self-guided tour of the city, pick up a *Seattle Tourmap* and a *Seattle Bicycling Guide Map* at the marina office.

FUN FACTS

Riding the Seattle Great Wheel is an exhilarating experience. This state-of-the-art Ferris wheel stands 175 ft tall, has fully enclosed gondolas and extends almost 40 ft beyond the end of Pier 57, over Elliott Bay.

Don't miss two quite diverse attractions: Chihuly Garden and Glass, a vibrant, multicolored exhibition that explores the inspiring work of Pacific Northwest artist Dale Chihuly, and Bill Speidel's fascinating Underground Tour, a unique historic tour of Seattle's hidden subterranean storefronts and sidewalks.

Not to be used for navigation. Depth contours are approximate and in fathoms.

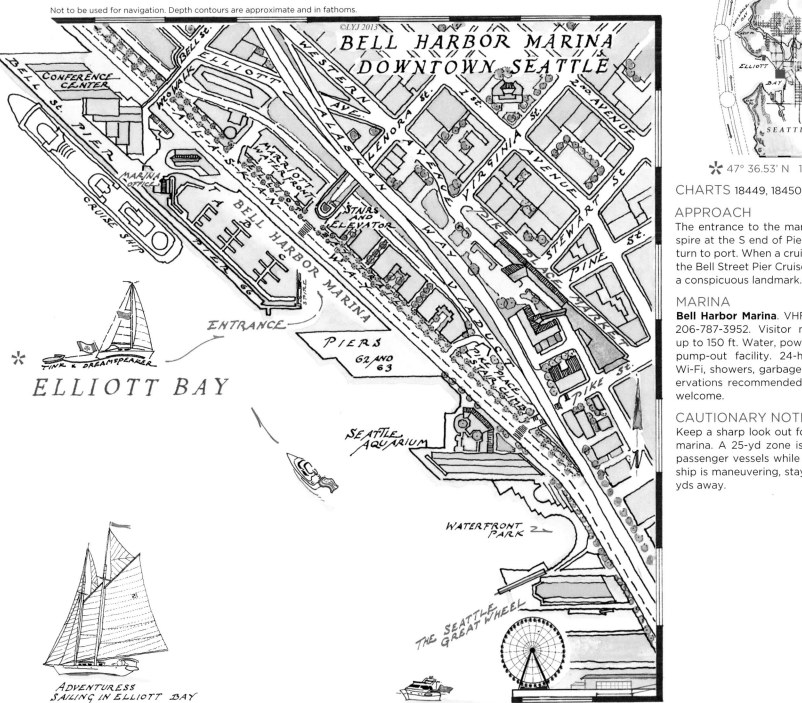

©LYJ 2013

BELL HARBOR MARINA DOWNTOWN SEATTLE

ELLIOTT BAY

TINK & DREAMSPEAKER

ADVENTURESS SAILING IN ELLIOTT BAY

CONFERENCE CENTER

MARINA OFFICE

BELL HARBOR MARINA

ENTRANCE

PIERS 62 AND 63

SEATTLE AQUARIUM

WATERFRONT PARK

THE SEATTLE GREAT WHEEL

✳ 47° 36.53' N 122° 21.00' W

CHARTS 18449, 18450

APPROACH

The entrance to the marina is marked by a spire at the S end of Pier 66. The run in is a turn to port. When a cruise ship is docked at the Bell Street Pier Cruise Terminal, it makes a conspicuous landmark.

MARINA

Bell Harbor Marina. VHF Channel 66A; call 206-787-3952. Visitor moorage for boats up to 150 ft. Water, power to 100 amps and pump-out facility. 24-hour security. Free Wi-Fi, showers, garbage and recycling. Reservations recommended. Groups and clubs welcome.

CAUTIONARY NOTE

Keep a sharp look out for boats exiting the marina. A 25-yd zone is in effect for large passenger vessels while moored. If a cruise ship is maneuvering, stay a minimum of 100 yds away.

4.2 ELLIOTT BAY MARINA

ELLIOTT BAY MARINA

www.elliottbaymarina.com

The fuel dock and check-in facility at Elliott Bay Marina.

Pleasure craft backed by towering cruise ships.

The sandy beach is just a stone's throw from the visiting cruise ships.

Elliott Bay Marina is tucked below the dramatic 200-foot-high expanse of Magnolia Bluff, just west of the Smith Cove Cruise Terminal. Extensive and well maintained, the marina is protected by a 2,700-foot rock breakwater. Slipping into the marina via the west entrance, we backed *Dreamspeaker* into our allotted berth minutes before the skies opened to welcome us with a grand Seattle downpour.

The marina grounds are built on fill and are artfully landscaped with trees and shrubs to create a parklike setting with walking and biking paths. Head west along the waterfront path to the sculptured granite bench and enjoy the views across Elliott Bay to Bainbridge Island and the Olympic Mountains. A stroll east from the marina office leads to a delightful white-sand beach and grassy park, just a stone's throw from the gigantic visiting cruise ships and downtown Seattle.

The marina office staff make visitors feel right at home and will provide concierge services and a list of on-site marine businesses. Call ahead of time to arrange transportation to downtown Seattle and the airport. Laurence and I took the marina's complimentary bikes and cycled to Whole Foods Market and QFC for a spot of provisioning. We then continued along the Elliott Bay Trail to downtown Seattle for a fun ride on the Seattle Great Wheel.

The upper-view level of the marina complex is home to the elegant Palisade Restaurant, with a reputation for fine dining. In partnership with the marina, they offer visitors a complimentary Town Car Service into Seattle and invite you to enjoy their pre-departure happy hour or a nightcap on your return. On the lower level, Maggie Bluffs cafe offers a casual, family-friendly menu, and its outdoor deck, shaded by colorful umbrellas, provides a sociable meeting place with a pleasant waterfront vista.

FUN FACTS

The spacious and pristine showers and restrooms at Elliott Bay Marina make "getting clean" a pleasure!

A water shuttle will transport you from the marina fuel dock to the viewing platform on the rock breakwater, specifically designed to protect the area's marine plant and animal life. The view is stupendous, and interpretative signs give the history of Elliott Bay and the eco-friendly construction of this privately owned marina.

It takes approximately one hour to bike (at a leisurely pace) along the Elliott Bay Trail to downtown Seattle. We had a most enjoyable time doing this, although the trail surface was a little bumpy in some spots, and our side trip to provision had to be navigated on busy roads.

Discovery Park, on the plateau of Magnolia Bluff, is Seattle's largest and most popular city park. Amenities include a Native American cultural center and well-maintained nature, hiking and biking trails. On summer weekends, the park runs a shuttle bus between the visitor center and the beach at West Point.

ELLIOTT BAY MARINA 4.2

Not to be used for navigation. Depth contours are approximate and in fathoms.

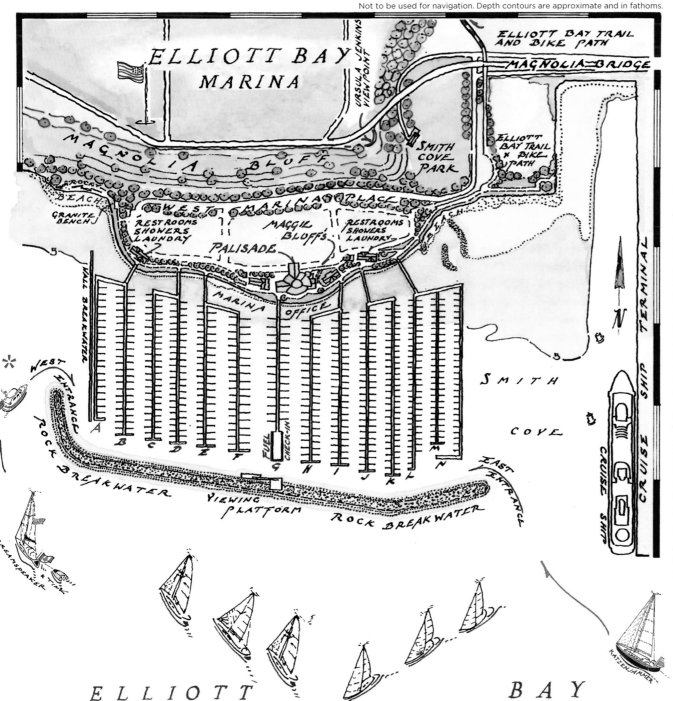

✳ 47° 37.73' N   122° 24.00' W

CHARTS 18449, 18450

APPROACH

The marina is conspicuous below Magnolia Bluff and W of the Smith Cove Cruise Terminal. Enter by rounding either end of the breakwater.

MARINA

Elliott Bay Marina. VHF Channel 78A; call 206-285-4817. Visitor moorage for boats up to 150 ft. Water, power to 100 amps and pump-out facility. Deckhand line assistance. 24-hour security. Free cable TV at each slip, and free Wi-Fi at the office. Showers, garbage, recycling and waste oil collection. Laundry facilities. On-site boat repair. Reservations recommended for boats 50 ft and up.

FUEL

The fuel dock is owned by Elliott Bay Marina. VHF Channel 78A; call 206-282-8424. Gasoline, diesel and pump-out facility. Convenient check-in. Store carries a good selection of staples, fresh and frozen meats, ice, wine, beer, boat supplies, tide tables and travel guides, snacks and bait.

CAUTIONARY NOTE

A 25-yd zone is in effect for large passenger vessels while moored. If a cruise ship is maneuvering, stay a minimum of 100 yds away.

4.3 SHILSHOLE BAY MARINA

SHILSHOLE BAY MARINA

A PORT OF SEATTLE PROPERTY

www.portseattle.org

The contemporary marina offices and plaza.

Generous fairways for large vessels.

The statue of Leif Erikson towers above Anne.

Located south of Golden Gardens Park, and with more than 1,400 slips, Shilshole Bay Marina has undergone major upgrades and offers first-rate moorage facilities, new concrete floats, generous fairways and a pleasantly landscaped foreshore, making this facility popular with boaters who require secure visitor, permanent and live-aboard moorage.

With *Dreamspeaker* neatly tucked into her reserved visitor slip, Laurence and I checked into the new, contemporary-style marina offices, where a sculptured plaza leads to a pocket garden edged with natural grasses and native plants. You can't miss the larger-than-life Leif Erikson statue as he surveys the modern facilities.

Shilshole Bay Marina is a popular destination with local residents for its splendid views out to Puget Sound and the Olympic Mountains, as well as over a mile of public promenade and a fishing pier at the north entrance. Stop for a legendary soft-serve ice cream at Little Coney before visiting the enchanting Golden Gardens Park. Alternatively, the Burke-Gilman Trail, east of Seaview Avenue, is a popular recreational trail for walkers, runners, cyclists and commuters.

It's a pleasant half-mile stroll south along the Seaview Avenue walking/biking path to Anthony's HomePort Restaurant and Ray's Boathouse & Cafe. Ballard Sails & Yacht Services and Purple Cow Espresso are located across the street from the small but busy Paseo restaurant. This Seattle institution serves mouth-watering Caribbean sandwiches, and the Onion Obsession Sandwich is a delicious experience – take-out and cash only!

A one-mile walk will take you to the lively neighborhood of Ballard, where shops, bookstores, restaurants, cafes and pubs abound, and provisioning is a pleasure. The Metro bus stop is located outside the marina building, and buses run regularly from Monday to Friday. When staff are available, the marina office will arrange a courtesy shuttle between 8 a.m. and 4:30 p.m.

SHILSHOLE BAY MARINA 4.3

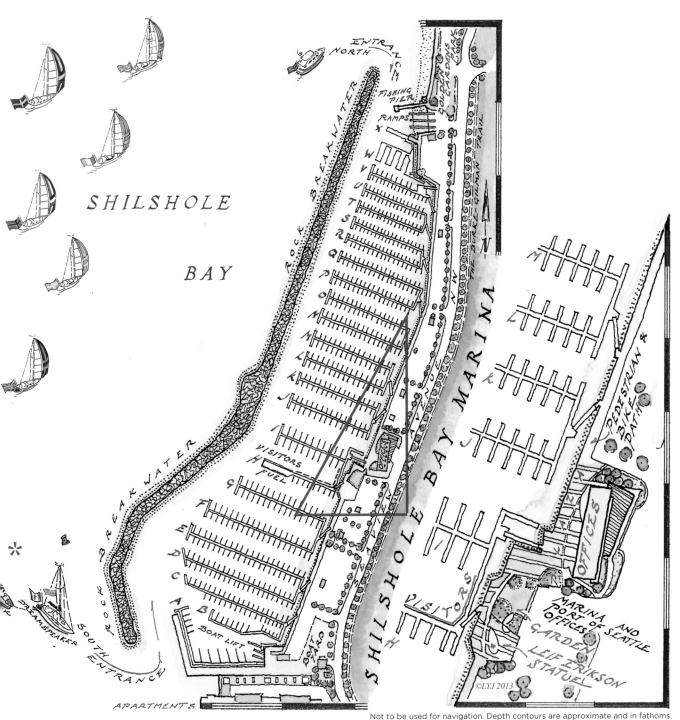

SHILSHOLE

BAY

✳ 12° 12.12'N   12°12.12'N

CHARTS 18449, 18450

APPROACH
An extensive rock breakwater runs parallel to the Shilshole Bay shoreline. Enter the marina by rounding either end of the breakwater.

MARINA
Shilshole Bay Marina. VHF Channel 17; call 206-787-3006, or after hours, 206-601-4089. Visitor moorage for boats up to 250 ft. Water, power to 100 amps and pump-out facility. 24-hour security. Free cable TV, garbage, recycling and waste oil and hazmat collection. Shower and laundry facilities. Reservations recommended.

FUEL
Shilshole Bay Fuel Dock. Open 7 days a week. VHF Channel 17; call 206-783-7555. Gasoline, diesel and CNG. The store carries ice, basic groceries, wine, beer and guidebooks. Free bilge and sewage pump-out. Seaview West is an on-site, full-service boatyard; call 206-783-6550. Propane and an excellent selection of marine supplies and parts are available at their chandlery.

CAUTIONARY NOTE
If approaching from the SW by rounding West Point, be aware of shoal
water off the shoreline of Discovery Park.

©LYJ 2013

Not to be used for navigation. Depth contours are approximate and in fathoms.

Burlington-Northern Railroad Bridge.

Anne signals Ballard Bridge.

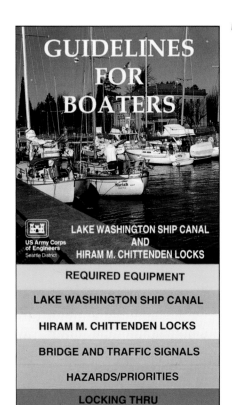
This invaluable brochure is courtesy of the U.S. Army Corps of Engineers.

The man-made, eight-mile-long Lake Washington Ship Canal is 100 feet wide and 30 feet deep and includes the Hiram M. Chittenden Locks, the Fremont Cut and the Montlake Cut. The locks form a permeable barrier between Lake Washington's freshwater ecosystem and the potentially damaging salt water of Puget Sound. Today, the canal provides a safe, navigable passage for commercial and government vessels, barges, recreational boats and kayaks. The locks, which are managed by the U.S. Army Corps of Engineers, consist of a large and a small lock that operate 24 hours a day and move over 70,000 vessels each year.

Innovatively designed by Hiram M. Chittenden and publicly dedicated in 1917, Lake Washington Ship Canal gives recreational vessels a unique opportunity to cruise through the urban metropolis of Seattle via Lake Union and Lake Washington. Transiting the locks is a fascinating experience that requires pre-planning to ensure a safe and stress-free passage.

The entrance to Lake Washington Ship Canal is in Shilshole Bay, south of the Shilshole Bay Marina, and is well marked. After passing through the locks into Lake Union, fuel, marine supplies and boat repair are readily available. Fishermen's Terminal offers overnight visitor moorage, and day moorage is possible at 24th Avenue Landing in Ballard.

To ensure a safe flow of traffic in the ship canal, a maximum speed limit of 7 knots is enforced; slow down to 2.5 knots or less when entering the locks. The canal passes under seven bridges before entering Lake Washington. If no bridge opening is required, it takes approximately half an hour to Lake Union and an hour to Lake Washington, after exiting the locks.

COMMUNICATION FACTS
VHF Channel 13 is for commercial vessels; pleasure vessels may only use it in an emergency or to listen in and monitor commercial traffic and bridge information.

BRIDGE RAISING
You must know the height of your mast, and be prepared to signal the bridge tender at least 100 yds from the bridge.

The SOUND SIGNAL to open bridges is ONE PROLONGED BLAST, followed by ONE SHORT BLAST of a whistle or horn. For all bridges across the Lake Washington Ship Canal, FIVE SHORT BLASTS of a whistle or horn from any bridge indicates that the draw is not ready to be opened immediately.

FUEL DOCKS
Covich-Williams Chevron (206-784-0171). Open Monday to Saturday. Diesel and gasoline. North side of Salmon Bay Canal. Commercial operation open to recreational vessels.

Ballard Oil Company (206-783-0241). Open Monday to Saturday. Diesel only. Just E of Chittenden Locks. Commercial operation open to recreational vessels.

Morrison's North Star Marine (206-284-6600). Open 7 days a week. Diesel and gasoline. This is a full-service fuel dock catering to commercial and recreational vessels. A grocery store carries ice, snacks, beer, wine and basic marine supplies and accessories. New bump rails installed in 2012.

Shilshole Bay Fuel Dock (see 4.3).

PUBLIC MOORAGE
24th Avenue Landing (no overnight moorage) is E of Fishermen's Terminal (see 4.6). The 300-ft dock is for dinghies and boats under 40 ft. The lively neighborhood of Ballard is a short walk from the dock.

Freemont Bridge commences opening.

Anne signals University Bridge.

Montlake Bridge and Cut.

✳ 47° 40.92' N 122° 25.08' W

CHART 18447

APPROACH
From Shilshole Bay. Run in aligned to the Shilshole Bay Entrance Range.

BRIDGES
Lake Washington Ship Canal is crossed by 5 bascule drawbridges and 2 fixed bridges:

1. **Burlington-Northern Railroad Bridge** (206-784-2976). Central vertical clearance is 41 ft. Open 24 hours. If drawbridge is closed, a train is due to cross.
2. **Ballard Bridge** (206-720-3048). Central vertical clearance is 30 ft. Closed 7 to 9 a.m. and 4 to 6 p.m. weekdays, and during special events.
3. **Fremont Bridge** (206-720-3048). Central vertical clearance is 30 ft. Closed 7 to 9 a.m. and 4 to 6 p.m. weekdays, and during special events.
4. **Aurora Bridge** (George Washington Memorial Bridge). Fixed span. Central vertical clearance is 135 ft.
5. **I-5 Ship Canal Bridge**. Fixed span. Central vertical clearance is 127 ft.
6. **University Bridge** (206-720-3048). Central vertical clearance is 42 ft. Closed 7 to 9 a.m. and 4 to 6 p.m. weekdays, and during special events.
7. **Montlake Bridge** (206-720-3048). Central vertical clearance is 46 ft. Opens on the hour and half hour 12:30 to 3:30 p.m. weekdays. Closed from 7 to 10 a.m. weekdays, and during special events. Closed 3:30 to 6:30 p.m. May through August, and 3:30 to 7 p.m. October through April.

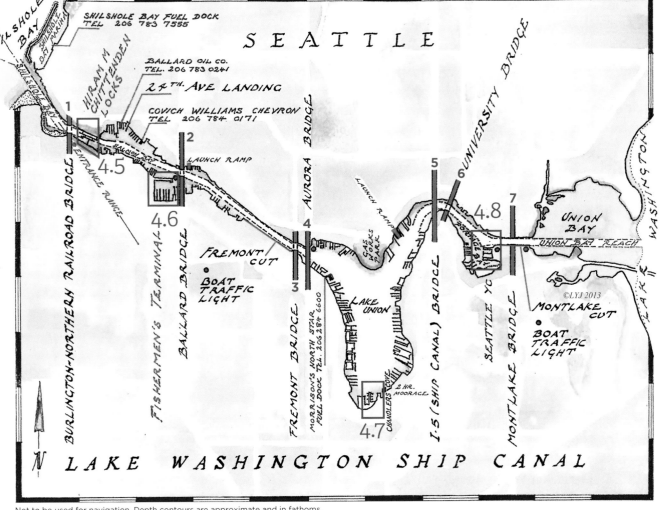

Not to be used for navigation. Depth contours are approximate and in fathoms.

4.5 HIRAM M. CHITTENDEN LOCKS

Anne tends the bow line.

Dreamspeaker exits the small lock.

CHITTENDEN LOCK FACTS
Completed in 1917, the Chittenden Locks are the link between the fresh water of Lake Washington Ship Canal and the salt water of Puget Sound. The locks are raised and lowered – from 20 to 22 feet – solely by the force of gravity.

If you are planning to lock through for the first time, pop into the visitor center, where you will find the essential *Guidelines for Boaters* booklet. The center also offers free locking-through workshops, an orientation video, which covers the history of the locks, and guided tours. Call 206-783-7059.

FUN FACTS
For those not locking through, it's great fun to watch those who are. Spectators are fascinated by the seemingly "magical" process of the raising and lowering of water levels in the locks. A walking path crosses the locks and Spillway Dam and leads to the fish ladder, which has a glass-fronted viewing gallery. This allows visitors to witness salmon migration throughout most of the year, which is a thrilling and educational experience for all ages.

Stroll through the beautiful, classic-style Carl S. English Jr. Botanical Garden. Filled with trees, shrubs and flowers from around the world, this is the perfect spot to relax and enjoy a picnic on the shaded, lush green lawns.

Boat exiting the small lock.

Locking through the Chittenden Locks is a straightforward experience if your boat has the required equipment, and your skipper and crew listen to the specific instructions given by the lock attendants. Recreational vessels will require adequate fenders attached to either side of the boat and two 50-foot mooring lines (bow and stern), each with a 12-inch eye-splice. When the signal lights to enter the lock are red, tie up at the waiting pier. When the lights turn green, listen for instructions over the public address system. The small lock is the primary one used by recreational vessels and kayaks. If the small lock is backed up, vessels will be directed to use the large one.

SMALL LOCK – The small lock has a floating guide wall to moor alongside. On entering, a lock attendant will indicate which side of the lock chamber to proceed to and the number of the yellow mooring button to loop your lines around. These must then be fastened securely around the boat cleat (stern line first). After the chamber is filled, keep your lines secured while the gates are being opened, but be prepared to release them in an emergency.

A little intimidating for small boats.

LARGE LOCK – Commercial and large vessels will be directed to moor alongside the dock walls, while smaller boats will be instructed to raft alongside these vessels. The large dock does not have a floating guide wall to tie up to. Listen for instructions, and pass your lines with the eye-splice to the attendant, who will attach them to the mooring buttons. The boater's end of the line should be held with a half figure eight so that it can be paid out or taken up smoothly. After the chamber is filled, keep your lines secured while the gates are being opened, but be prepared to release them in an emergency.

HIRAM M. CHITTENDEN LOCKS 4.5

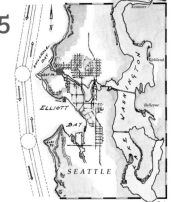

LOCK DIMENSIONS
Small Lock: 30 x 150 ft
Large Lock: 80 x 820 ft

NOTE
VHF Channel 13 is for commercial traffic and is to be used only in an emergency.

At first you're up ...

Then you're down!

LEGEND		TRAFFIC LIGHTS		
		Salt water barrier		
Salt	Salt water barrier light	Lights Off	○	Down
L	Large Lock light	Lights On	○	Up
S	Small Lock light	Lock lights		
	Storm warning	Red	●	Stop
C	Control Tower	Green	●	Proceed

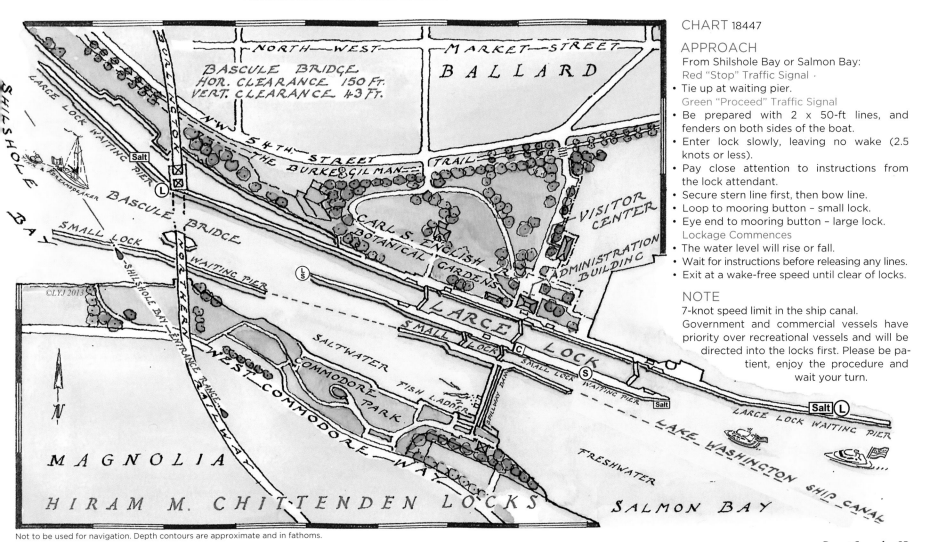

Not to be used for navigation. Depth contours are approximate and in fathoms.

CHART 18447

APPROACH
From Shilshole Bay or Salmon Bay:
Red "Stop" Traffic Signal ·
- Tie up at waiting pier.
Green "Proceed" Traffic Signal
- Be prepared with 2 x 50-ft lines, and fenders on both sides of the boat.
- Enter lock slowly, leaving no wake (2.5 knots or less).
- Pay close attention to instructions from the lock attendant.
- Secure stern line first, then bow line.
- Loop to mooring button – small lock.
- Eye end to mooring button – large lock.
Lockage Commences
- The water level will rise or fall.
- Wait for instructions before releasing any lines.
- Exit at a wake-free speed until clear of locks.

NOTE
7-knot speed limit in the ship canal.
Government and commercial vessels have priority over recreational vessels and will be directed into the locks first. Please be patient, enjoy the procedure and wait your turn.

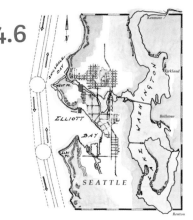

Fishermen's Terminal. Port of Seattle Photo.

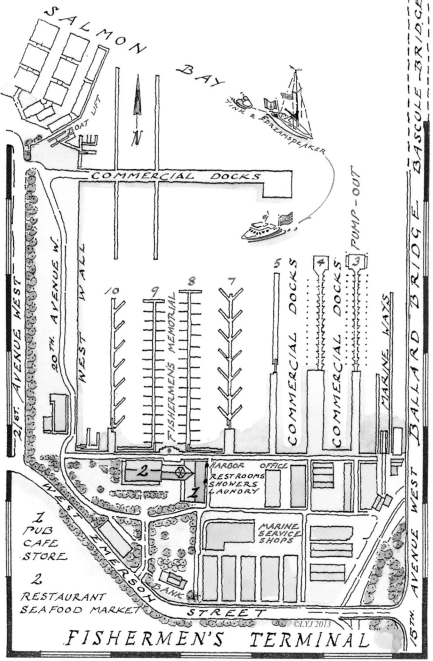

Home port of the North Pacific fishing fleet since 1914, historic Fishermen's Terminal has recently undergone major upgrades, which include new concrete floating docks and wide fairways. Just one mile east of the Hiram M. Chittenden Locks, this is the perfect spot to tie up and enjoy the marina's moorage facilities and welcoming on-site eateries and stores, as well as visit the lively district of Ballard by water – it's only a short trip to 24th Avenue Landing, where free day moorage is available (see 4.4).

Fishermen's Terminal is a popular location, where the Bay Cafe serves hearty breakfast dishes, Chinook's menu includes inviting happy hour drinks and appetizers and the newly renovated Highliner pub specializes in craft-brewed ales. The Fishermen's Green Market & Deli stocks organic produce, and we are told that Seattleites will drive for miles to shop at the Wild Salmon Seafood Market.

CHART 18447

APPROACH
From the W out of Salmon Bay. The entrance is adjacent to Ballard Bridge. Enter by rounding the outer commercial dock.

MARINA
Fishermen's Terminal. VHF Channel 17; call 206-787-3395 for slip assignment. Visitor moorage for boats up to 125 ft. Water, power to 50 amps (rates inclusive of power) and pump-out facility. 24-hour security. Free 4-hour visitor moorage, garbage, recycling and waste oil disposal. Shower and laundry facilities. Repair facilities on site.

FISHERMEN'S TERMINAL

A PORT OF SEATTLE PROPERTY

www.portseattle.org

Not to be used for navigation. Depth contours are approximate and in fathoms.

The scene on Lake Union – colorful catamarans and luxury yachts.

A university scull cuts past the Seattle Yacht Club Optimist fleet in Portage Bay.

4.7 CHANDLER'S COVE,
Lake Union

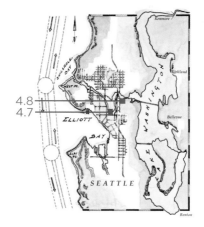

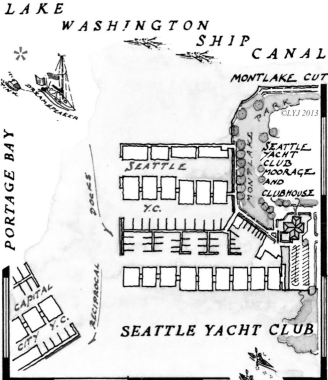

©LYJ 2013

Not to be used for navigation. Depth contours are approximate and in fathoms.

A choice of first-rate restaurants, the superb Museum of History and Industry (MOHAI), the inspiring Center for Wooden Boats and the expanded Lake Union Park are all accessible to boaters from Chandler's Cove. Providing public access to the water, the park celebrates the region's rich maritime and cultural heritage and includes 12 acres of imaginatively landscaped green space, a restored shoreline habitat, a tree grove and picnic area, grassy mounds and a 300-foot interactive fountain.

4.8 SEATTLE YACHT CLUB, Portage Bay

Fortunate to find space at the Seattle Yacht Club reciprocity dock, Laurence and I decided to join in the club's weekly family night sailing event. We managed a good number of thrilling tacks and jibs across Portage Bay, trying not to capsize our 17-foot dinghy or add more bruises to our knees. We were also inspired by fellow boaters who were enjoying a biking and boating cruise, as Seattle has an extensive network of well-maintained hiking and biking trails.

4.7

✳ 47° 37.77' N   122° 20.09' W

CHART 18447

APPROACH
From the N – the run in is clear. Keep in mind that Lake Union is busy with boat activity, especially on weekends.

ANCHOR
2-hour visitor moorage for restaurant patrons and visitors to the museum, the park and The Center for Wooden Boats.

4.8

✳ 47° 38.82' N   122° 18.79' W

CHART 18447

APPROACH
Portage Bay lies S between University Bridge and Montlake Bridge. It is shoal S of the marinas.

ANCHOR
Reciprocal moorage at the Seattle Yacht Club and Capital City Yacht Club.

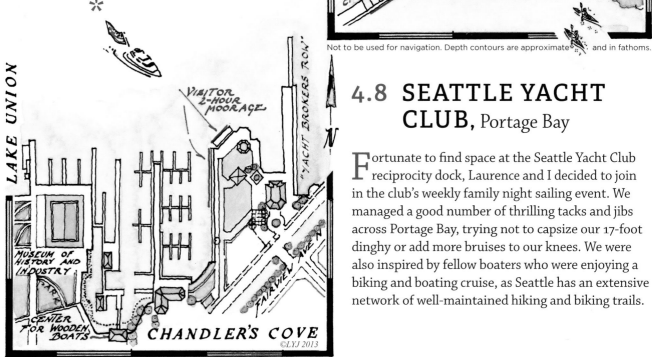

©LYJ 2013

Not to be used for navigation. Depth contours are approximate and in fathoms.

KIRKLAND, Lake Washington

Not to be used for navigation. Depth contours are approximate and in fathoms.

Kirkland's Thursday evening summer concerts in Marina Park are well attended by local boaters; we squeezed *Dreamspeaker* into the last empty spot on the dock and joined in the festivities. Welcoming and cosmopolitan, with an easygoing personality, downtown Kirkland made us feel right at home.

Pedestrian-friendly streets offer a variety of clothing and lifestyle stores, art galleries, espresso bars, wine-tasting rooms and a choice of fun eateries serving happy hour specials. Well-manicured parks abound, and the picturesque waterfront has a delightful swimming beach.

For provisioning, QFC is a pleasant 15-minute walk up Kirkland Avenue to 6th Street, and the Kirkland Wednesday Market is located on Park Lane from 2 to 7 p.m. Rococo Coffee Roasting serves fine coffee and teas and has free Wi-Fi, and the Cactus restaurant and Santorini Greek Grill are local favorites.

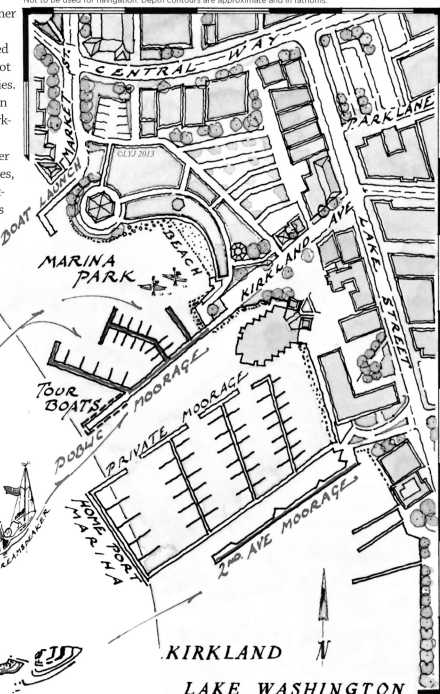

4.9

✳ 47° 40.36' N 122° 12.54' W

CHART 18447

APPROACH
From the W for Marina Park and 2nd Avenue visitor moorage. Although the run in is clear, keep a look out for small craft maneuvering in and out of the slips.

MARINA
Moss Bay is open to the N and S. Marina Park and 2nd Avenue dock visitor moorage is operated by the City of Kirkland on a first-come basis. Public pay stations are at the head of both docks. You cannot reserve your slip if you leave and wish to return. Power to 20 amps on the S side of Marina Park dock only. Inside slips primarily for small boats.

LAUNCH
Operated by the City of Kirkland; call 425-587-3332 for information.

NOTE
Boat activity in Moss Bay can make moorage at the docks rather bumpy.

Not to be used for navigation. Depth contours are approximate and in fathoms.

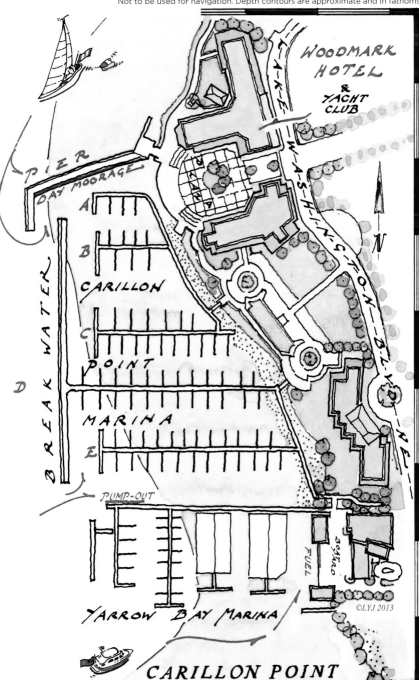

Carillon Point's Woodmark Hotel is the perfect lunch stop. Treat yourself to a meal at one of their two lakeside restaurants. Bin on the Lake serves Mediterranean-inspired Pacific Northwest dishes in a stylish yet relaxed atmosphere, while the Beach Cafe specializes in more casual fare in a friendly and fun setting. Both establishments have magnificent waterfront views and offer happy hour specials. The hotel spa provides an alternative indulgence – relax with a hot stone massage, European facial or a pampering manicure and pedicure.

The upscale shopping complex adjacent to the hotel includes clothing and jewelry boutiques, a hair and makeup salon and a relaxed coffee shop with free Wi-Fi.

✴ 47° 39.26' N 122° 12.57' W

CHART 18447

APPROACH
Carillon Point Marina and Yarrow Bay Marina and fuel dock from the SW. Carillon Point Marina and public pier from the NW. The guest pier offers complimentary 2-hour visitor moorage on a first-come basis. Boats over 36 ft are required to use the outside of the pier.

MARINAS
Carillon Point Marina; call 425-822-1700. Visitor moorage on a first-come basis, when available; call ahead. Power to 50 amps on the docks. Free Wi-Fi and showers are available.

Yarrow Bay Marina and fuel dock; call 425-822-6066. Gasoline, diesel and marine parts. Pump-out and haulout facilities, and repairs, are available. The marina is private.

BELLEVUE, Meydenbauer Bay

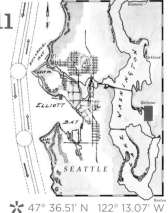

✳ 47° 36.51' N 122° 13.07' W

CHART 18447

APPROACH
Meydenbauer Bay from the SW – there are no obstructions. Depths of 30 - 40 ft in the bay.

ANCHOR
We found comfortable anchorage for the night off Meydenbauer Bay Park, in line with the speed-limit marker buoys and out of the way of local traffic. Good holding in mud, in 20+ ft.

PUBLIC DOCK
No shore access from the park or street ends (2013). Proposed visitor day moorage, located at the S end of Bellevue Place and provided by the City of Bellevue, will be available in late 2013/early 2014. All marinas are private. The Meydenbauer Bay Yacht Club in Whalers Cove offers reciprocal moorage.

NOTE
Dinghy access to the park and downtown Bellevue will be available at the new public docks in late 2013/early 2014.

In the 1940s Bellevue was one of the last active whaling ports in the United States. Today, what remains of the pier and warehouse are now owned by the city and will become an integral part of the new visitor moorage and park development proposed for late 2013/early 2014.

We enjoyed our evening anchored in Meydenbauer Bay, lazing in *Dreamspeaker's* cosy cockpit, surrounded by lavish homes with luxurious landscaped gardens and stylish private docks. Fascinated by the general feeling of opulence, we explored Whalers Cove in *Tink*,

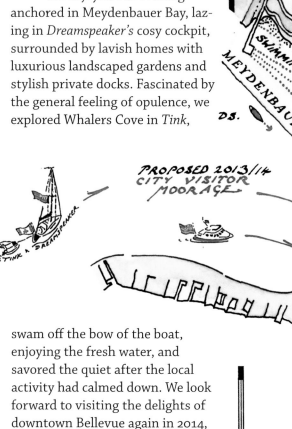

swam off the bow of the boat, enjoying the fresh water, and savored the quiet after the local activity had calmed down. We look forward to visiting the delights of downtown Bellevue again in 2014, which will be accessible from the new public dock.

©LYJ 2013

Not to be used for navigation. Depth contours are approximate and in fathoms.

Situated on the northeast end of Mercer Island, 77-acre Luther Burbank Park is beautifully landscaped and features sweeping green lawns and grassy knolls, spectacular views of Lake Washington, a community and events center, well-tended flower gardens, an excellent kids' play area, tennis courts and maintained trails for walking and running.

Dropping anchor adjacent to the park's grassy shoreline and small pebble beach, we rowed to the wooden park dock. The park has two public docks, a designated fishing pier and an inviting swimming beach. This is an exceptionally dog-friendly park, and Calkins Point is an official off-leash area. Happily, much of the park has been left undeveloped to foster a variety of wildlife, many of which live in the wetlands that occupy the north and south ends of the park.

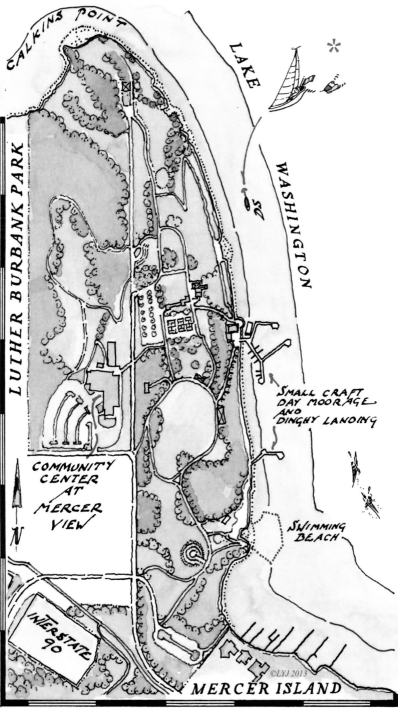

Not to be used for navigation. Depth contours are approximate and in fathoms.

✻ 47° 35.68' N 122° 13.28' W

CHART 18447

APPROACH
The park is situated along the NE tip of Mercer Island, below Calkins Point. The run in is clear.

ANCHOR
Luther Burbank Park confirmed that day anchorage is in fact available along the E shore of the park, N of the public docks. Good holding in mud, in 20+ feet.

PUBLIC DOCKS
The visitor docks are for day moorage only and are designed mainly for small craft, dinghies and kayaks, although larger boats can be accommodated. Call 206-275-7609.

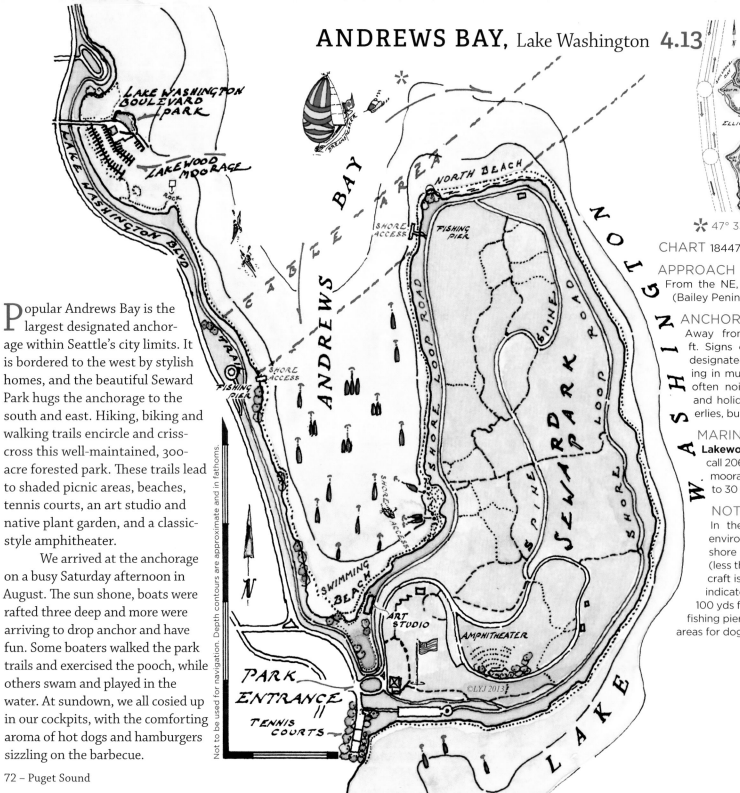

ANDREWS BAY, Lake Washington 4.13

✳ 47° 33.89' N 122° 15.34' W

CHART 18447

APPROACH
From the NE, off the tip of Seward Park (Bailey Peninsula). The run in is clear.

ANCHOR
Away from the cabled area in 20+ ft. Signs on shore indicate the bay's designated anchoring zone. Good holding in mud. This is an extremely busy, often noisy anchorage on weekends and holidays. Open to summer northerlies, but well protected from the S.

MARINA
Lakewood Moorage; call 206-722-3887. Some visitor moorage available; call ahead. Power to 30 amps and laundry facilities.

NOTE
In the interest of protecting the environmentally sensitive areas, onshore landing of small powerboats (less than 10 hp) and non-motorized craft is permitted ONLY at two sites indicated on the chart. Please stay 100 yds from the swimming beach and fishing pier. The park has many off-leash areas for dogs.

Popular Andrews Bay is the largest designated anchorage within Seattle's city limits. It is bordered to the west by stylish homes, and the beautiful Seward Park hugs the anchorage to the south and east. Hiking, biking and walking trails encircle and crisscross this well-maintained, 300-acre forested park. These trails lead to shaded picnic areas, beaches, tennis courts, an art studio and native plant garden, and a classic-style amphitheater.

We arrived at the anchorage on a busy Saturday afternoon in August. The sun shone, boats were rafted three deep and more were arriving to drop anchor and have fun. Some boaters walked the park trails and exercised the pooch, while others swam and played in the water. At sundown, we all cosied up in our cockpits, with the comforting aroma of hot dogs and hamburgers sizzling on the barbecue.

Not to be used for navigation. Depth contours are approximate and in fathoms.

Chapter 5

BAINBRIDGE ISLAND
& BLAKE ISLAND State Park

Eagle Harbor & Blakely Harbor to Port Madison

A sailboat glides into Eagle Harbor.

Eagle Harbor & Blakely Harbor to Port Madison

Young Optimist sailors take a lesson in Eagle Harbor.

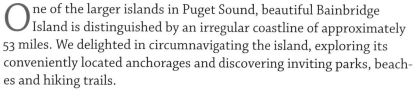

One of the larger islands in Puget Sound, beautiful Bainbridge Island is distinguished by an irregular coastline of approximately 53 miles. We delighted in circumnavigating the island, exploring its conveniently located anchorages and discovering inviting parks, beaches and hiking trails.

Close to Seattle and central Puget Sound, Eagle Harbor provides a handy hopping-off point for destinations north and south. A short cruise south took us from the bustling harbor to the more laid-back Blakely Harbor, with its spectacular views of the Seattle skyline and the Cascade Mountains to the east. Although close to major urban centers, the harbor, which has a pristine forested backdrop and natural wildlife areas, offers a feeling of tranquility.

Once again following the path of Captain Vancouver, we rounded the southern tip of Restoration Point through to Rich Passage, Port Orchard and the inner shores of Bainbridge Island. Tucked into the northwest corner, Manzanita Bay is a peaceful spot to drop anchor. Every Memorial Day weekend there is a gathering of beautifully restored wooden motor boats in the bay that is well worth seeing. Then, heading north, we tucked into protected Port Madison, where we located road access to the magnificent Bloedel Reserve. "Inner Port Madison," as locals call it, also has a small dock that allows access to charming Hidden Cove Park.

Blake Island, which is only accessible by boat, lies in the middle of Puget Sound, just seven nautical miles from Seattle. The island has been a refuge for bootleggers smuggling alcohol from Canada, the private residence of Seattle industrialist William Trimble and a U.S. army garrison. Today, it is a popular state park, and Tillicum Village, on the island's northeast end, is a showcase for Northwest Coast Indian arts, culture and food.

TIDES
Tide Height Station: Seattle

CURRENTS
Tidal Current Station: Bush Point

WEATHER
NOAA Weather Radio WX4: Puget Sound
NOAA VHF Weather Channel 1 or 3
www.nws.noaa.gov/nwr

FACTS
Once only accessible by boat, Bainbridge Island is connected to the Kitsap Peninsula by the Agate Pass Bridge. Washington State Ferries offers regular service between Eagle Harbor and Pier 52 in Seattle. Made up of farms, artisan wineries and distinctive galleries, shops and restaurants, the island is frequented by a steady stream of visitors and day trippers. It has, however, become somewhat of an affluent bedroom community of Seattle, with much of its population commuting there each day. Fortunately, the local Island Land Trust has kept a tight control over development and is maintaining the island's natural, open green spaces.

The handy *Bainbridge Island Map: A Guide to Destinations by Foot, Bike and Kayak* is a must-have for those who want to explore the island by walking or by using alternative transportation. Rent a bike at Barn Rentals, June to October; call 206-842-3434. Classic Cycle rents bikes from October to the second week in June; call 206-842-9191.

Kitsap Tours will pick boaters up from the City Dock or the marinas. They offer scheduled tours that explore Bainbridge Island and its colorful communities, as well as the beautiful Bloedel Reserve. Custom tours can also be arranged; call 877-877-1950.

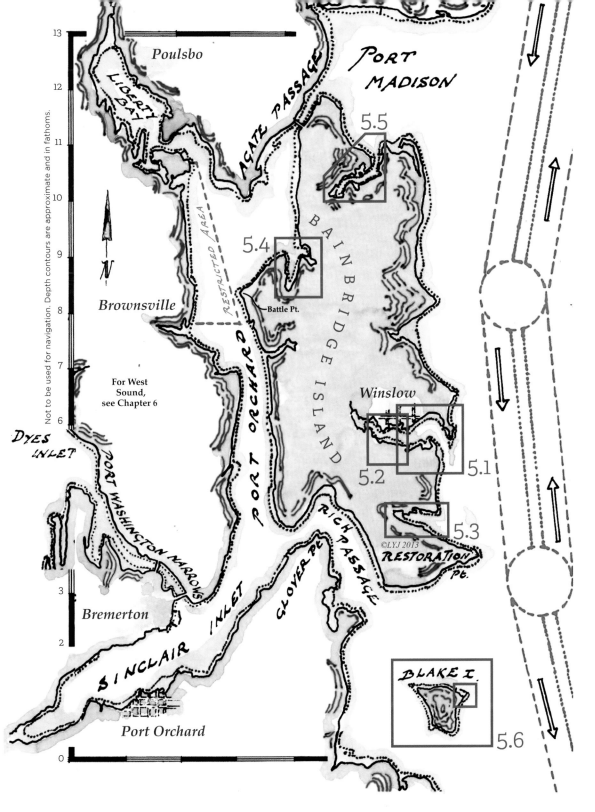

5 BAINBRIDGE ISLAND &BLAKE ISLAND
State Park

FEATURED DESTINATIONS

FUEL
There are no fuel facilities. Closest are Elliott Bay Marina (see 4.2), and Port of Brownsville Marina, Port Orchard (see 6.4)

PUMP-OUT FACILITIES
5.2 Eagle Harbor City Dock; 5.6 Blake Island Marina

CAUTIONARY NOTE
Restricted area Port Orchard. Flashing red lights on Navy range vessels between Keyport and Brownsville and atop a building at the seaward end of the southern buildings at Keyport Naval Undersea Warfare Center indicates that the restricted area is operational. Stay inshore along the Bainbridge Island shore to Battle Pt.

The Bainbridge-Seattle ferry departs Eagle Harbor.

Not to be used for navigation. Depth contours are approximate and in fathoms.

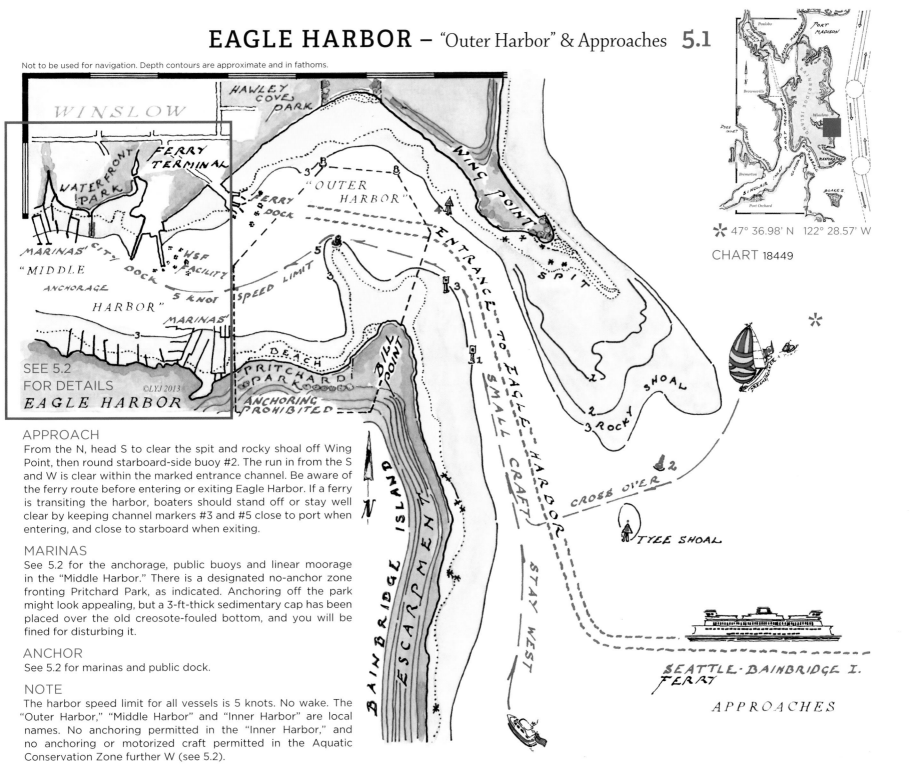

47° 36.98' N   122° 28.57' W

CHART 18449

APPROACH

From the N, head S to clear the spit and rocky shoal off Wing Point, then round starboard-side buoy #2. The run in from the S and W is clear within the marked entrance channel. Be aware of the ferry route before entering or exiting Eagle Harbor. If a ferry is transiting the harbor, boaters should stand off or stay well clear by keeping channel markers #3 and #5 close to port when entering, and close to starboard when exiting.

MARINAS

See 5.2 for the anchorage, public buoys and linear moorage in the "Middle Harbor." There is a designated no-anchor zone fronting Pritchard Park, as indicated. Anchoring off the park might look appealing, but a 3-ft-thick sedimentary cap has been placed over the old creosote-fouled bottom, and you will be fined for disturbing it.

ANCHOR

See 5.2 for marinas and public dock.

NOTE

The harbor speed limit for all vessels is 5 knots. No wake. The "Outer Harbor," "Middle Harbor" and "Inner Harbor" are local names. No anchoring permitted in the "Inner Harbor," and no anchoring or motorized craft permitted in the Aquatic Conservation Zone further W (see 5.2).

5.2 EAGLE HARBOR – *"Middle Harbor"* & Winslow Village

The Winslow waterfront has a village-like ambience.

Anne finally finds her destiny!

A bell tower adds to Winslow's character.

Eagle Harbor and the small-town charm of Winslow Village are only a 35-minute ferry ride from downtown Seattle and even less by private motorized craft, making the protected harbor a popular boating destination in the summer months. To the north, south and west, the harbor is surrounded by an abundance of marinas and private docks, luxurious homes and the scenic Waterfront Trail. To the east, the impressive panorama of Seattle's towering skyline looms large.

With *Dreamspeaker* snugly at anchor, Laurence and I rowed to the City Dock, which is backed by the lawns, tennis courts and children's playground of Waterfront Park. Securing *Tink*, we set off to locate the local visitor center to pick up biking maps and brochures, as Bainbridge Island has also become a popular cycling destination.

Winslow is a very walkable and friendly town, with easy provisioning at the Town & Country Market (across the street from the playground) and an overwhelming choice of tasteful shops and specialty stores (including Churchmouse Yarns & Teas, a fabulous yarn store), art galleries, bookstores, cafes, cosy lunch spots, bakeries, handcrafted confectionary and ice cream stops, waterfront pubs, one-of-a-kind restaurants and wine shops with tasting rooms.

After a delicious lunch on the shaded patio of Pegasus Coffee House, we joined the waterfront's West Loop Trail. Landscaped with native plants, grasses and trees, the trail twists around the marina district and harbor-view eateries. We dropped into Chandlery Marine at Winslow Wharf for our favorite boating magazines, before continuing up Madison Avenue S to Waterfront Park. Here the trail continues east along the shoreline, past the groves of madrona trees, picnic tables and benches to a footbridge that crosses a wooded ravine. The trail turns south to the site of the old Hall Brothers Shipyard, where traces of the marine railway can be seen at low water.

LOCAL FACTS

At the Bainbridge Island Chamber of Commerce and visitor center on Winslow Way E and Bjune Drive SE, pick up a *Walking Tour of Historic Winslow* brochure, which features a guide to Winslow's many historic homes and buildings, as well as interesting information on the history of the founding families of Bainbridge Island. The small brochure titled *Bathrooms of Bainbridge* could also come in handy!

Take time to visit the Bainbridge Island Historical Museum in the renovated 1908 schoolhouse on Erickson Avenue NE and Winslow Way E. Their new long-term exhibit, "An Island Story," takes visitors on a multimedia voyage through island history. Open Wednesday to Sunday, 1 to 4 p.m.

The Bainbridge Island Farmers' Market runs at the Town Square at City Hall, off Madison Avenue N, every Saturday from 9 a.m. to 2 p.m., April through November.

FUN FACTS

Enjoy a walkable wine-tasting tour along Winslow Way E. Sip a glass of delicious Bainbridge Island wine at Eagle Harbor Wine Company, Eleven Winery, Harbor Square Wine Shop & Tasting Room and Island Vintners.

Take in a show at Bainbridge Performing Arts, located on Madison Avenue N. This is community theater at its best.

©LYJ 2013

WINSLOW

BAINBRIDGE ISLAND FERRY TERMINAL

WINSLOW WAY

WINSLOW GREEN

MADISON AVE

B. JOHN DRIVE

O'BRIEN DRIVE

SHANNON DR.

POST OFFICE

PROVISIONS

WATERFRONT PARK

OLYMPIC DRIVE

FERRY DOCK

HARBOUR PUBLIC HOUSE

PARFITT WAY

BOAT LAUNCH

FERRY MAINTENANCE FACILITY

CITY DOCK

PILES STAY CLEAR

DREAMSPEAKER & TINK

WINSLOW WHARF

HARBOUR MARINA

OPEN WATER MARINA

LINEAR MOORAGE

EAGLE HARBOR "MIDDLE HARBOR"

EAGLE HARBOR MARINA

BAINBRIDGE I. MARINA

BAINBRIDGE ISLAND

Not to be used for navigation. Depth contours are approximate and in fathoms.

CHART 18449

APPROACH
After clearing the "Outer Harbor," the run in to the "Middle Harbor" is clear.

ANCHOR
The city regulates the Open Water Marina in the protected "Middle Harbor," which operates on a first-come basis. Tie up at their 400 ft of linear moorage, or pick up one of the 4 public buoys. Pay at the City Dock. Ample anchorage in the area, as indicated. Keep a short scope, because of local boats on permanent buoys. Good holding in mud, in 3+ ftm (18+ ft).

PUBLIC DOCK
The City Dock offers 250 ft of visitor moorage for boats up to 70 ft, on a first-come basis. Call the harbormaster at 206-780-3733. No power or water. Showers and a pump-out facility. Visitor kiosk. Moorage limited to 48 hours per week. Shallow depths at N end of dock.

MARINAS
Bainbridge Island Marina & Yacht Club; call 206-953-6767. **Eagle Harbor Marina**; call 206-842-4003. **Winslow Wharf Marina**; call 206-842-4202. **Harbour Marina**; call 206-550-5340. Complimentary tie-up available for Harbour Public House patrons. All private marinas listed offer visitor moorage, if slips are available. Call in advance for availability and reservations.

LAUNCH
The public boat launch is adjacent to the City Dock.

BLAKELY HARBOR

CHART 18449

APPROACH
The run in to Blakely Harbor from the SE is clear, although be aware of the shallow area that dries on the S shore. From the N, a reef extends seaward from an unnamed point and should be given ample clearance.

ANCHOR
E of Blakely Harbor Park and the cabled area. Good holding in mud, in 3+ ftm (18+ ft). Good protection from the N and S. All buoys and docks are private. Public shore access to Blakely Harbor Park; otherwise, all other tidelands are private.

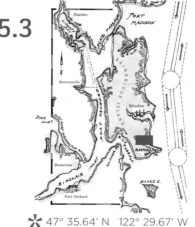

✳ 47° 35.64' N   122° 29.67' W

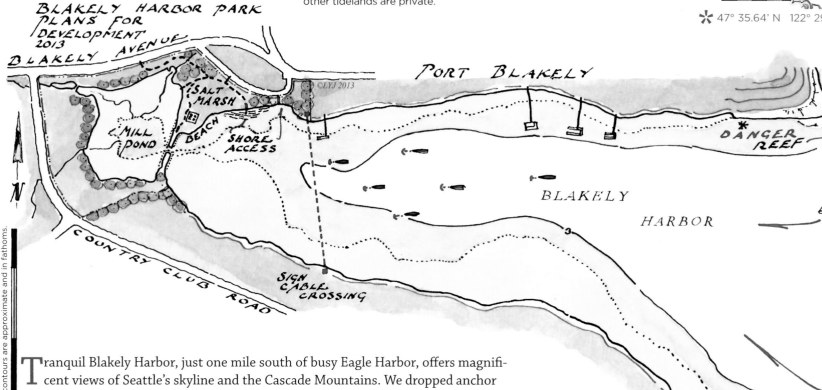

Tranquil Blakely Harbor, just one mile south of busy Eagle Harbor, offers magnificent views of Seattle's skyline and the Cascade Mountains. We dropped anchor west of Port Blakely and spent a pleasant day picnicking on the beach and exploring the stone causeway, Mill Pond and the saltwater marsh that make up Blakely Harbor Park. A half-mile trail winds through the woodlands to Blakely Avenue. Hikers can cross Country Club Road at the southwest corner of the Blakely meadow to pick up the one-mile trail to Fort Ward State Park.

Blakely Harbor Park is on the former site of Port Blakely Mill, which was one of the world's largest sawmills in the late 1800s. The 40-acre park is currently being developed for recreational use, including picnicking, hiking, kayaking and bird-watching.

Not to be used for navigation. Depth contours are approximate and in fathoms.

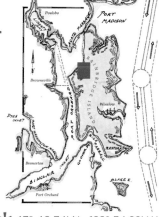

Manzanita Bay provided a peaceful over-night anchorage, with convenient shore access. Laurence and I woke to the shrill chirping of dozens of barn swallows resting and preening on our spreaders and lifelines. One inquisitive bird flew through our forward hatch and departed through the rear companionway!

©LYJ 2013

✳ 47° 40.74' N   122° 34.22' W

CHART 18446

APPROACH
The run in to Manzanita Bay from the way-point is clear.

ANCHOR
As indicated, in Manzanita Bay, with good protection from the S. Good holding in mud, in 3+ ftm (18+ ft). Shore access is best at mid-tide to high water, especially when anchored in Port Orchard.

NOTE
Shore access to the half-mile Fairy Dell Trail and Battle Point Park is possible from the temporary anchorage W of Arrow Point, in Port Orchard. Keep in mind that the shore shelves rapidly to the drying mud flats.

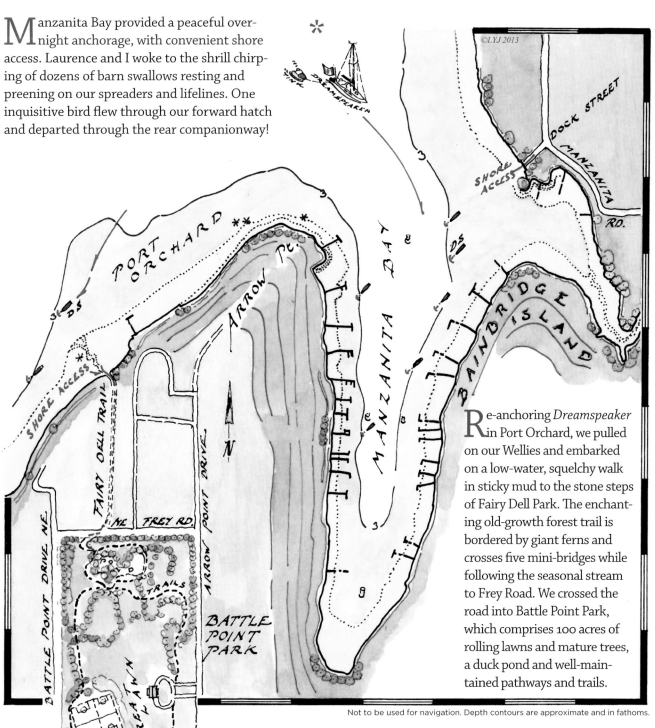

Re-anchoring *Dreamspeaker* in Port Orchard, we pulled on our Wellies and embarked on a low-water, squelchy walk in sticky mud to the stone steps of Fairy Dell Park. The enchanting old-growth forest trail is bordered by giant ferns and crosses five mini-bridges while following the seasonal stream to Frey Road. We crossed the road into Battle Point Park, which comprises 100 acres of rolling lawns and mature trees, a duck pond and well-maintained pathways and trails.

Shore access to Fairy Dell Trail.

Not to be used for navigation. Depth contours are approximate and in fathoms.

A ketch at anchor in "Inner Port Madison."

PORT MADISON

Surrounded by lovely homes, with lush land-scaped gardens and mature trees, tranquil Port Madison, and its mile-long stretch of water, maintains an air of laid-back opulence. On our first visit, we enjoyed a picnic in the cockpit, soaking in the relaxed ambience.

During our second visit, we discovered public road access at Euclid Avenue NE, and another at Broom Street, that leads to the magnificent Bloedel Reserve, an internationally renowned public garden and forest preserve that includes a Japanese moss garden, reflection pool and bird refuge pond. Further south, a small dock allows access to charming Hidden Cove Park, with picnic tables overlooking the water and a short trail leading to another two-mile, multi-use trail.

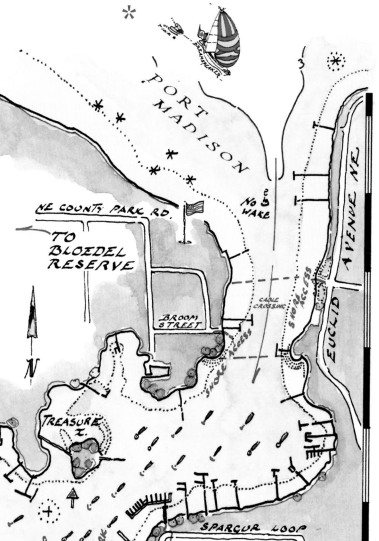

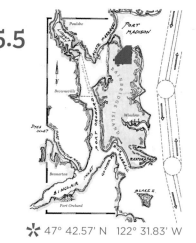

✳ 47° 42.57' N   122° 31.83' W

CHART 18446

APPROACH
When approaching the cabled area from Port Madison to "Inner Port Madison" (local name), keep to the center channel and leave no wake.

ANCHOR
S of the cabled area, and between local boats at anchor or on private buoys. Short scope advised. Good holding in mud, in 1 - 3 ftm (6 - 18 ft). Good all-round protection.

PARK DOCK
A 100-ft, shallow-water dinghy dock provides access to Hidden Cove Park.

MARINA
No visitor moorage available (2013). Port Madison Yacht Club offers reciprocal moorage.

CAUTIONARY NOTE
Shoals extend N of Treasure Island, and a submerged rock lies SW of the island. The head of Port Madison, known locally as "Hidden Cove," shallows to less than 1 ftm (6 ft).

Not to be used for navigation. Depth contours are approximate and in fathoms.

BLAKE ISLAND State Park

Seven nautical miles from Seattle and only accessible by private boat or water taxi, Blake Island was once an ancestral camping ground of the Suquamish Tribe, and legend has it that Chief Seattle was born there. Logged in the mid-1800s and home to the Trimble family until 1936, today 475-acre Blake Island State Park offers moorage, camping, glorious beaches and a network of walking trails through shaded second-growth forest.

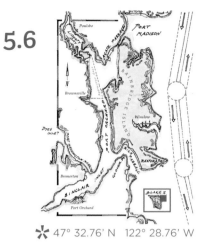

5.6

✳ 47° 32.76' N   122° 28.76' W

CHART 18449

APPROACH
The run in from all quarters is clear. The run in to Blake Island Marina is well marked – turn SE and keep in the marked channel.

ANCHOR
Pick up a park buoy (over 20 are positioned around the island). Buoys to the W and E are popular but exposed to the S. Buoys to the N have good protection from the S. All buoys have a 45-ft limit. Rafting limits are posted on the buoys. Anchoring between the buoys should be undertaken with care, as the bottom shelves rapidly. Moderate holding in mud and sand, in 3+ ftm (18+ ft).

MARINA
Blake Island Marina. VHF Channel 16; call 360-731-8330. Operated by Washington State Parks. Moorage on a first-come basis. Water and power to 30 amps. Free pump-out facility. Docks have 4 fingers, with moorage on either side of each. The linear moorage is made up of buoys for bow and stern tying.

NOTE
It has been reported by the state park that the minimum depth in the marina area at mean low tide is 10 ft.

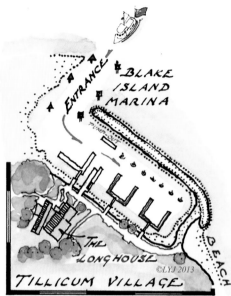

After a magical stroll along the interpretative nature trail, Laurence and I arrived at Tillicum Village and its impressive cedar longhouse, restaurant and performance area. We warmed ourselves around the reception fire pit, where whole salmon were being cooked in the traditional Northwest Coast Indian style for the daily salmon bake. As we relaxed by the cosy fire, we admired the stunning view of Seattle's twinkling skyline and were struck by this remarkable juxtaposition of urban life and indigenous history.

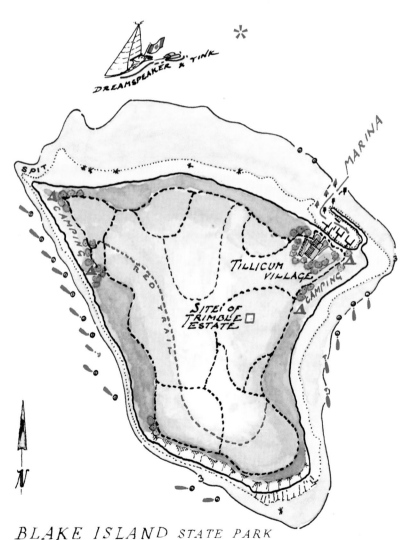

BLAKE ISLAND STATE PARK
Not to be used for navigation. Depth contours are approximate and in fathoms.

Looking south from the spit.

Chapter 6
POULSBO & WEST SOUND
Brownsville, Bremerton & Port Orchard to Silverdale

Out for an evening sail, backed by downtown Poulsbo and the First Lutheran Church.

CHAPTER 6 POULSBO & WEST SOUND
Brownsville, Bremerton & Port Orchard to Silverdale

www.cityofpoulsbo.com

Poulsbo waterfront with the Olympic Mountains aglow in the distance.

CAUTIONARY NOTE
Be aware of the Keyport Range Site in Port Orchard, charted as a Restricted Area on NOAA Navigation Chart 18446. If active, transit via the Port Orchard Channel on the Bainbridge Island side (see 6.2).

West Sound is made up of Liberty Bay in the north and Sinclair and Dyes inlets in the south, connected by the waters of Port Orchard and Port Washington Narrows. The sound's northern entrance is via Agate Passage, while its southern entrance is through Rich Passage. Take a leisurely cruise of the area and enjoy the rich combination of Scandinavian and maritime heritage.

Our first stop is Poulsbo. Tucked into the end of Liberty Bay and known as "Little Norway," Poulsbo was originally settled by Norwegian immigrants, who likened the fjord-like landscape to their homeland. Scandinavian hospitality and old-world charm abound along Front Street, with its unique shops and eateries, European bakery and Viking murals.

Don't miss the Naval Undersea Museum in Keyport. Situated on a small peninsula, "Torpedo Town U.S.A." is also home to the Naval Undersea Warfare Center. The Port of Brownsville Marina offers a warm welcome to visiting boaters and is a favorite spot for club rendezvous, while Illahee State Park offers fishing and a quiet refuge.

Divided into east and west by Point Washington Narrows, Bremerton is the largest city on the Kitsap Peninsula. At the north end of the marina, the *USS Turner Joy* is a worthwhile educational diversion. A short hop on the foot ferry takes you across the waters of Sinclair Inlet to the slow-paced charm of Port Orchard. Browse through the choice of antique stores and interesting shops, or visit the small Log Cabin Museum.

Finally, it's a warm Scandinavian *velkommen* in Old Town Silverdale, with its panoramic views of peaceful Dyes Inlet. While Clear Creek Trail winds through Silverdale's urban area, then meanders for five miles through sensitive wetlands, the Old Mill Site on Bucklin Hill hints at the town's origins as an agriculture and timber center.

TIDES
Tide Height Station: Bremerton

CURRENTS
Tidal Current Station: Bush Point
Travel with the direction of the current when transiting Port Washington Narrows.

WEATHER
NOAA Weather Radio WX4: Puget Sound
NOAA VHF Weather Channel 1 or 3
www.nws.noaa.gov/nwr

HISTORIC FACTS
Poulsbo's strong Norwegian heritage began in the late 1880s, when Jorgen Eliason immigrated from Fordefjord, Norway. He is credited with founding the town. Not long after, Ivar B. Moe arrived from Paulsbo, Norway, and settled with his family at the head of the bay (their farm has since become Poulsbo Village Shopping Center).

More Norwegian and Scandinavian immigrants soon arrived, and for many years, Norwegian was the town's official language. Due to a misprint, the new town of Paulsbo became Poulsbo, and within a span of five generations, it has become a thriving community, with a deep sense of heritage and an ambient small-town charm.

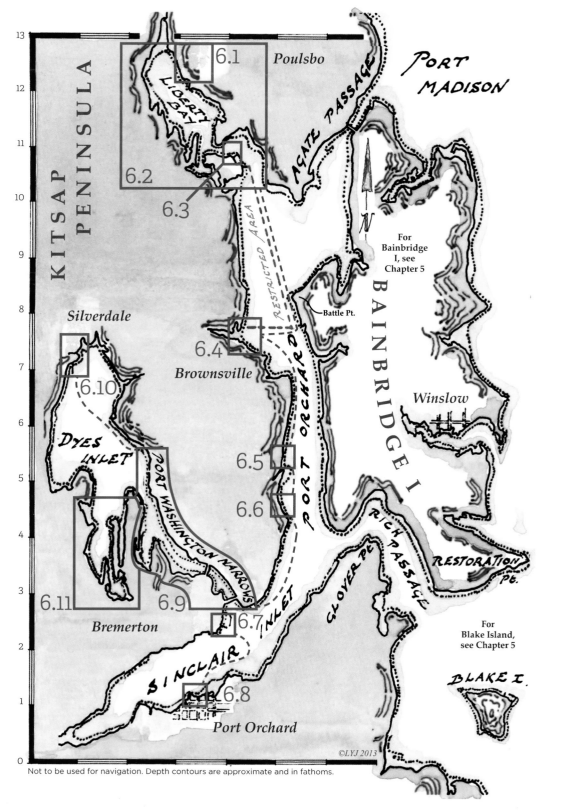

6 POULSBO & WEST SOUND

FEATURED DESTINATIONS

FUEL
6.1 Poulsbo Marina; 6.4 Port of Brownsville Marina; 6.8 Port Orchard Marina

PUMP-OUT FACILITIES
6.1 Poulsbo Marina; 6.4 Port of Brownsville Marina; 6.7 Bremerton Marina; 6.8 Port Orchard Marina; 6.10 Silverdale Marina

CAUTIONARY NOTE
Restricted area Port Orchard. Flashing red lights on Navy range vessels between Keyport and Brownsville and atop a building at the seaward end of the southern buildings at Keyport Naval Undersea Warfare Center indicates that the restricted area is operational. Stay inshore along the Bainbridge Island shore to Battle Pt.

Not to be used for navigation. Depth contours are approximate and in fathoms.

The Poulsbo Marina and anchorage waterfront alive with visiting boats.

Located in the heart of downtown Poulsbo and only minutes from bustling Front Street, the well-managed Poulsbo Marina is backed by lawns and the mature trees of Muriel Iverson Williams Waterfront Park. The impressive First Lutheran Church, which was built in 1886, sits commandingly on the hill above the historic waterfront and downtown; it is the oldest standing building in Poulsbo and is still in use today.

Vibrant downtown Poulsbo is filled with enticing storefronts and friendly businesses that welcome visitors from land and sea. You are never far from an espresso bar, cosy cafe, waterfront restaurant or pub, serving Poulsbo craft beer, or wine shops offering local tastings. The neighborhood bagelry and Scandinavian-inspired bakery offer fresh, homemade goodies to go.

Front Street offers an abundance of interesting shopping possibilities, from antiques, apparel, gift and specialty stores to art studios and galleries, an excellent bookstore and consignment and thrift stores. Longship Marine has almost all of your boating needs, and the Marina Market has a great selection of provisions, including basic groceries, imported foods, fresh produce, beer, wine and ice. The farmers' market sets up every Saturday, with fresh, locally grown produce.

After a day of exploring, shopping and visiting the science center and aquarium, our favorite spot to relax and take it easy is under the dappled shade of the 100-year-old magnolia tree, standing tall in the courtyard of Sogno di Vino restaurant. Sipping on a chilled drink and sharing one of their delicious, wood-fired pizzas and calzone treats is a wonderful way to relax and enjoy the old-world charm of downtown Poulsbo.

A charming city with a strong Scandinavian heritage.

Dreamspeaker and Tink *at the port's fuel dock.*

LOCAL FACTS

The Poulsbo Farmers' Market takes place on Saturdays from 9 a.m. to 1 p.m. at the Poulsbo Village Medical/Dental Center at the corner of 7th Avenue NE and Iverson Street (April to December).

Albertsons and a mix of 50 retail stores are located in the Poulsbo Village Shopping Center, located on 7th Avenue NE, just off Iverson Street.

FUN FACTS

Enjoy a stroll from the marina along the shaded waterfront park and boardwalk to American Legion Park, with its wooded trails and views of Liberty Bay.

The Poulsbo Marine Science Center and Aquarium has a touchy-feely intertidal pool, tanks with sea creatures and a gray whale skeleton. This is a treat for the whole family.

LOCAL EVENTS

The hospitable city is proud of its 105-year Norwegian heritage and invites visitors to share in its Scandinavian traditions. Don't miss the three-day Viking Fest on the third weekend in May, with entertainment, a festive parade and a 1500 A.D. Viking Village.

The St. Hans/Mid-sommer Festival, put on by the Sons of Norway, is celebrated on the June summer solstice in the waterfront park from 4 to 8 p.m. Enjoy the Viking Parade, folk dancing and lighting of the bonfire.

Begin your Fourth of July celebration with an afternoon of food and entertainment at the waterfront park, and be sure to stay for an excellent fireworks display at 10 p.m.

www.portofpoulsbo.com

Not to be used for navigation. Depth contours are approximate and in fathoms.

✳ 47° 43.70' N   122° 38.97' W

CHART 18446

APPROACH
For approaches to Liberty Bay, see 6.2.

ANCHOR
Ample anchorage in the area, as indicated. Good protection from the N. Moderate protection from the S. Good holding in mud, in 2 - 3 ftm (12 - 18 ft).

MARINA
Poulsbo Marina. VHF Channel 66A; call 360-779-3505. Operated by the Port of Poulsbo. Visitor moorage on "E" and "F" docks for boats up to 76 ft. Reservations for first 10 slips only; 120 slips on a first-come basis. Water, power to 30 amps and free pump-out facility and portable cart. Free Wi-Fi, garbage drop and recycling. Shower and laundry facilities. Tidal maintenance grid. Designated dinghy and floatplane dock. Club and group rendezvous welcome; multipurpose room available for groups.

FUEL
Fuel dock operated by the port. Gasoline and diesel are available.

LAUNCH
The boat launch is accessed from the corner of Front Street.

NOTE
In a strong southerly, anchor tucked in between Poulsbo Marina and Poulsbo Yacht Club, or N of the two marinas. Shelter can also be found in SE and SW Liberty Bay (see 6.2).

FUEL

6.1 Poulsbo Marina; 6.4 Port of Brownsville Marina; 6.8 Port Orchard Marina

PUMP-OUT FACILITIES

6.1 Poulsbo Marina; 6.4 Port of Brownsville Marina; 6.7 Bremerton Marina; 6.8 Port Orchard Marina; 6.10 Silverdale Marina

CAUTIONARY NOTE

Restricted area Port Orchard. Flashing red lights on Navy range vessels between Keyport and Brownsville and atop a building at the seaward end of the southern buildings at Keyport Naval Undersea Warfare Center indicates that the restricted area is operational. Stay inshore along the Bainbridge Island shore to Battle Pt.

www.portofpoulsbo.com

The Naval Undersea Museum is a must!

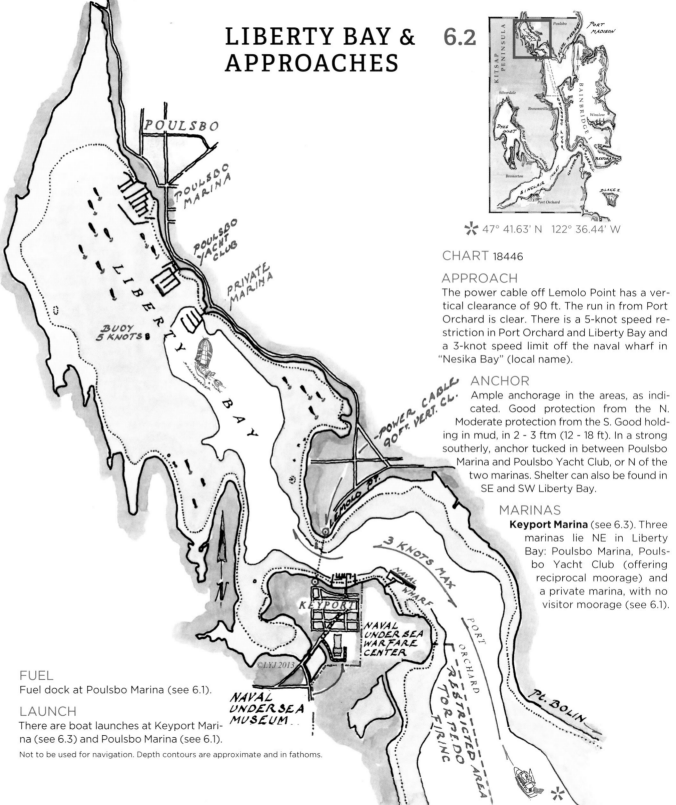

LIBERTY BAY & APPROACHES 6.2

✳ 47° 41.63' N   122° 36.44' W

CHART 18446

APPROACH

The power cable off Lemolo Point has a vertical clearance of 90 ft. The run in from Port Orchard is clear. There is a 5-knot speed restriction in Port Orchard and Liberty Bay and a 3-knot speed limit off the naval wharf in "Nesika Bay" (local name).

ANCHOR

Ample anchorage in the areas, as indicated. Good protection from the N. Moderate protection from the S. Good holding in mud, in 2 - 3 ftm (12 - 18 ft). In a strong southerly, anchor tucked in between Poulsbo Marina and Poulsbo Yacht Club, or N of the two marinas. Shelter can also be found in SE and SW Liberty Bay.

MARINAS

Keyport Marina (see 6.3). Three marinas lie NE in Liberty Bay: Poulsbo Marina, Poulsbo Yacht Club (offering reciprocal moorage) and a private marina, with no visitor moorage (see 6.1).

FUEL

Fuel dock at Poulsbo Marina (see 6.1).

LAUNCH

There are boat launches at Keyport Marina (see 6.3) and Poulsbo Marina (see 6.1).

Not to be used for navigation. Depth contours are approximate and in fathoms.

KEYPORT, Liberty Bay

Keyport Marina and its small, friendly community make this an appealing boating destination. The original wharf was used as a landing for the Mosquito Fleet steamboats, and the welcoming Keyport Mercantile & Diner, just up from the marina, has been in operation since 1903.

Open for breakfast, lunch and dinner, the diner is famous for its excellent "Merc Made" soups, sandwiches and hand-rolled pizza. If you're craving something lighter, sit under the shade of an umbrella and enjoy an espresso or a traditional ice cream soda. The store also stocks groceries, beer and wine.

Just a 15-minute walk from the marina, a relaxed dinner at the Whiskey Creek Steakhouse is a welcome treat. Alternative waterfront accommodation for non-boating friends is available at the well-appointed Grandview Gardens Bed and Breakfast.

✳ 47° 42.36' N   122° 37.35' W

CHART 18446

APPROACH
From the W, having observed the 3-knot speed limit off the naval wharf. The run in to Keyport Marina from Port Orchard is clear. Refer to 6.2 for the navigable channel E of the restricted area and naval wharf.

MARINA
Keyport Marina. Operated by the Port of Keyport. Visitor moorage on a first-come basis; check in at the Keyport Mercantile & Diner, just south of the dock on Washington Avenue. Well-maintained concrete slips. 250 ft of visitor moorage in 5 50-foot slips. First 6 hours free. Water and power to 30 amps.

LAUNCH
The boat launch is adjacent to the pier.

LOCAL FACT
Keyport is known locally as "Torpedo Town U.S.A." and has an impressive Naval Undersea Museum on Garnett Way, which invites visitors to experience the fascinating history of undersea warfare. It is open every day in the summer months from 10 a.m. to 4 p.m., and admission is free!

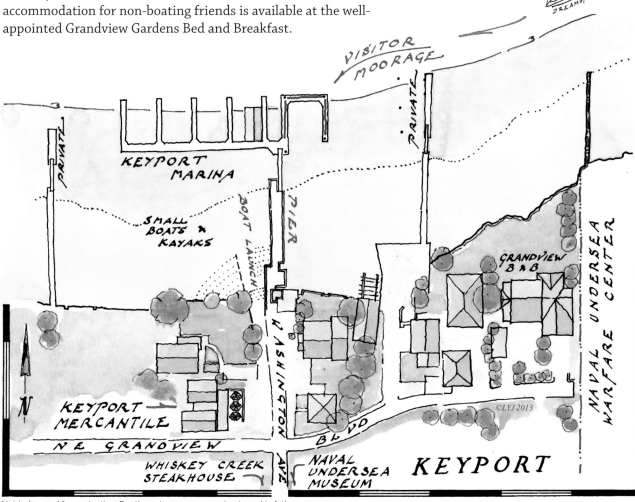

Not to be used for navigation. Depth contours are approximate and in fathoms.

BROWNSVILLE, Port Orchard

Popular with group rendezvous, the welcoming Port of Brownsville Marina is a pleasant destination in a rural setting. Amenities include clean showers, an on-the-water covered pavilion and a park picnic area with barbecues, a fire pit and great views to Port Orchard. Well patronized by locals, The Deli at the marina offers a bit of everything, including good espresso, Italian sodas, tasty sandwiches and salads, as well as a decent selection of beer and wine.

A welcome and surprise discovery was Sweeney's Country Style Meats & Seafood, just west of the marina. The family-owned smokehouse has been in business for 30 years and is famed for its homemade sausages, smoked salmon, buffalo jerky and elk pepperoni, to name just a few delicious choices. TheDaily Stop Grocery has an ATM and carries a good selection of boating provisions, some fresh produce and ice.

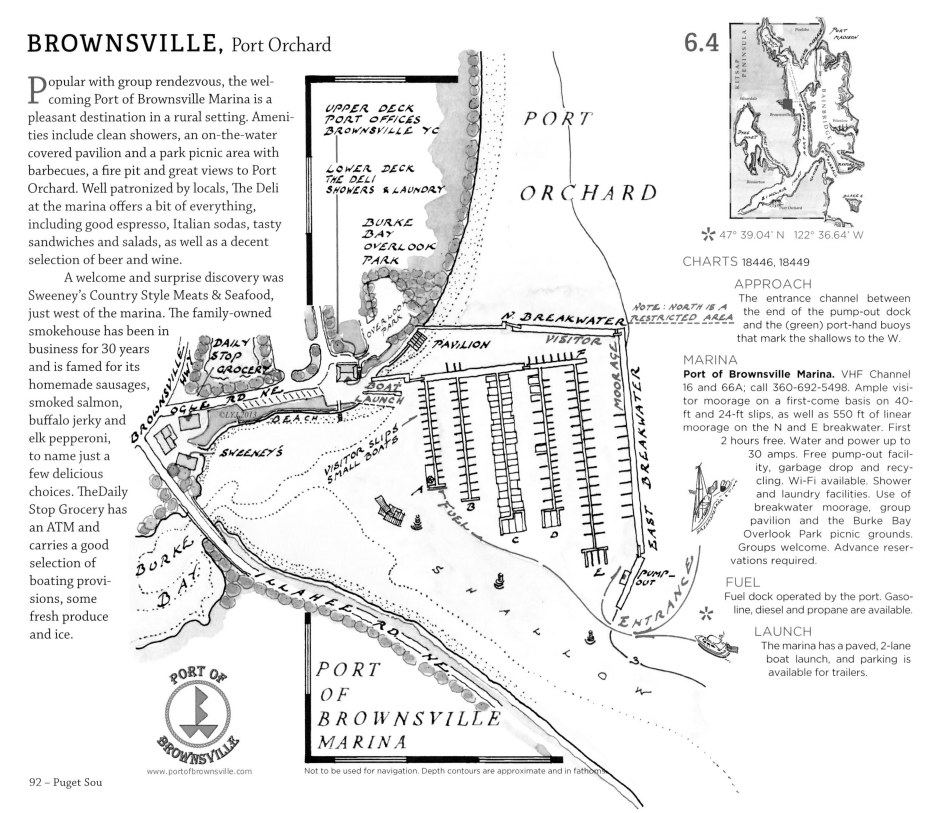

✱ 47° 39.04' N 122° 36.64' W

CHARTS 18446, 18449

APPROACH
The entrance channel between the end of the pump-out dock and the (green) port-hand buoys that mark the shallows to the W.

MARINA
Port of Brownsville Marina. VHF Channel 16 and 66A; call 360-692-5498. Ample visitor moorage on a first-come basis on 40-ft and 24-ft slips, as well as 550 ft of linear moorage on the N and E breakwater. First 2 hours free. Water and power up to 30 amps. Free pump-out facility, garbage drop and recycling. Wi-Fi available. Shower and laundry facilities. Use of breakwater moorage, group pavilion and the Burke Bay Overlook Park picnic grounds. Groups welcome. Advance reservations required.

FUEL
Fuel dock operated by the port. Gasoline, diesel and propane are available.

LAUNCH
The marina has a paved, 2-lane boat launch, and parking is available for trailers.

www.portofbrownsville.com

Not to be used for navigation. Depth contours are approximate and in fathoms.

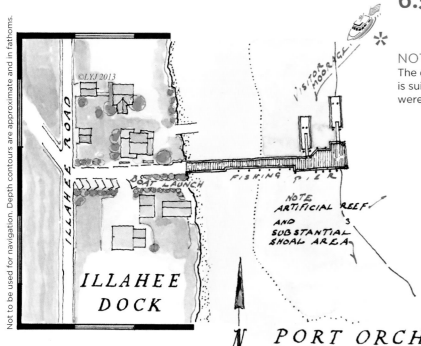

©LYJ 2013

ILLAHEE DOCK

BOAT LAUNCH

ILLAHEE ROAD

FISHING PIER

NOTE ARTIFICIAL REEF AND SUBSTANTIAL SHOAL AREA

3

N

PORT ORCHARD

6.5 ILLAHEE DOCK,
Port Orchard

VISITOR MOORAGE

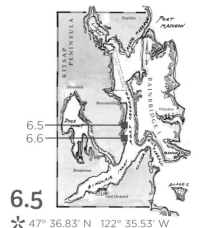

NOTE
The dock is exposed to boat wake and weather and is suitable for a short stopoff. When we visited, there were no facilities within walking distance (2013).

6.5

✳ 47° 36.83' N   122° 35.53' W

CHART 18449

APPROACH
The run in from the N is clear.

PUBLIC DOCK
The Illahee Dock is managed by the Port of Illahee and is made up of 2 substantial floats, with visitor moorage on either side for boats up to 40 ft. Moorage limited to 3 days on a first-come basis. No reservations.

LAUNCH
The boat launch is adjacent to the fishing pier.

6.6 ILLAHEE STATE PARK, PORT ORCHARD

Illahee State Park is a 75-acre marine camping park with 1,785 feet of saltwater frontage on Port Orchard Bay. Popular with the locals, who enjoy fishing off the park pier, this is a fun destination, especially on a warm, sunny day. Laze on the sandy beach, picnic in the lower park or enjoy a good hike up the steep trails through old-growth fir and cedar stands to the campground in the upper portion of the park.

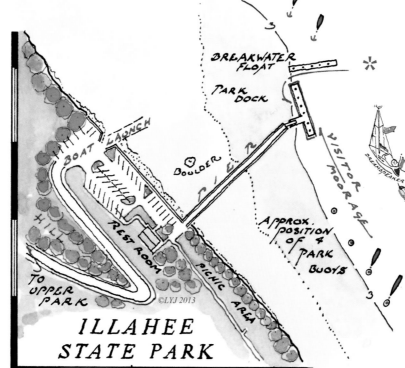

BOAT LAUNCH

HILL

TO UPPER PARK

REST ROOM

PIER

PICNIC AREA

BOULDER

BREAKWATER FLOAT

PARK DOCK

VISITOR MOORAGE

Approx. position of 4 park buoys

DREAMSPEAKER & TINK

3

3

✳

©LYJ 2013

ILLAHEE STATE PARK

6.6

✳ 47° 36.08' N   122° 35.54' W

CHART 18449

APPROACH
The run in from Port Orchard is clear.

ANCHOR
Pick up one of the 4 park buoys, or anchor N of the breakwater. Good holding in mud, in 3+ ftm (18+ ft). Good protection from the S, but exposed to the N.

PARK DOCK
The park dock is protected from the N by a floating concrete breakwater and offers 356 ft of visitor moorage. No water or power. Cold shower facilities near the beach and hot showers in the campground, a 1-mile hike up the hill.

LAUNCH
A 1-lane boat launch lies N of the pier.

KITSAP PENINSULA

PORT MADISON

Poulsbo

PORT ORCHARD

BAINBRIDGE I

Silverdale

Brownsville

Winslow

Dyes

6.5
6.6

Bremerton

SINCLAIR

Port Orchard

RESTORATION

BLAKE I

Bremerton's Fountain Park is quite a splash for visitors.

BREMERTON, Sinclair Inlet

The Bremerton Marina, with its squeaky-clean facilities, provided us with a much-needed hot shower. After a tasty sandwich from Boogaloo's Barbeque Pit on the boardwalk, we set off on a fascinating tour of the destroyer *USS Turner Joy*, on permanent display as a Navy Memorial Museum Ship.

A city where history, public art and fountains abound, downtown Bremerton is easy to enjoy. Pick up some walking maps at the marina office and look for the many artistic banners that are hanging from street lamps along Pacific and Washington avenues.

Fronting the majestic Puget Sound Naval Museum, Harborside Fountain Park features impressive copper-ringed fountains and wading pools in a landscaped setting, while the PSNS Plaza displays striking rock-and-water sculptures that illustrate three eras of naval shipyard history. With our heads filled with local history, Laurence and I flopped into the patio chairs at Anthony's HomePort and indulged in their happy hour specials.

Not to be used for navigation. Depth contours are approximate and in fathoms.

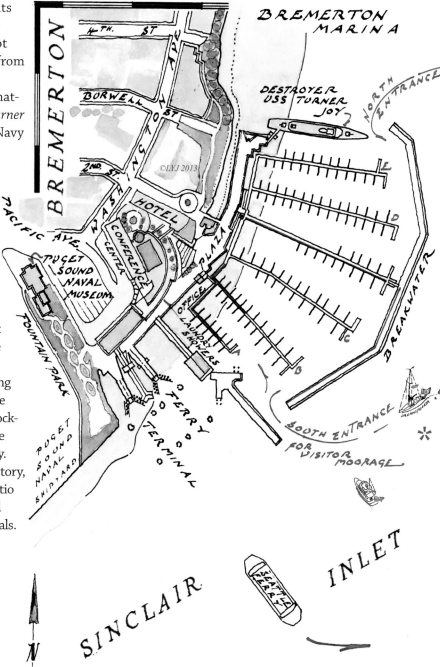

✳ 47° 33.77' N   122° 37.18' W

CHARTS 18452, 18449

APPROACH

The N entrance is conspicuous by the presence of the destroyer *USS Turner Joy*. For the S entrance and visitor moorage, enter by rounding the S end of the breakwater. Be aware of the Seattle-Bremerton ferry, and the frequent foot ferry that runs between Bremerton and Port Orchard.

MARINA

Bremerton Marina. VHF Channel 66A; call 360-373-1035. Operated by the Port of Bremerton. Ample visitor moorage for boats up to 100+ ft. Reservations accepted. Water, power to 50 amps and a free pump-out facility at the end of "C" dock. Free shower facilities, Wi-Fi, garbage and recycling. Laundry facilities. Activity tent on "A" dock and the breakwater. Shuttle service when staff is available. For line handling assistance, call ahead. Groups welcome, with advance reservations.

FUEL

Fuel and Full service repair yards see Port Orchard 6.8

LAUNCH

Evergreen Park in Bremerton has a 2-lane, surfaced boat launch.

LOCAL FACTS

The Bremerton Farmers' Market (on the boardwalk) takes place on Sundays from 10:30 a.m. to 2:30 p.m. (May to mid-October). For the Port Orchard Farmer's Market, see 6.8.

PORT ORCHARD, Sinclair Inlet

PORT OF Bremerton *Washington*

www.portofbremerton.org

Located on the pristine waters of Sinclair Inlet, welcoming Port Orchard Marina is a 10-minute ferry ride, or a one-mile crossing by boat, from the City of Bremerton. The town has the slow-paced ambience of a small tourist village, and we spent a leisurely morning shopping at the farmers' market and browsing through the choice of antique and vintage stores and assortment of interesting shops.

Good breakfast and lunch spots include the Hideaway Cafe, serving hearty fare, and the Home Made Cafe off Bay Street, offering lighter dishes and a shaded courtyard. Don't miss the charming two-story Log Cabin Museum nearby. Built in 1913, it is filled with fascinating artifacts and furniture.

Port Orchard has a good selection of restaurants and bistros dotted around town. Taking a break from the galley, we warmed to the cosy, local atmosphere at the Bay Street Bistro and enjoyed sampling their fresh menu choices.

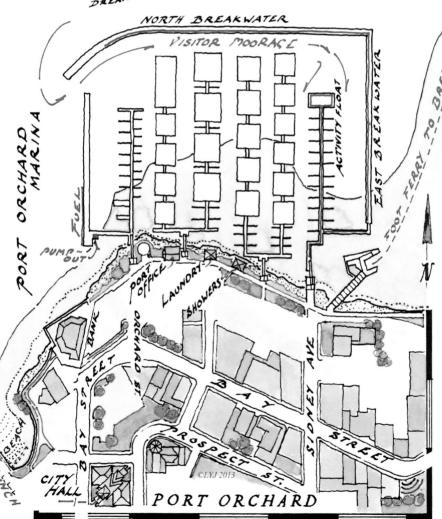

Not to be used for navigation. Depth contours are approximate and in fathoms.

* 47° 32.85' N 122° 38.25' W

CHARTS 18452, 18449

APPROACH
The run in is clear when rounding the W end of the breakwater. The fairway between the breakwater and the end of the covered moorage is relatively narrow – proceed with caution. The foot ferry makes frequent runs between Bremerton and Port Orchard.

MARINA
Port Orchard Marina. VHF Channel 66A; call 360-876-5535. Operated by the Port of Bremerton. Ample visitor moorage for boats up to 100 ft. First 4 hours free. Water and power to 50 amps. Free shower facilities, Wi-Fi, garbage and recycling. Laundry facilities. Covered activity float and tent. Shuttle service when staff is available. For line handling assistance, call ahead. Groups welcome, with advance reservations.

FUEL
The fuel dock has gasoline and diesel and a free pump-out facility. Call 360-876-5535. Full-service repair yards available at Port Orchard.

LAUNCH
The Water Street public boat launch is a 2-lane, surfaced launch, located W of the marina, off Bay Street.

LOCAL FACT
The Port Orchard Farmers' Market takes place on Saturdays from 9 a.m. to 3 p.m. (April to mid-October). For the Bremerton Farmer's Market, see 6.7.

PORT WASHINGTON NARROWS

6.9

DYES INLET

BOAT LAUNCH
TRACYTON

TIDE RIPS

ROCKY PT.

©LYJ 2013

N

BREMERTON YC

PHINNEY BAY

BOAT LAUNCH

LIONS PARK

CAUTION

WARREN AVENUE BRIDGE

FIXED BRIDGE
HOR CL 220 FT
VERT CL 80 FT

POWER CABLE CL 90 FT.

ANDERSON COVE

PORT WASHINGTON MARINA

CAUTION

POWER CABLE CL 80 FT.

BOAT LAUNCH
EVERGREEN PARK

MANETTE BRIDGE

FIXED BRIDGE
VERT CL 82 FT.

BREMERTON

HERRON

SINCLAIR INLET

BREMERTON MARINA

Not to be used for navigation. Depth contours are approximate and in fathoms.

12° 12.12' N   12° 12.12' N

CHART 18449

APPROACH

Sinclair and Dyes inlets are connected by the Port Washington Narrows, with a navigable width of 500 yds (the deepest water is mid-channel). The narrows are spanned by 2 bridges and 2 power cables, with a minimum vertical clearance of 80 ft. The run in is clear, except for 4 areas of shoal water, indicated on the chart with *Caution*.

ANCHOR

The quiet anchorage in Phinney Bay is well protected but loses the evening light early. Holding unrecorded. Be aware of the charted reef and submerged rock.

Three-mile-long Port Washington Narrows is the connecting waterway between Sinclair and Dyes inlets, and because boat traffic is heavy, boaters are requested to maintain a minimum speed to reduce wake damage to the shoreline and moored boats.

Located under the Manette Bridge on the southeast shore of the narrows, the Boat Shed restaurant has a dock for boating customers, but don't forget to check your current tables (see Cautionary Note)!

Surrounded by a wooded shoreline, Phinney Bay, on the northwest shore, offers a tranquil anchorage away from the bustling narrows and is a good overnight stop. Once the narrows have been navigated, your reward is peaceful Dyes Inlet and a view of the impressive Olympic Mountains. At the entrance to the inlet is Tracyton, with road access to a gas station, pub and well-stocked convenience store.

MARINAS

Port Washington Marina in Anderson Cove has no visitor moorage. Bremerton Yacht Club in Phinney Bay has reciprocal moorage.

LAUNCH

Evergreen Park in Bremerton has a 2-lane, surfaced boat launch. There is a 3-lane, surfaced boat launch at the W end of Lions Park and a 1-lane, surfaced boat launch at Tracyton.

CAUTIONARY NOTE

Check current tables before navigating Port Washington Narrows, as currents can average speeds of over 4 knots, which ebb SE and flood NW. Expect tide rips around Rocky Point.

Silverdale Marina docks – the art of fun boating is knowing how to keep cool.

SILVERDALE, Dyes Inlet

Docking at Silverdale Marina on a hot summer afternoon, Laurence and I were amused to find our boating neighbors relaxing beside their inflatable pool, cocktails in hand!

The marina is backed by the shaded picnic lawns and kids' play area of Silverdale Waterfront Park. The Clear Creek Trail led us along the shoreline and sandy beach to Lowell Street, then past heritage homes and gardens to the Clear Creek Sa'qad Interpretive Center. Turning into Bayshore Drive, and happy to cool off on the Yacht Club Broiler's patio, we took in the fine views across Dyes Inlet.

Old Town Silverdale has a few good finds, including Monica's Waterfront Bakery & Cafe and the Old Town Pub. It is also home to a Tuesday farmers' market (May to September) and the annual Whaling Days festival, held on the last weekend in July.

www.portofsilverdale.com

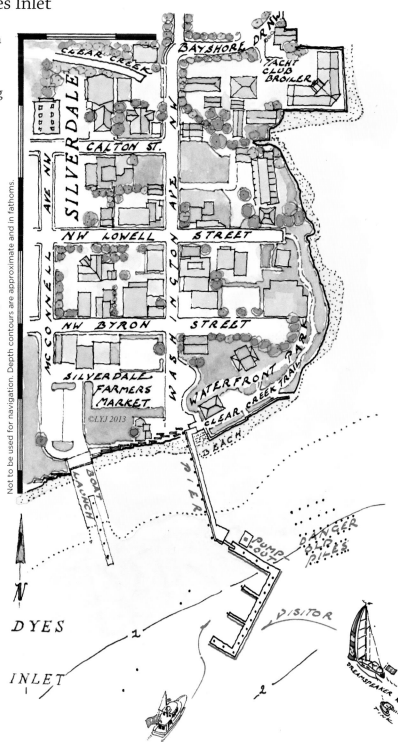

* 47° 38.38' N   122° 41.62' W

CHART 18449

APPROACH
Silverdale lies at the head of Dyes Inlet on the W shore. The run in is clear.

MARINA
Silverdale Marina. Call 360-698-4918. Operated by the Port of Silverdale. Ample visitor moorage (1,300 ft), with wide and sturdy, timber-decked, concrete docks. Potable water, power to 30 amps and a free pumpout facility. Shower and laundry facilities. 3-night maximum stay. Moorage payment at the head of the pier. Reservations possible for a fee. For boaters' safety, the pier has both security cameras and random foot patrols.

LAUNCH
A 2-lane, concrete launch ramp, operated by the port, is W of the pier.

LOCAL FACTS
For provisions, the Silverdale Grocery Outlet on Silverdale Way is a 15- to 20-minute walk from the marina, opposite Silverdale Village Shopping Center. Safeway is a little further, at NW Bucklin Hill Road.

The Kitsap Transit #35 Old Town Shuttle will transport you to the Kitsap Mall (no provisions). For Alpha Transportation's Super Kab, call 360-536-4361.

*

OSTRICH & OYSTER BAYS, Dyes Inlet

47° 35.74' N   122° 40.86' W

CHART 18449

APPROACH
From Dyes Inlet, the run in to Ostrich Bay is clear. Oyster Bay lies to the S. The approach channel, which begins at Madrona Point, has shallow areas and is bordered by private homes.

ANCHOR
Anchor, as indicated, in Ostrich and Oyster bays, in 2 - 3 ftm (12 - 18 ft). Good holding in mud.

CAUTIONARY NOTES
A large rock lies N of the abandoned navy wharf.

While Oyster Bay got its name from the multitude of oysters once found in its waters, today shellfish gathering is prohibited as a result of the pollution caused by development along its shoreline.

Once the shallows of Port Washington Narrows have been successfully navigated, the protected bays of lake-like Dyes Inlet welcome the cruising boater to stay awhile and enjoy their peaceful anchorages.

We dropped anchor in the quiet of NAD Marine Park at the head of Ostrich Bay, the largest anchorage in the one-and-a-half-mile inlet, and rowed to shore. Concrete steps led us into the undeveloped Bremerton city park, with its public access at the end of Shorewood Drive. From here, we took an exploratory walk north along the disused road, enjoying the views across Dyes Inlet, until we reached the private navy housing development and a rocky beach.

After departing Ostrich Bay, we slipped through the narrow channel into Oyster Bay's pocket anchorage, cosied up in *Dreamspeaker's* cockpit with cups of hot tea and simply took in the afternoon tranquility.

Not to be used for navigation. Depth contours are approximate and in fathoms.

DYES INLET

NAVAL HOSPITAL ELWOOD Pt.

NAVAL PROPERTY

OSTRICH BAY

NAVAL WHARF

NAD MARINE PARK

SHOREWOOD DR.

MADRONA Pt.

ROCKS

APPROACH CHANNEL

OYSTER BAY

CABLE AREA

N

©LYJ 2013

TACOMA & CENTRAL SOUND

Des Moines, Vashon Island & Maury Island

The Tacoma Museum of Glass, with its iconic dome, is a great attraction in the "Lower" Thea Foss Waterway.

CHAPTER 7 TACOMA & CENTRAL SOUND
Des Moines, Vashon Island & Maury Island

The City of Tacoma, like its suspension bridge, links old and new.

TIDES
Tide Height Station: Tacoma

CURRENTS
Tidal Current Station: Tacoma Narrows

WEATHER
NOAA Weather Radio WX4: Puget Sound
NOAA VHF Weather Channel 1 or 3
www.nws.noaa.gov/nwr

NOTE
We have divided Thea Foss Waterway into "Upper" (7.1) and "Lower" (7.2), with the dividing line being the Murray Morgan Bridge.

HISTORIC FACTS
Tacoma was incorporated in 1875 following the merger of Old and New Tacoma. It is the third-largest city in the northwestern United States, with approximately 200,678 residents and a total of 1 million inhabitants in the South Sound region. The Port of Tacoma is an independent seaport in the deep-water harbor of Commencement Bay and is the largest port in Washington State.

Since the 1990s, Tacoma's downtown core development has included the University of Washington, the first modern electric light-rail service in the state (Tacoma Link) and a restored urban waterfront on the west side of Thea Foss Waterway. Tacoma also has the highest density of art and history museums in Washington State.

CAUTIONARY NOTES
Be aware of the large commercial craft that use the shipping lanes in East Passage and in Commencement Bay, where vessels enter or depart from the Port of Tacoma, the busiest port in Puget Sound.

A reef extends from the SE shore of Maury Island into Quartermaster Harbor.

Vashon and Maury islands reside comfortably together in central Puget Sound, with tranquil Quartermaster Harbor between them. Having voyaged south via Colvos Passage, we planned to visit the metropolis of Tacoma before traveling north, via East Passage.

From Commencement Bay, Tacoma's Thea Foss Waterway, a 1.5-mile deep-water inlet, follows the city's edge, while an expansive stretch of railway and highway separates the revitalized waterfront from uptown and downtown Tacoma.

The Museum of Glass and its iconic stainless steel cone is the city's centerpiece, while the Chihuly Bridge of Glass connects the waterfront with the downtown museums and businesses, and the light rail links the Museum District to the Theater District. The result is an interesting cultural mix, which we enjoyed exploring.

Leaving New Town Tacoma, we found day moorage at the upgraded Old Town Dock, just a short walk from the historic Old Town district, with its inviting coffee shops, eateries and engaging museum. At Point Defiance, we had our faulty starter motor repaired and spent a day exploring magnificent Point Defiance Park, which includes a zoo and an aquarium.

Having exhausted our urban curiosity, we headed across Delco Passage to the protection of spacious Quartermaster Harbor. Stopping at Dockton Beach Park, we hiked the trails and swam in the refreshing water, before spending a quiet evening at anchor, with plenty of privacy and room to swing.

Convenient day moorage at Des Moines Marina allowed provisioning at the Saturday Downtown Farmers' Market and a stroll into town for a loaf of fresh bread and picnic treats. We completed our Central Sound explorations anchored off Point Heyer, where we joined the Vashon Island locals on a lovely stretch of beach and spent a blissful afternoon with sand between our toes.

7 TACOMA & CENTRAL SOUND

FEATURED DESTINATIONS

FUEL
7.1 Foss Harbor Marina & Tacoma Fuel Dock; 7.4 Breakwater Marina & Point Defiance Marina; 7.7 Des Moines Marina

PUMP-OUT FACILITIES
7.1 Foss Harbor Marina & Tacoma Fuel Dock; 7.2 Dock Street Marina; 7.4 Breakwater Marina & Point Defiance Marina; 7.5 Dockton Beach Park; 7.7 Des Moines Marina

Map labels:

COLVOS PASSAGE

VASHON I.

HEYER PT.

7.8

7.6

Des Moines
7.7

PT. ROBINSON

EAST PASSAGE

THREE TREE PT

QUARTERMASTER HR.

MAURY I.

7.5

POVERTY BAY

For Harbor, Chapter 8

DALCO PASSAGE

PT. DEFIANCE

7.4

BROWNS PT.

COMMENCEMENT BAY

THE NARROWS

For Narrows Marina, see Chapter 8

7.3

7.1

7.2

TACOMA

©LYJ 2013

Not to be used for navigation. Depth contours are approximate and in fathoms.

7.1 TACOMA – "Upper" Thea Foss Waterway

The old City Hall sits on the bluff.

Take a walk via the Spanish Steps.

"My girl, talking about my girl!" Aloha Cabs.

The City of Tacoma's waterfront greets boating visitors with a large painted welcome sign on a storage tank at the entrance to Thea Foss Waterway. Laurence and I were captivated by the grandness of the urban Victorian architecture, commanding the escarpment and uptown district to the west. Looking forward to exploring uptown Tacoma by foot and light rail, we checked in at Foss Harbor Marina, donned comfortable hiking shoes and took the esplanade walkway north past the impressive Foss Waterway Seaport and Maritime Museum to lovely Thea's Park.

An expansive stretch of railway and the 705 Highway separate the west side of Thea Foss Waterway from uptown and downtown Tacoma. It's a steep hike to Schuster Parkway (not many people take this route!) and a short walk along the highway to the Spanish Steps, Old City Hall, Antique Row and the Theater District. We relaxed in the tranquility of Fireman's Park, with its restored 1903 totem pole and expansive views of Commencement Bay, Mt. Rainier and the Port of Tacoma.

The Tacoma Link light-rail transit system is a very pleasant way to get around the city, and it's free! Serving six key destinations between the Theater District and Tacoma Dome stations, the Link runs approximately every 15 minutes, seven days a week. If you happen to be visiting on a Thursday, don't miss the superb Tacoma Farmers' Market (hop off at Commerce and 11th Street).

Broadway Farmers' Market, Tacoma's original market since 1990, offers a selection of local, farm-fresh vegetables, fruits, cheeses, eggs, fish, meat, herbs, cut flowers, preserves and baked goods. It's a friendly community-gathering place to meet for lunch, watch chef demonstrations and enjoy live family entertainment. We indulged in a variety of treats before stopping in at the City Grocer IGA (on the corner of Pacific and 13th Street) to complete our boat provisioning.

FUN FACTS

The Broadway Farmers' Market takes place every Thursday on Broadway, between 9th and 11th Street. It runs from 9 a.m. to 2 p.m., mid-May to mid-October.

The Foss Waterway Seaport and Working Waterfront Maritime Museum is housed in a historic waterfront warehouse and was founded in 1996 to "celebrate the art, culture, crafts and skills of Puget Sound's maritime community." They have a significant collection of historic marine artifacts, interactive exhibits and a boat-building shop dedicated to wooden boat restoration and education.

The Theater District offers three very distinct theaters. The Pantages and the Rialto are historic icons, while the Theater on the Square is a newer addition. All three are managed by the Broadway Center for Performing Arts, which partners with international and local performing arts groups, including the Tacoma City Ballet and the Tacoma Symphony Orchestra. Grand Cinema, a nonprofit art-house theater, is another Tacoma favorite, located close to the Theater District.

FOOD FACTS

Over the Moon Cafe: Hidden from the theaters down an alleyway, the cafe has an intimate dining atmosphere and focuses on Pacific Northwest cuisine.

The Harmon Hub: A casual and local brew pub, famous for its unique pizzas, beer and warm atmosphere.

Amocat Cafe: This coffeehouse is the perfect spot to grab a latte in the day or sip a local microbrew in the evening. A favorite among many of Tacoma's urban residents.

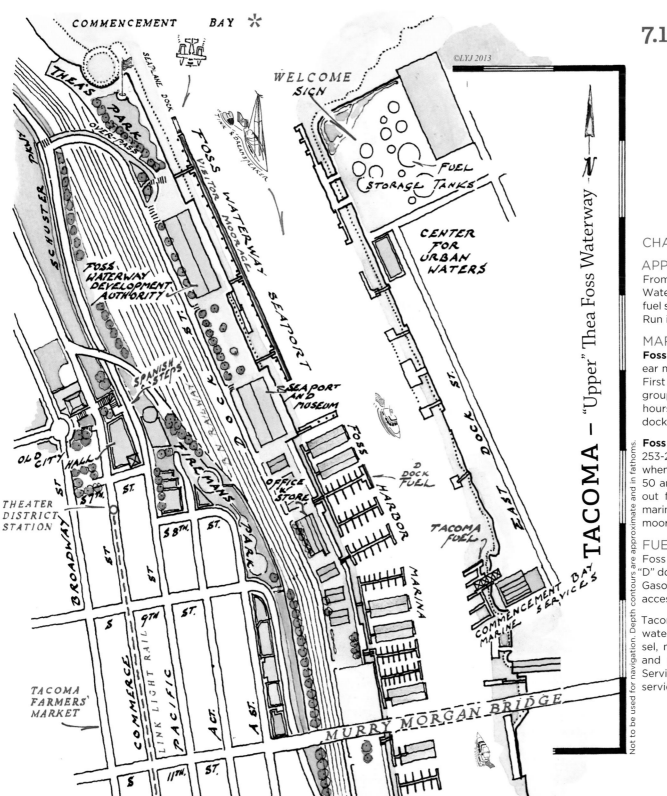

COMMENCEMENT BAY ✳

THEA'S PARK

SEAPLANE DOCK

LINK & DREAMSHAKER

FOSS WATERWAY SEAPORT

VISITOR MOORAGE

WELCOME SIGN

©LYJ 2013

FUEL STORAGE TANKS

CENTER FOR URBAN WATERS

FOSS WATERWAY DEVELOPMENT AUTHORITY

SCHUSTER PKWY

OVERPASS

15TH. ST.

SPANISH STEPS

OLD CITY HALL

7TH ST.

SEAPORT AND MUSEUM

FIREMAN'S PARK

THEATER DISTRICT STATION

S 8TH. ST.

OFFICE 'N' STORE

FOSS HARBOR MARINA

D DOCK FUEL

EAST DOCK ST.

TACOMA FUEL

BROADWAY ST.

9TH. ST.

COMMERCE ST.

PACIFIC AV.

1ST. AV.

LINK LIGHT RAIL

TACOMA FARMERS' MARKET

COMMENCEMENT BAY MARINE SERVICES

S 11TH. ST.

MURRY MORGAN BRIDGE

TACOMA – "Upper" Thea Foss Waterway – N

Not to be used for navigation. Depth contours are approximate and in fathoms.

7.1

TACOMA

Des Moines

COMMENCEMENT BAY

TACOMA

✳ 47° 15.8′ N 122° 26.34′ W

CHART 18453

APPROACH

From Commencement Bay into Thea Foss Waterway. A welcome sign painted on a fuel storage tank is a highly visible landmark. Run in along the city shoreline.

MARINAS

Foss Waterway Seaport has 1,200 ft of linear moorage for visitors; call 253-272-2750. First 4 hours free. Reservations for boating groups. Pay at the office, or drop box after hours. Power to 50 amps and water on the docks. Fee for pump-out. No other facilities.

Foss Harbor Marina. VHF Channel 71; call 253-272-4404. Visitor moorage up to 90 ft when slips are available; call ahead. Power to 50 amps, shower, laundry, Wi-Fi and pump-out facility. Groceries, beer, wine, ice and marine supplies at the store. Reciprocal moorage at Totem and Fircrest yacht clubs.

FUEL

Foss Harbor Marina Fuel Dock at the end of "D" dock. VHF Channel 71; call 253-272-4404. Gasoline, diesel and marine supplies, with access to the marina store.

Tacoma Fuel Dock is on the "E" side of the waterway; call 253-572-2666. Gasoline, diesel, marine supplies, pump-out facility, ice and snacks. Commencement Bay Marine Services sells parts and offers full marine services and haulout.

www.traveltacoma.com

Tacoma's revitalized waterfront comes complete with visitor moorage at Dock Street Marina.

The city abounds with artwork.

The Tacoma Link is modern, efficient and free.

With plans to visit the Museum District in "Lower" Thea Foss Waterway, we reserved moorage at Dock Street Marina, with a quick stop at Johnny's Seafood Co. for fresh halibut. The marina's visitor moorage is backed by the prominent Museum of Glass (MOG), with its dramatic, tilting stainless-steel cone, three reflecting pools and the 500-foot-long Chihuly Bridge of Glass. Designed by acclaimed architect Arthur Erickson, the 90-foot-tall cone tilts 17 degrees to the north and references the old wood-burning sawmills of the region.

Visit the MOG, the Washington State History Museum (WSHM) and the Tacoma Art Museum (TAM) for one low price of $25 with the Tacoma Museum Pass, available at any of the three museums. Watch artists work with molten glass at the MOG Hot Shop, and at the TAM, be inspired by Pacific Northwest and international artists, or buy an amusing "knit your own dog" kit by Muir & Osborne. The WSHM is a must-visit for the whole family, with interactive exhibits, theatrical storytelling and high-tech displays. The museum gift stores all offer a diverse selection of merchandise, from affordable to collectable. After museum-hopping, if time and energy permit, take a look at the Chihuly displays at the renovated Union Station.

The historic Proctor District is located just west of the museums. A favorite with Tacoma locals, the area has cultivated an urban village atmosphere and offers visitors unique sidewalk shopping and eateries, including Grassi's Garden Cafe and Anthem Coffee & Tea.

A day of visiting museums can be exhausting, and happily The Social Bar and Grill on the waterfront came to our rescue. Their welcoming shaded patio and cosy fire pit are perfect for outdoor dining. We were happy to relax with a selection of delicious appetizers and cocktails, a front row view of the bustling waterway and the soothing cascade of the Chihuly glass fountains just across from our table.

LOCAL FACTS

The Tacoma Visitor Information Center is located in the Marriott Hotel; take the Link to the Convention Center Station.

The MOG is open seven days a week, Monday to Saturday, 10 a.m. to 5 p.m., and Sunday, 12 to 5 p.m., from Memorial Day to Labor Day. Open until 8 p.m. on the third Thursday of each month, with free entry from 5 to 8 p.m. Open five days a week only in fall, winter and spring.

The TAM is open Wednesday to Sunday, 10 a.m. to 5 p.m. Open until 8 p.m. on the third Thursday of each month, with free entry from 5 to 8 p.m.

The WSHM is open Tuesday to Sunday, 10 a.m. to 5 p.m. Open until 8 p.m. on the third Thursday of each month, with free entry from 2 to 8 p.m.

For the most uplifting and entertaining taxi ride in Tacoma, call Aloha Cab (253-428-9999). The city's original karaoke cab (yes, your driver will do karaoke on every ride!) is efficient, friendly and affordable.

FOOD FACTS – MUSEUM DISTRICT

Choripan by Asado: Located inside the MOG, here you can enjoy lunch Argentinian style.

Bite: This Hotel Murano restaurant offers a locally sourced menu featuring Pacific Northwest-inspired dishes. Serves breakfast, lunch and dinner (and dessert!).

Pacific Grill: Across the street from the Children's Museum of Tacoma, this fine-dining restaurant and lounge is noted for their all-day happy hour menu and noodle bar.

CHART 18453

APPROACH
Proceed S, passing under the Murray Morgan Bridge.
Vertical Lift Bridge:
- Horizontal CL. 200 ft
- Vertical CL. 64 ft closed
- Vertical CL. 139 ft open

MARINA
Dock Street Marina; call 253-250-1906. Visitor moorage at "H" and "G" docks for boats up to 120 ft. Power to 100 amps, slip-side pump-out and hazmat disposal. 24-hour security. Free cable TV and Wi-Fi. Laundry facilities and free showers. Reservations recommended; call well ahead for group bookings.

Johnny's Dock Restaurant & Marina has visitor moorage for restaurant guests, and overnight moorage is also possible; call 253-627-3186.

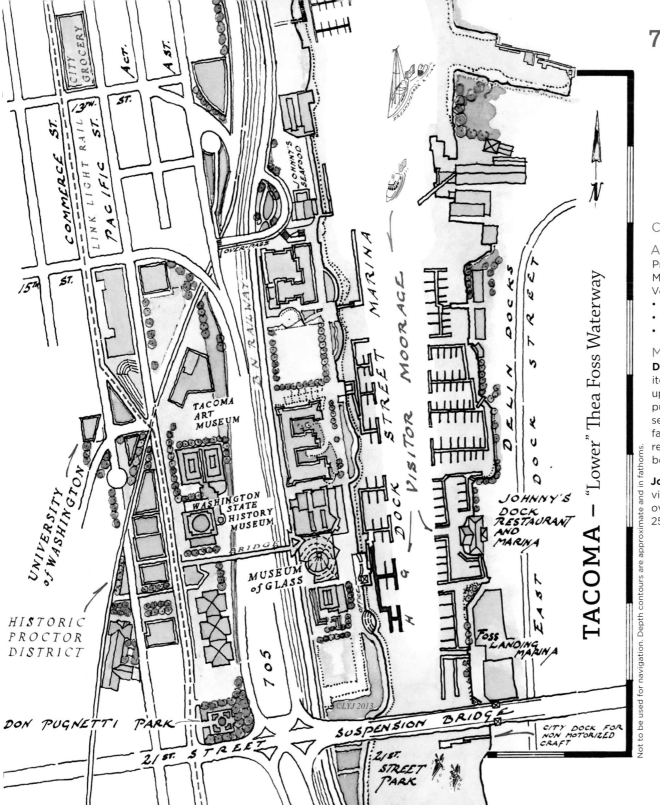

TACOMA – "Lower" Thea Foss Waterway

Not to be used for navigation. Depth contours are approximate and in fathoms.

TACOMA – Old Town Dock

The refurbished dock off Ruston Way offers excellent visitor moorage and the convenience of visiting Tacoma's charming Old Town.

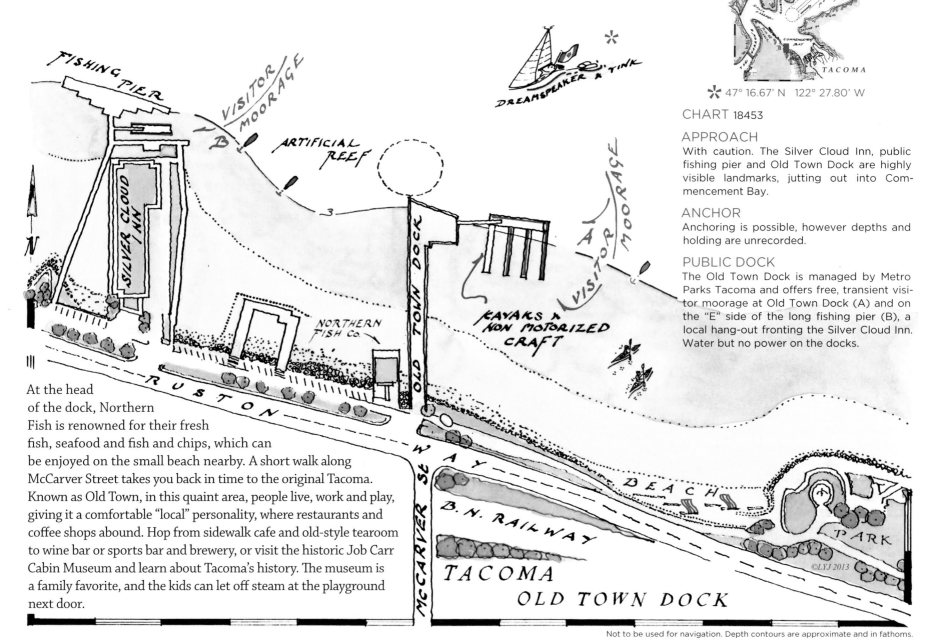

✳ 47° 16.67' N 122° 27.80' W

CHART 18453

APPROACH
With caution. The Silver Cloud Inn, public fishing pier and Old Town Dock are highly visible landmarks, jutting out into Commencement Bay.

ANCHOR
Anchoring is possible, however depths and holding are unrecorded.

PUBLIC DOCK
The Old Town Dock is managed by Metro Parks Tacoma and offers free, transient visitor moorage at Old Town Dock (A) and on the "E" side of the long fishing pier (B), a local hang-out fronting the Silver Cloud Inn. Water but no power on the docks.

At the head of the dock, Northern Fish is renowned for their fresh fish, seafood and fish and chips, which can be enjoyed on the small beach nearby. A short walk along McCarver Street takes you back in time to the original Tacoma. Known as Old Town, in this quaint area, people live, work and play, giving it a comfortable "local" personality, where restaurants and coffee shops abound. Hop from sidewalk cafe and old-style tearoom to wine bar or sports bar and brewery, or visit the historic Job Carr Cabin Museum and learn about Tacoma's history. The museum is a family favorite, and the kids can let off steam at the playground next door.

Not to be used for navigation. Depth contours are approximate and in fathoms.

Thea's Park overlooks Commencement Bay and is perfect for viewing commercial vessels entering or leaving the Port of Tacoma.

The water in Puget Sound is rarely rough in summer, and a light breeze will get you sailing.

✳ 47° 18.52' N   122° 30.87' W

CHART 18453

APPROACH
From the N. An unnamed cove lies behind a man-made rock-and-gravel spit, SE of Point Defiance; the Tacoma Yacht Club sits prominently on the end of the spit. The Vashon Island Ferry Terminal defines the cove entrance channel to the W.

MARINAS
Breakwater Marina; call 253-752-6663. Visitor moorage in unoccupied slips; call ahead. Power to 30 amps, Wi-Fi and pump-out facility available on the docks. Shower and laundry facilities. Repair service available.

Point Defiance Marina; call 253-591-5325. Public 8-lane launch ramp and visitor moorage with a pump-out facility to the E of the ferry terminus (up to 72 hrs). Free visitor moorage on the E side, fronting the boathouse store, is for day/evening only – no overnight stays. Tacoma Yacht Club has designated reciprocal moorage.

FUEL
Breakwater Marina Fuel Dock. Gasoline, diesel and propane. Their store stocks marine-related parts and accessories, ice, pop and snacks.

Point Defiance Marina Gas Dock. Gasoline only. Their boathouse store sells bait and tackle, marine supplies, food and beverages.

CAUTIONARY NOTE
Be aware that the cove's ferry and boat traffic from the marinas and 8-lane boat launch makes the entrance very busy.

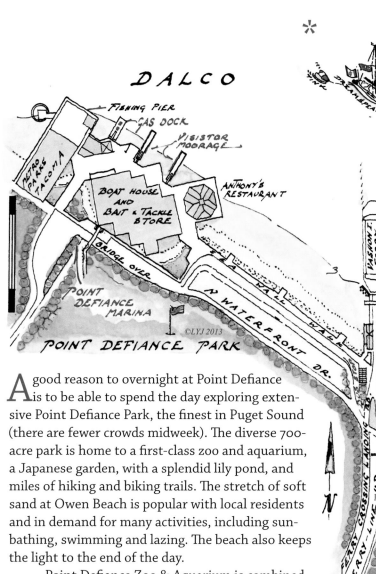

DALCO   PASSAGE

FISHING PIER
GAS DOCK
VISISTOR MOORAGE
ANTHONY'S RESTAURANT
METRO PARKS TACOMA
BOAT HOUSE AND BAIT & TACKLE STORE
BRIDGE OVER
POINT DEFIANCE MARINA
©LYJ 2013
POINT DEFIANCE PARK
N WATERFRONT DR.
VASHON I. FERRY
PUBLIC VISITOR MOORAGE
TACOMA YACHT CLUB
T.Y.C. RECIPROCAL
BREAKWATER
FUEL DOCK
8 LANE BOAT LAUNCH
PUMP OUT
OFFICE
FERRY CROSSING LANDING
FERRY LINE UP
N WATERFRONT DRIVE
MARINA

TACOMA
POINT
DEFIANCE

A good reason to overnight at Point Defiance is to be able to spend the day exploring extensive Point Defiance Park, the finest in Puget Sound (there are fewer crowds midweek). The diverse 700-acre park is home to a first-class zoo and aquarium, a Japanese garden, with a splendid lily pond, and miles of hiking and biking trails. The stretch of soft sand at Owen Beach is popular with local residents and in demand for many activities, including sunbathing, swimming and lazing. The beach also keeps the light to the end of the day.

Point Defiance Zoo & Aquarium is combined, and it's large enough to offer a remarkable selection of animals yet small enough to view them up close. Almost all of the animals at the zoo are from the Pacific Rim, although the Kids' Zone features animals from around the world.

Not to be used for navigation. Depth contours are approximate and in fathoms.

Quartermaster Harbor, Maury Island

This is a real family park with a swim-float and roped-off swimming area, showers, a playground and grassy picnic spots, as well as nine miles of hiking, biking and horseback riding trails in the Dockton Forest and Natural Area. The park offers excellent visitor moorage, which is well used by locals. We dropped our hook east of the docks and held well in very sticky mud. It was a sunny Friday afternoon, and boats filled with kids, dogs and coolers began arriving in rapid succession.

In search of the nearby forest trailhead, Laurence and I rowed over to the park, crossed the road and, after hiking the initial steep path, had a lovely walk along the loop trails in the shade of a second-growth forest. Later, it was pure bliss diving off the swim platform prior to happy hour in *Dreamspeaker's* cockpit.

* 47° 22.47' N   122° 27.32' W

CHART 18474

APPROACH
The park moorage from the NW, out of the center of Quartermaster Harbor, because obstructions line the inshore route along the Dockton community shoreline.

ANCHOR
As indicated in sticky mud, in 2+ ftm (12+ ft). Good protection from the SE. NOAA Navigation Chart 18474 indicates that the bottom is foul further to the NE.

PARK DOCK
Dockton Beach Park, managed by King County Parks, has moorage at the park dock (designated for visitors), with concrete floats, a pump-out facility and ample room for visiting boaters. There is a 3-day moorage limit. This is a popular weekend spot for locals.

LAUNCH
A public boat launch is SW of the park moorage.

Not to be used for navigation. Depth contours are approximate and in fathoms.

BURTON ACRES PARK,

Quartermaster Harbor,
Vashon Island

Quartermaster Harbor is a peaceful, five-mile expanse of water, where locals and visiting boaters find their favorite spots within the roomy anchorage. We spent a quiet evening anchored in four fathoms of water, with plenty of privacy and room to swing. North and northeast of the Burton Peninsula affords the best protection and easy shore access to Burton Acres Park.

The park is an island gem that protects mature second-growth woodlands. Beach your dinghy or kayak on the shell and pebble beach adjacent to the boat launch, where you will find a map of the park trails. Local residents and park visitors have established a system of walking, hiking and horseback riding trails that traverse and loop around the park. After an invigorating hike, enjoy a picnic in the shade of a large madrona tree or on the lawn above the beach.

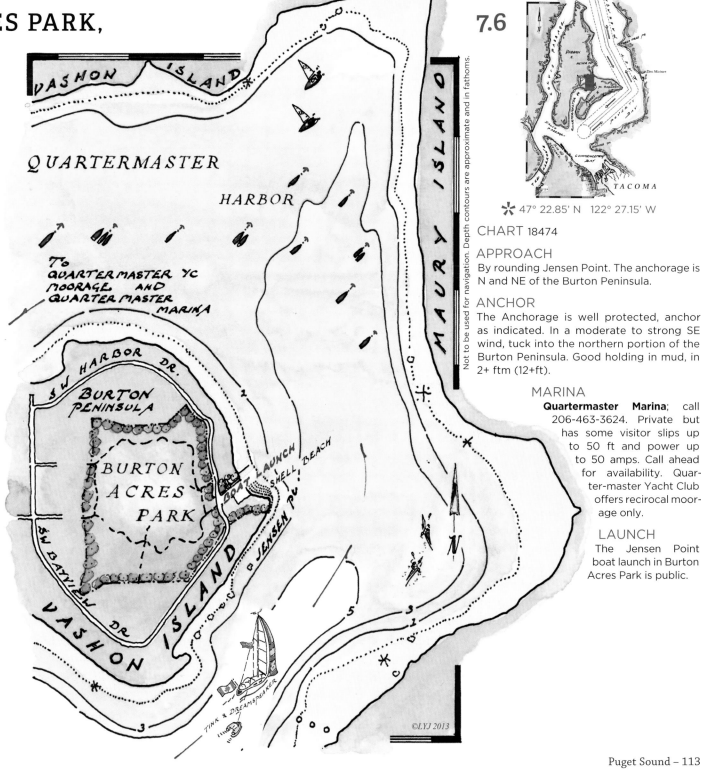

✳ 47° 22.85' N   122° 27.15' W

CHART 18474

APPROACH
By rounding Jensen Point. The anchorage is N and NE of the Burton Peninsula.

ANCHOR
The Anchorage is well protected, anchor as indicated. In a moderate to strong SE wind, tuck into the northern portion of the Burton Peninsula. Good holding in mud, in 2+ ftm (12+ft).

MARINA
Quartermaster Marina; call 206-463-3624. Private but has some visitor slips up to 50 ft and power up to 50 amps. Call ahead for availability. Quartermaster Yacht Club offers recirocal moorage only.

LAUNCH
The Jensen Point boat launch in Burton Acres Park is public.

The Des Moines Marina fuel dock fronts the visitor moorage.

DES MOINES MARINA & APPROACHES

❊ 47° 24.05' N 122° 20.17' W

Saturday morning at Des Moines Marina is a festive affair with the Waterfront Farmers' Market in full swing. The market is filled with a bounty of local and fresh vegetables, fruit, honey, cheeses, crafts, flowers, meat and fish. Since its successful inception, it has become a community-gathering place with lively entertainment.

A stroll along Cliff Avenue leads to charming Des Moines Beach Park, which overlooks East Passage and Point Robinson Lighthouse. Kayaks line the sand and gravel beach, kids play in the cool water and families picnic on the lawns. A pleasant walk to downtown Des Moines via Marine View Drive reveals a fascinating variety of retail stores, yarn and craft shops, restaurants and coffee bars. We were delighted to discover the Blue Vanilla Bakery & Cafe, B & E Meats and Seafood (great homemade sausages) and Auntie Irene's for espresso and ice cream.

LOCAL FACT
The Waterfront Farmers' Market takes place every Saturday, 10 a.m. to 2 p.m., from June to the end of October.

CHART 18474

APPROACH
S of the fishing pier and port-hand buoy (green). Enter the marina by rounding the rock breakwater and inner timber breakwater.

MARINA
Des Moines Marina. VHF Channel 16, switch to 68; call 206-824-5700. Ample visitor moorage. Slips for boats up to 50 ft, and side tie for boats up to 100 ft on a first-come basis. Check for availability at the fuel dock. Reservations for boats 32+ ft and groups of 5+ boats. Power to 150 amps and free pump-out and shower facilities. The marina offers a shuttle into town for laundry and grocery shopping. QFC is at the nearby plaza.

Des Moines Yacht Club offers reciprocal moorage.

ANCHOR
At the marina. Gasoline, diesel and propane available. CSR Marine provides a full-service boatyard; call 206-878-4414.

CAUTIONARY NOTE
Dead-slow speed on entering. Be aware of boats exiting and maneuvering around the fuel dock.

Not to be used for navigation. Depth contours are approximate and in fathoms.

It was a blue-sky, sunny day as we crossed East Passage from Des Moines Marina into Tramp Harbor and headed towards Point Heyer and a spot known locally as "KVI Beach." An appealing stretch of fine sand, backed by sun-bleached driftwood, invited us to investigate further. Anchoring off the point, we packed our beach gear and rowed over to join Vashon Islanders basking in the sunshine, while dogs and kids romped in the water.

The sand and driftwood spit forms a natural pool as the tide begins to rise, providing blissful warm-water bathing. An entertaining local dog spent hours "fishing" in the pool, although his owner couldn't confirm if he had caught anything to date! At high water, the beach disappeared, visitors made their way home and we rowed to *Dreamspeaker* to wash off in the cockpit.

Not to be used for navigation. Depth contours are approximate and in fathoms.

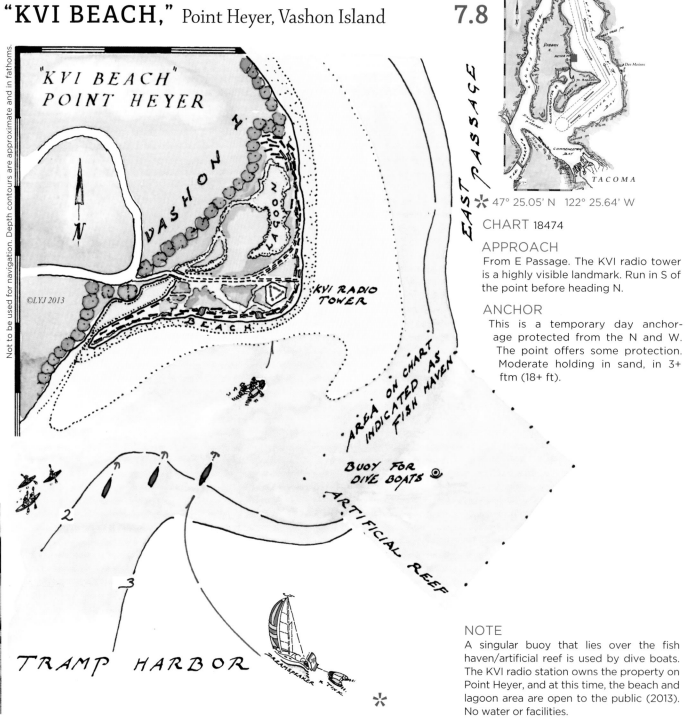

Anne felt at home in a hat.

✳ 47° 25.05' N   122° 25.64' W

CHART 18474

APPROACH
From E Passage. The KVI radio tower is a highly visible landmark. Run in S of the point before heading N.

ANCHOR
This is a temporary day anchorage protected from the N and W. The point offers some protection. Moderate holding in sand, in 3+ ftm (18+ ft).

NOTE
A singular buoy that lies over the fish haven/artificial reef is used by dive boats. The KVI radio station owns the property on Point Heyer, and at this time, the beach and lagoon area are open to the public (2013). No water or facilities.

GIG HARBOR & SOUTH SOUND "EAST"

Tacoma Narrows & Carr Inlet to Johnson Point

Gig Harbor is one of Puget Sound's great natural harbors and a paradise for all who venture onto the water. Mike Martin photo.

CHAPTER 8 GIG HARBOR & SOUTH SOUND "EAST"

Tacoma Narrows & Carr Inlet to Johnson Point

The twin suspension bridges span Tacoma Narrows, the gateway to South Sound.

www.cityofgigharbor.net

CAUTIONARY NOTE
The depth and width of the entrance channel to Gig Harbor are restricted at low water and on a minus tide.

After rounding the curved spit into Gig Harbor, the narrow entrance opens to reveal one of the most extensive and sheltered anchorages in Puget Sound, and this merited a few days' exploration! Buzzing with activity, the generous bay is filled with a vibrant array of watercraft, and the lively shoreline is dense with marinas, docks and boats. A convenient downtown public dock fronts pedestrian-friendly streets, with a pleasant mix of coffee bars, restaurants and shops that we enjoy, before traveling south to the enchanting state parks and anchorages of Carr Inlet and Nisqually Reach.

Slipping out of Gig Harbor after an enjoyable weekend, we transited the Narrows on a flooding current, watching the twin bridges pass swiftly overhead. At Narrows Marina, we topped up our tanks and headed into Hale Passage, where we dropped anchor in Wollochet Bay for a picnic lunch. Taking advantage of the fresh breeze, we enjoyed an afternoon sail in Carr Inlet, anchoring in sheltered Horsehead Bay for the night. This became our base camp as we hiked in Kopachuck State Park and swam off the sand spit at unspoiled Cutts Island State Park.

A misty morning in Mayo Cove revealed families and their dogs digging for clams on the long spit off Penrose Point State Park. That afternoon we navigated Pitt Passage and dropped anchor in Filucy Bay, one of the loveliest destinations to spend a laid-back few days rowing, swimming and just lazing in the cockpit.

Prior to anchoring for the night in Oro Bay on Anderson Island, Laurence and I took advantage of the low tide and had a pleasant walk around the shoreline of small Eagle Island State Park. As we headed south to Olympia the following day, we anchored off Tolmie State Park to hike the trails, then popped into friendly Zittel's Marina for fuel, water and ice cream.

TIDES
Tide Height Station: Tacoma

CURRENTS
Tidal Current Station: Tacoma Narrows

WEATHER
NOAA Weather Radio WX4: Puget Sound
NOAA VHF Weather Channel 1 or 3
www.nws.noaa.gov/nwr

NOTE
Be aware of the police-enforced 5 mph, no-wake speed limit in Gig Harbor. The harbor is patrolled on a regular basis and violation tickets are handed out.

FACTS
Incorporated in 1946, the City of Gig Harbor experienced its most notable population growth in the mid-1990s. There are approximately 7,500 residents within the city limits, and a total of 66,000 inhabitants in the Gig Harbor/Key Peninsula area. Centrally situated, Gig Harbor is an hour's drive from Seattle, and 45 minutes from Sea-Tac International Airport in the north and the state capital of Olympia in the south.

Fondly referred to as "The Maritime Village," Gig Harbor has preserved its heritage and celebrates its history of commercial fishing and boat-building, which reaches back to the mid-1800s, when immigrants, mostly Croatian, followed by Norwegians and Swedes, settled here.

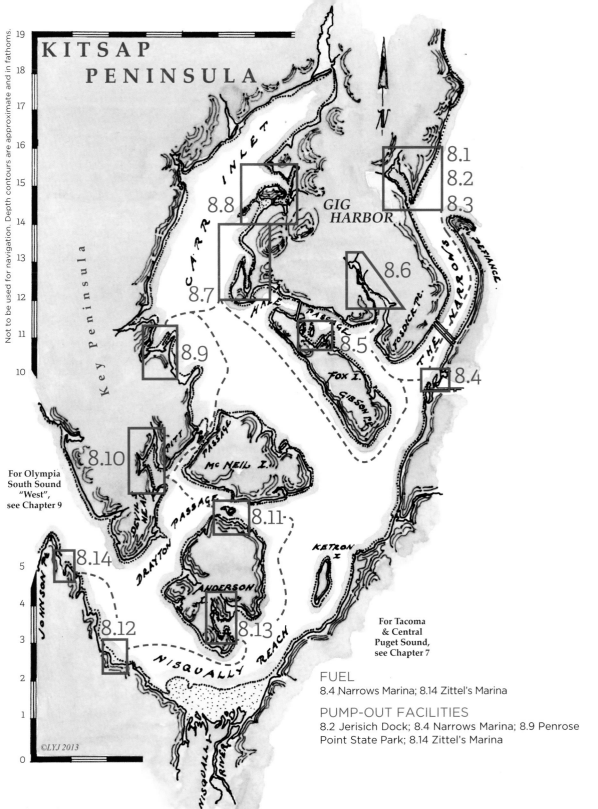

8 GIG HARBOR
& SOUTH SOUND "EAST"

FEATURED DESTINATIONS

FUEL
8.4 Narrows Marina; 8.14 Zittel's Marina

PUMP-OUT FACILITIES
8.2 Jerisich Dock; 8.4 Narrows Marina; 8.9 Penrose Point State Park; 8.14 Zittel's Marina

For Olympia South Sound "West", see Chapter 9

For Tacoma & Central Puget Sound, see Chapter 7

©LYJ 2013

8.1 GIG HARBOR & APPROACHES

The light on the spit welcomes boaters to Gig Harbor.

A breeze to sail, and warm water for swimming.

The panorama east over Gig Harbor from the view climb.

Sailing on a good northerly breeze, we approached the Gig Harbor light under full sail and learned first-hand that our speed was no match for the strong outgoing tidal current that sweeps around the tip of the spit. It was time to furl in *Dreamspeaker's* sails and start the motor. The narrow entrance into the harbor opens to reveal an extensive anchorage filled with a vibrant array of watercraft, as well as a lively shoreline dense with marinas, docks and boats.

We dropped anchor northeast of Jerisich Dock, with plans to explore the harbor by dinghy and foot for a few days. The large bay is bustling with activity, from paddleboarders, kayakers and sailing dinghies crisscrossing the bay to classic wooden boats out for a jaunt and local sailboat races weaving through vessels at anchor. The harbor is blessed with a cool, thermal breeze during hot days, and the tip of the spit has an inviting sandy beach to dig your toes into.

Gig Harbor derived its name from the longboat, or captain's "gig," during the Wilkes Expedition of 1841. Since the late 1880s, the harbor has established a rich history of fishing, logging, boat-building and farming. Most of the Croatian settlers of the mid-1800s were commercial fishermen, which along with boat-building, dominated the local economy for the next 100 years. Although reduced in size, the town's commercial fishing fleet is still alive today.

Homes along the residential east shore maintain landscaped lawns and flower gardens shaded by a profusion of trees. Private docks provide moorage for even more boats and the occasional working tug. Dotted with public parks and historic net sheds, the harbor's western shoreline is divided into the downtown and working waterfronts, the Museum District and the historic Finholm District.

EVENTS

The Maritime Gig Festival, which is held every year during the first weekend of June, is a fun community event that includes the traditional Blessing of the Fleet, a parade, music and local booths.

The Gig Harbor Summer Arts Festival takes place on the third Saturday and Sunday in July, with hundreds of Pacific Northwest artists on hand – an exuberant outdoor fair.

LOCAL FACTS

Just up from the "City Dock," the highly popular Summer Sounds at Skansie Brothers Park presents fun-for-all outdoor concerts every Tuesday night, as well as family movie nights on Fridays and Saturdays.

The Gig Harbor Art Walk takes place on the first Saturday of each month from 1 to 5 p.m. Pick up a map and enjoy a self-guided tour of interesting downtown art galleries and studios. Many galleries serve refreshments, and artists are often in attendance.

For fresh local and organic produce, homemade jams, preserves and crafts, visit the colorful Downtown Farmers' Market at Skansie Brothers Park on Wednesdays and Sundays, from 11 a.m. to 4 p.m. (June to September).

Pick up the *Waterfront Walking, Boating and Shopping Guide*, published by the Downtown Waterfront Alliance and available at the Gig Harbor Visitor Information Center, or one of the many kiosks around town.

Pierce Transit offers a convenient trolley service from Gig harbor's downtown waterfront to the uptown shopping area. The 30-minute service will run daily from 11 a.m. to 7:30 p.m. with extended service to 9:30 p.m. on Tuesday, Friday and Saturday.

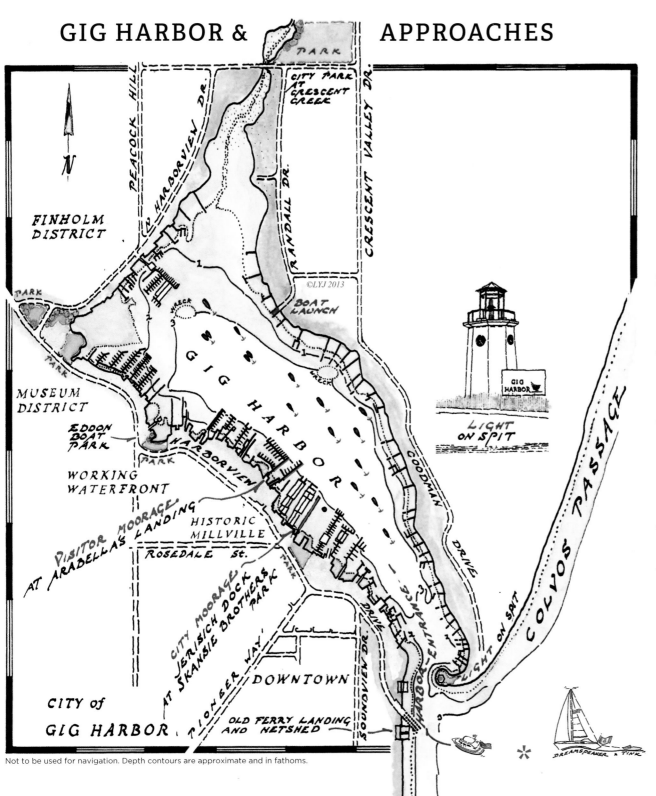

FINHOLM
DISTRICT

MUSEUM
DISTRICT

EDDON
BOAT
PARK

WORKING
WATERFRONT

Visitor Moorage
at Arabella's Landing

HISTORIC
MILLVILLE

ROSEDALE St.

City Moorage
Jerisich Dock
at Skansie Brothers Park

GIG HARBOR

PEACOCK HILL

N HARBORVIEW DR.

PARK

CITY PARK
AT CRESCENT
CREEK

RANDALL DR.

CRESCENT VALLEY DR.

©LYJ 2013

BOAT
LAUNCH

HARBORVIEW DR.

SOUNDVIEW DR.

PIONEER WAY

DOWNTOWN

CITY of
GIG HARBOR

OLD FERRY LANDING
AND NETSHED

HARBOR ENTRANCE

GOODMAN DRIVE

LIGHT ON SPIT

COLVOS PASSAGE

GIG
HARBOR

LIGHT
ON SPIT

DREAMSPEAKER & TINK

Not to be used for navigation. Depth contours are approximate and in fathoms.

KISAP
PENINSULA

✳ 47° 19.50' N   125° 34.40' W

CHART 18445

APPROACH
The harbor entrance is marked by a red light on an octagonal, lighthouse-style tower. Stay well S of the spit. A strong tidal current sweeps around the tip of the spit.

ANCHOR
Well-protected anchorage is possible throughout the harbor, as indicated. Good holding in mud, in depths of 2+ ftm (12+ ft).

PUBLIC DOCK
Visitor moorage and a dinghy dock are available at the Jerisich Dock, known locally as the "City Dock."

FUEL
Currently not available in the harbor (2013).

LAUNCH
A public boat launch is situated on the NE shore, at the S end of Randall Drive.

NOTE
There is a police-enforced 5 mph, no-wake speed limit in the harbor.

In the heart of downtown Gig Harbor, Jerisich Dock fronts pedestrian-friendly streets with a pleasant mix of coffee bars, cafes, shops, bookstores, vintage stores and specialty gift shops. Begin your day with a good coffee and pastry at Java & Clay Cafe, or with breakfast at Netshed No. 9, just north of Skansie Brothers Park. For a traditional breakfast, juicy hamburger or sinful ice cream, Kelly's is a local family favorite. From here, it's a short walk to Judson Street, where the visitor center, West Marine and popular 7 Seas Brewing and Tap Room are located. Tides Tavern, adjacent to the Maritime Pier, is a well-known South Sound waterfront pub and restaurant that also offers ample complimentary customer moorage.

Heading west, Ship to Shore is an excellent full-service marine chandlery that also carries ice and basic groceries. Further along, Suzanne's Bakery & Deli produces delicious loaves of bread and fine pastries, and they serve lunch on the shaded outdoor patio.

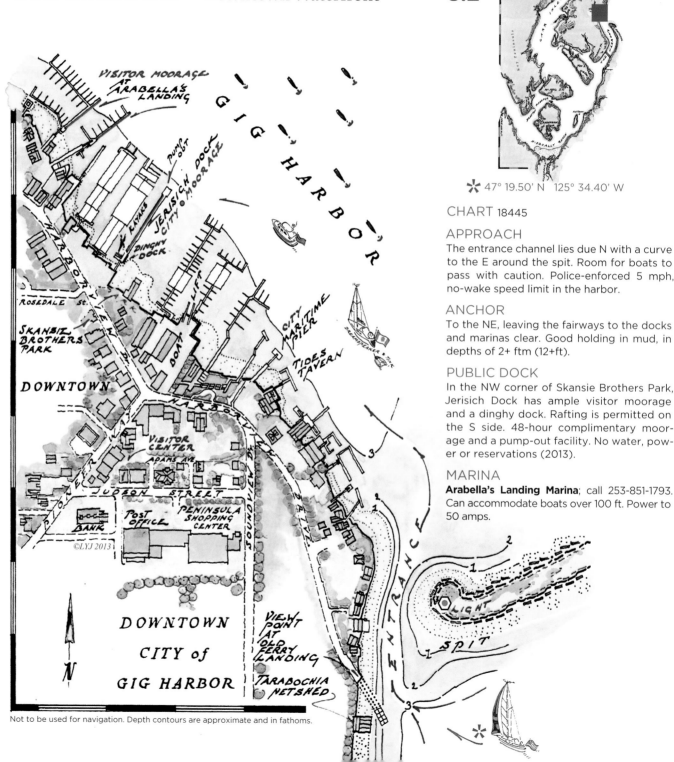

Not to be used for navigation. Depth contours are approximate and in fathoms.

✳ 47° 19.50' N   125° 34.40' W

CHART 18445

APPROACH
The entrance channel lies due N with a curve to the E around the spit. Room for boats to pass with caution. Police-enforced 5 mph, no-wake speed limit in the harbor.

ANCHOR
To the NE, leaving the fairways to the docks and marinas clear. Good holding in mud, in depths of 2+ ftm (12+ft).

PUBLIC DOCK
In the NW corner of Skansie Brothers Park, Jerisich Dock has ample visitor moorage and a dinghy dock. Rafting is permitted on the S side. 48-hour complimentary moorage and a pump-out facility. No water, power or reservations (2013).

MARINA
Arabella's Landing Marina; call 253-851-1793. Can accommodate boats over 100 ft. Power to 50 amps.

Sailing past Skansie Brothers Park and Jerisich Dock, downtown Gig Harbor.

The Finholm's Market and Grocery predates the first Volkswagen Beetle of 1938.

With *Dreamspeaker* anchored near the head of Gig Harbor, we explored the northwest shoreline by dinghy. It was a wonderful surprise to discover the charming, historic waterfront of Finholm. Provisioning at Finholm's Market was an added bonus, as they carry just about anything that you might need, including a selection of groceries, fresh produce, ice, beer and wine. Treat yourself to lunch at the Devoted Kiss Cafe, or fresh halibut and chips from the friendly Marketplace Grille. End the day at Morso – a welcoming wine bar with a view.

The Finholm View Climb, built to honor the area's pioneering brothers, John and Edward Finholm, leads you up 98 wooden steps to the viewpoint, where the quintessential panorama of Gig Harbor and Mt. Rainier is your reward.

At high water, non-motorized craft can beach at Austin Estuary Park to visit the Harbor History Museum, which offers custom exhibitions, hands-on programs and the *Shenandoah*, a 65-foot fishing vessel built by the renowned Skansie Ship Building Company.

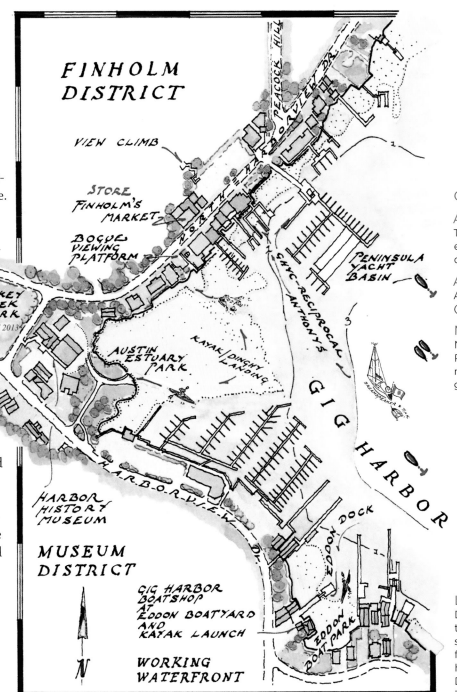

Not to be used for navigation. Depth contours are approximate and in fathoms.

CHART 18445

APPROACH
The NW corner of Gig Harbor is the quiet end, but stay clear of the fairways to the docks and marinas.

ANCHOR
Anchorage is possible in depths of 2+ ftm (12+ ft), with good holding in mud.

MARINAS
No visitor moorage available (2013). The Peninsula Yacht Basin has 80 ft of reciprocal moorage. Anthony's at Gig Harbor provides guest moorage for patrons of the restaurant.

LOCAL FACTS
Dinghy and kayak access to the Finholm District can be found off the small beach and stairs below the Ruth M. Bogue Viewing Platform. A kayak landing and temporary (two-hour) dinghy tie-up is possible at Eddon Boat Dock. Visit the renovated Eddon Boatyard, home of the classic Thunderbird sailboats.

NARROWS MARINA,
Tacoma Narrows

www.narrowsmarina.com

A welcoming, family owned and operated facility, Narrows Marina has been serving boaters since 1949. They now offer visitor moorage, marine services, a refurbished bait and tackle store and a restaurant with a generous deck and microbrewery, all on one site.

The Bait & Tackle store also sells a wide selection of marine supplies and hardware, and their convenience section carries ice, snacks, sandwiches and salads, fresh coffee and beer and wine. Boathouse 19 Bar & Grill is a lively restaurant that serves casual seasonal and local fare, either indoors or on the wooden deck, which is shaded by large white umbrellas. Narrows Brewing Company, with its fine selection of beer on tap, is a cosy spot to enjoy a pint of the good stuff.

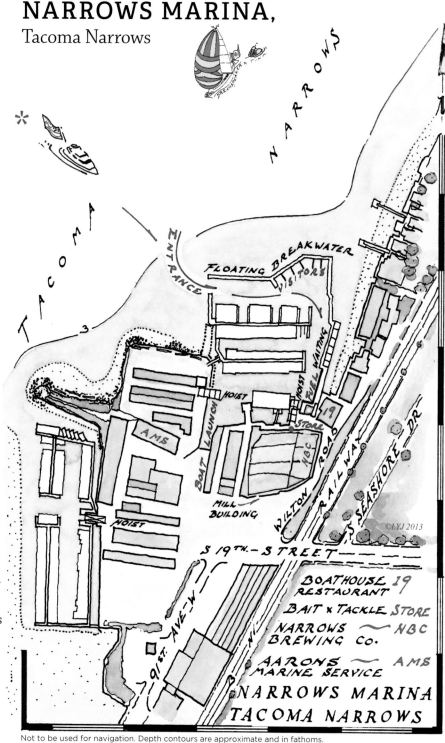

Not to be used for navigation. Depth contours are approximate and in fathoms.

✳ 47° 14.50' N   122° 33.67' W

CHART 18448

APPROACH
The marina lies S of the Tacoma Narrows Bridge (twin suspension bridges) and N of Day Island on the mainland shore. Approach from the NW, being mindful of the current in Tacoma Narrows.

MARINA
Narrows Marina; call 253-564-3032. Full-service facility with visitor slips for boats up to 26 ft and side-tie moorage for the restaurant and brewery. Docks have surveillance cameras and security gates, water, power to 30 amps and a pump-out facility.

FUEL
Gasoline, diesel and water are available at the fuel dock. Aarons Marine Service is an on-site marine repair and full-service shop; call 253-564-1644.

NOTE
Overnight side-tie moorage for larger boats can be arranged – no power. Call ahead for information.

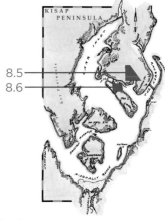

Map labels (top map):
WOLLOCHET BAY ESTUARY PARK
LAUNCH RAMP
1½
TACOMA Y.C. OUTSTATION
WOLLOCHET HARBOR CLUB
4
3
N
WOLLOCHET BAY
©LYJ 2013

Not to be used for navigation. Depth contours are approximate and in fathoms.

8.5 "ECHO BAY," Fox Island

Locally named "Echo Bay" provided us with a pleasant lunch stop, just west of the forested foreshore of Tanglewood Island, which is private. Although there is no shore access to Fox Island and the charming waterfront chapel, this sheltered anchorage is perfect for a picnic and a nap in the cockpit.

8.5

⚓ 47° 16.33' N   122° 57.97' W

CHART 18448

APPROACH
"Echo Bay" (local name) lies to the E of the Fox Island Bridge, off Hale Passage. The run in around Tanglewood Island is clear, except for an aquaculture raft, charted as an obstruction.

ANCHOR
Anchorage is possible to the E or W of Tanglewood Island. Stay clear of the cable area and oyster floats. Good holding in mud, in depths of 5+ ftm (30+ ft).

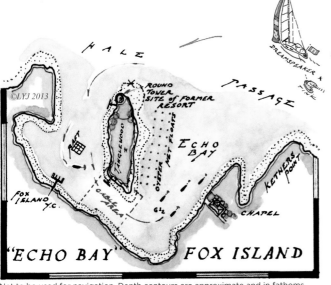

Map labels (bottom map):
HALE PASSAGE
ROUND TOWER SITE OF FORMER RESORT
TANGLEWOOD I.
ECHO BAY
OYSTER NET FLOATS
KETNERS POINT
FOX ISLAND Y.C.
CABLE AREA
6½
CHAPEL
"ECHO BAY"   FOX ISLAND
DREAMSPEAKER
©LYJ 2013

Not to be used for navigation. Depth contours are approximate and in fathoms.

8.6 WOLLOCHET BAY, HALE PASSAGE

Although the private foreshore is lined with elegant homes and docks, Wollochet Bay, known as "the bay of squirting clams," provides sheltered anchorage between Wollochet Harbor Club and the public launch ramp. The winds in the outer bay offer perfect dinghy sailing conditions, and at high tide, it is possible to explore the estuary and take the pooch for a walk in Wollochet Bay Estuary Park.

8.6

⚓ 47° 16.65' N   122° 35.76' W

CHART 18448

APPROACH
Wollochet Bay branches N from Hale Passage, and the run in is clear.

ANCHOR
As indicated, N of the 3-ftm contour. Good holding in mud, in depths of 1.5+ ftm (9+ ft).

KOPACHUCK STATE PARK,

Carr Inlet

✳ 47° 18.12' N   122° 41.70' W

CHART 18474

APPROACH
The approach waypoint is due W of the entrance to Horsehead Bay. The run in is clear to both the buoys off Kopachuck State Park and Horsehead Bay. The spit to the W is private.

ANCHOR
The anchorage and buoys off Kopachuck State Park are open to the SE. Horsehead Bay provides good protection from SE winds and is the preferred overnight anchorage. Good holding in mud, in depths of 2+ ftm (12+ ft).

Open views to the Olympic Mountains, a fine public beach and a shaded trail through the park make Kopachuck State Park an attractive destination for the whole family. At high tide, explore the mounds of driftwood deposited by winter storms, or set up a picnic on the wooden tables overlooking the beach. When the tide is out, dig your toes into the stretch of soft sand, and on a rising tide, the shallows and sloping beach provide the opportunity for an enticing warm-water dip. Showers are available at the campsite.

Overnight anchorage can be found in sheltered Horsehead Bay, which is protected by a long, fingerlike spit. Although the bay is surrounded by private homes with docks and swimming rafts, our overnight stay was most enjoyable, and the Olympic Mountain Range, silhouetted by a watercolor afterglow, was stunning.

CARR INLET

ARTIFICIAL REEF

PARK BUOYS

CLAMMING BEACH

CMT CAMPSITE

KOPACHUCK STATE PARK

KOPACHUCK DRIVE NW

56TH St. NW

©LYJ 2013

TINK & DREAMSPEAKER

SPIT

HORSEHEAD BAY

BOAT RAMP

36TH St.

36TH St. N.W

HORSEHEAD BAY DRIVE

N

Not to be used for navigation. Depth contours are approximate and in fathoms.

CUTTS ISLAND STATE PARK, Carr Inlet

With uninterrupted views across the Key Peninsula to the Olympic Mountains, unspoiled Cutts Island State Park is a Puget Sound gem accessible only by water; the small island is easily identified by a cluster of fir trees atop its precipitous sandstone cliff.

On a very low tide, an extensive sand spit on the island's northeast point almost stretches to the tide flats of Raft Island. Speckled with crushed shell, the spit and sand beach, with warm-water swimming on a rising tide, is a delight for all ages.

The small urban cove behind Raft Island provides sheltered overnight anchorage, and the Island View Market customer dock (no access at low water) is a short dinghy ride away. Gasoline and diesel are available, and they carry a good selection of basic groceries, some fresh produce, ice, beer, wine and tasty homemade salsa.

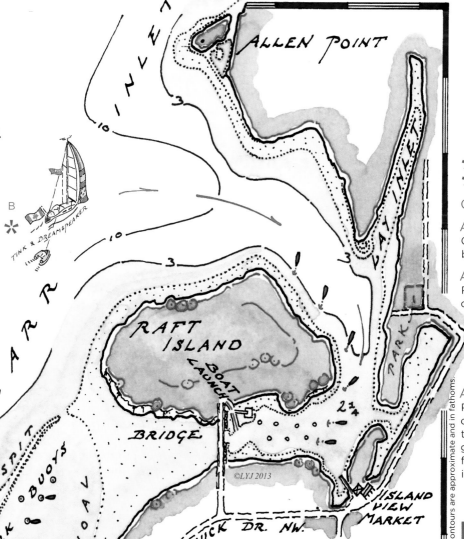

✳ (A) 47° 18.92' N 122° 41.72' W
✳ (B) 47° 18.80' N 122° 41.52' W

CHART 18474

APPROACH A
Cutts Island from the SW. A line of park buoys extend N on its E side.

APPROACH B
Raft Island from the N. Protected anchorage can be found to the N and SE of the island.

ANCHOR
Pick up a park buoy or anchor E of the buoys off Cutts Island State Park, which is open to the SE. The Raft Island anchorage provides good protection from SE winds and is the preferred overnight anchorage. Holding is good in mud and sand, in depths of 2+ ftm (12+ ft).

Cutts Island has a distinct profile.

PENROSE POINT STATE PARK, Carr Inlet

Arriving in Mayo Cove at low water, we dropped anchor south of the boats on park buoys and west of the half-mile spit that runs parallel to Penrose Point. Although it was a misty morning, the shallows were already busy with families digging for clams, beachcombing and walking their pooches.

Sunny weather brought out swimsuits, beach blankets, picnic lunches and colorful water toys. On a rising tide, the water heats up over the shallows, and the sandy beach off the park's picnic lawns is a favorite spot for swimming. The beach opposite the park dock is popular with the sunbathing crowd. Over two miles of trails loop through the park and campgrounds. Pick up a map and take a leisurely stroll through shady second-growth forests filled with a diversity of wildlife.

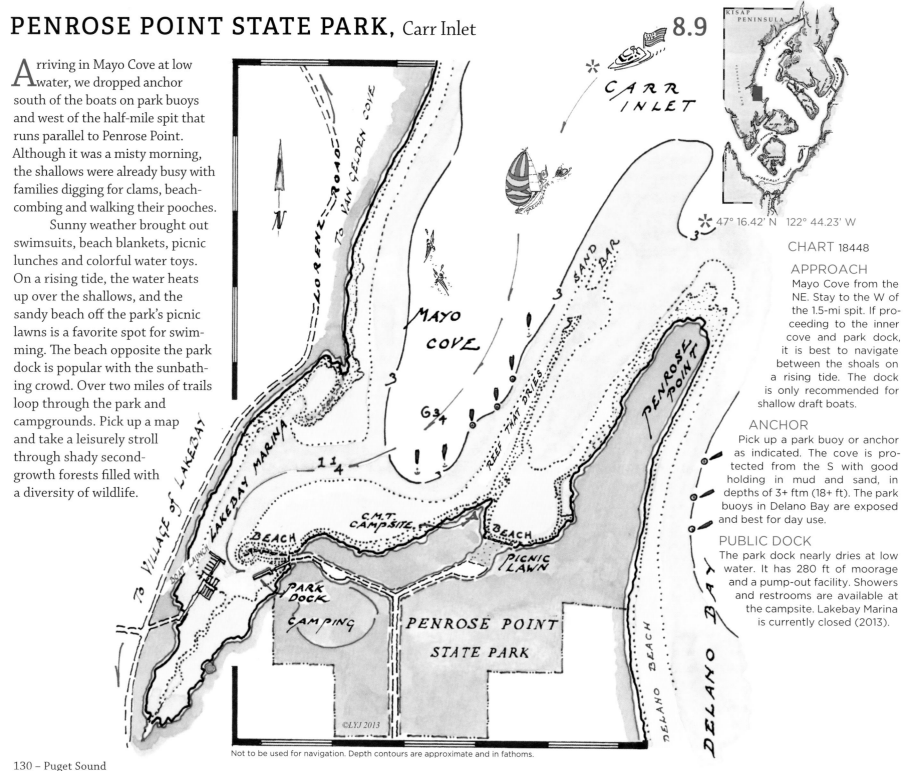

8.9

47° 16.42' N 122° 44.23' W

CHART 18448

APPROACH
Mayo Cove from the NE. Stay to the W of the 1.5-mi spit. If proceeding to the inner cove and park dock, it is best to navigate between the shoals on a rising tide. The dock is only recommended for shallow draft boats.

ANCHOR
Pick up a park buoy or anchor as indicated. The cove is protected from the S with good holding in mud and sand, in depths of 3+ ftm (18+ ft). The park buoys in Delano Bay are exposed and best for day use.

PUBLIC DOCK
The park dock nearly dries at low water. It has 280 ft of moorage and a pump-out facility. Showers and restrooms are available at the campsite. Lakebay Marina is currently closed (2013).

Not to be used for navigation. Depth contours are approximate and in fathoms.

"Echo Bay," Fox Island, is a quiet and picturesque anchorage.

Dreamspeaker meets Chemistry at Longbranch Marina in Filucy Bay.

FILUCY BAY & LONGBRANCH MARINA,
Key Peninsula

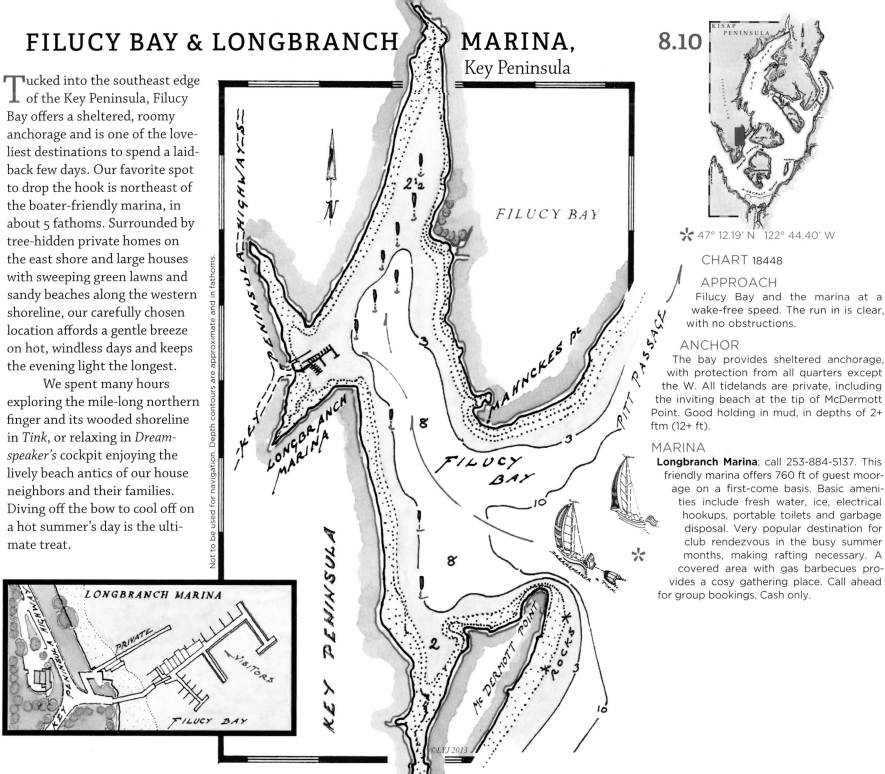

Tucked into the southeast edge of the Key Peninsula, Filucy Bay offers a sheltered, roomy anchorage and is one of the loveliest destinations to spend a laid-back few days. Our favorite spot to drop the hook is northeast of the boater-friendly marina, in about 5 fathoms. Surrounded by tree-hidden private homes on the east shore and large houses with sweeping green lawns and sandy beaches along the western shoreline, our carefully chosen location affords a gentle breeze on hot, windless days and keeps the evening light the longest.

We spent many hours exploring the mile-long northern finger and its wooded shoreline in *Tink*, or relaxing in *Dreamspeaker's* cockpit enjoying the lively beach antics of our house neighbors and their families. Diving off the bow to cool off on a hot summer's day is the ultimate treat.

Not to be used for navigation. Depth contours are approximate and in fathoms.

LONGBRANCH MARINA

PRIVATE

VISITORS

FILUCY BAY

KITSAP PENINSULA

KEY PENINSULA

FILUCY BAY

MAHNCKES Pt

PITT PASSAGE

FILUCY BAY

McDERMOTT POINT

ROCKS

©LYJ 2013

KITSAP PENINSULA

* 47° 12.19' N   122° 44.40' W

CHART 18448

APPROACH
Filucy Bay and the marina at a wake-free speed. The run in is clear, with no obstructions.

ANCHOR
The bay provides sheltered anchorage, with protection from all quarters except the W. All tidelands are private, including the inviting beach at the tip of McDermott Point. Good holding in mud, in depths of 2+ ftm (12+ ft).

MARINA
Longbranch Marina; call 253-884-5137. This friendly marina offers 760 ft of guest moorage on a first-come basis. Basic amenities include fresh water, ice, electrical hookups, portable toilets and garbage disposal. Very popular destination for club rendezvous in the busy summer months, making rafting necessary. A covered area with gas barbecues provides a cosy gathering place. Call ahead for group bookings. Cash only.

8.11 EAGLE ISLAND STATE PARK, Balch Passage

Laurence and I had a very pleasant walk around Eagle Island's shoreline and gravel beach at low water. We met families digging for clams and found a sandy pocket beach, misshapen firs and clusters of knotted madrona trees. Picnicking on the park's west side, we were entertained by diving seals and their young, who love to haul out and sunbathe on the nearby reef.

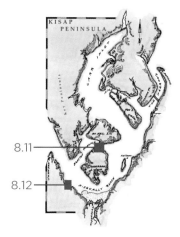

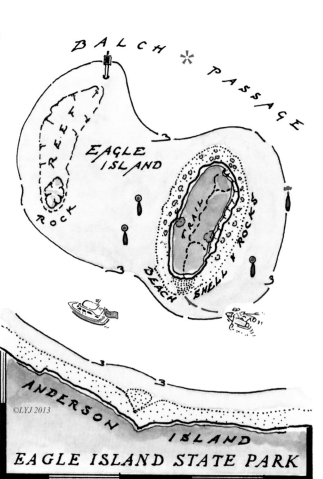

Not to be used for navigation. Depth contours are approximate and in fathoms.

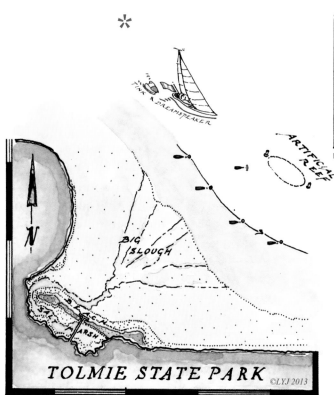

Not to be used for navigation. Depth contours are approximate and in fathoms.

8.11

✳ 47° 11.50' N 122° 41.75' W

CHART 18448

APPROACH
From Balch Passage or the channel off Anderson Island.

ANCHOR
Beware of a strong current around the island when picking up a park buoy or anchoring off. Fair holding on a mixed bottom, in depths of 3+ ftm (15+ ft). Not recommended for overnight anchorage, as there is little protection from any wind and the wake of passing boats.

8.12 TOLMIE STATE PARK, Nisqually Reach

At low water, the park buoys seem a long way from the park itself. At mid to high water, the perception changes, and taking a kayak or dinghy to explore Tolmie State Park seems less daunting. The park, close to the protected Nisqually National Wildlife Refuge, supports the biodiversity of a 100-acre saltwater marsh, over two miles of hiking trails and a welcoming sandy beach for swimming.

8.12

✳ 47° 07.42' N 122° 45.55' W

CHART 18448

APPROACH
From the NE. The bottom shelves rapidly W of the park buoys to the slough that dries, then gently rises to the shoreline of Tolmie State Park. The inside park buoys are in shallower water.

ANCHOR
Drop the hook NE of the park buoys in 3+ ftm (15+ ft). Nisqually Reach is open to all quarters except the SE.

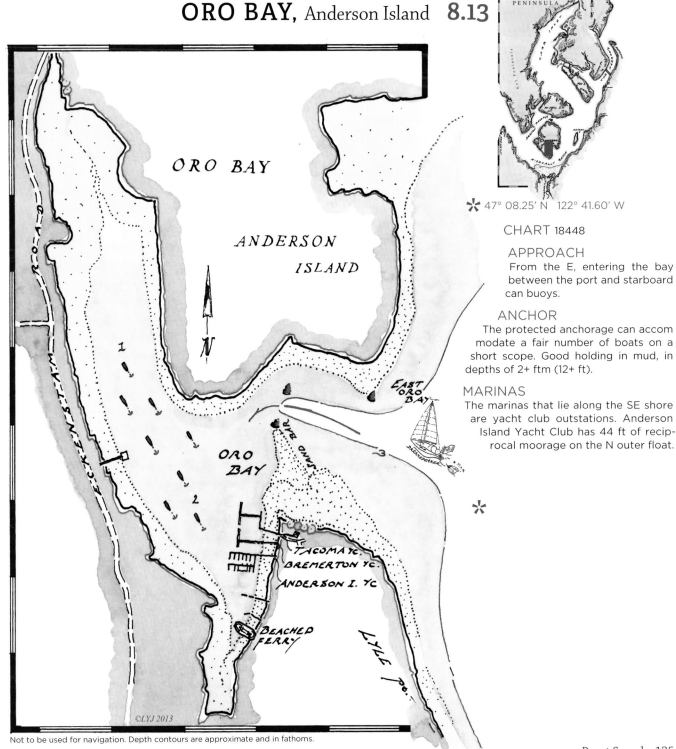

Plenty of room to swing in Oro Bay.

With a superb view of Mt. Rainier, Oro Bay is the most protected anchorage on Anderson Island and an excellent base for a motor-powered dinghy excursion to the Nisqually National Wildlife Refuge at high water.

It is approximately two and a half miles from the bay to the head of the Nisqually River Delta. Here, the fresh water of the Nisqually River merges with the salt water of Puget Sound to form an estuary rich in nutrients that supports an elaborate diversity of sea life. While most of the major estuaries in Washington State have been filled, dredged or developed, the Nisqually River Estuary was restored in 2009, and it now protects the area's abundance of fish and wildlife habitats – a significant step in the revitalization of Puget Sound.

NOTE
The surrounding tidelands of Oro Bay are private.

✱ 47° 08.25' N 122° 41.60' W

CHART 18448

APPROACH
From the E, entering the bay between the port and starboard can buoys.

ANCHOR
The protected anchorage can accommodate a fair number of boats on a short scope. Good holding in mud, in depths of 2+ ftm (12+ ft).

MARINAS
The marinas that lie along the SE shore are yacht club outstations. Anderson Island Yacht Club has 44 ft of reciprocal moorage on the N outer float.

Not to be used for navigation. Depth contours are approximate and in fathoms.

©LYJ 2013

Family owned and operated for over 50 years, friendly Zittel's Marina is dotted with colorful flower containers and has the sweetest filtered well water in Puget Sound. The marina's latest fishing and crabbing reports are just a phone call away.

The well-stocked tackle shop and store carry fishing gear, bait, ice, marine accessories, groceries, ice cream and beverages, including beer and wine. There is a snack bar, where you can buy a fresh cup of coffee, pastries and a variety of sandwiches. In the summer, visitors can enjoy views across Nisqually Reach on the small patio, which is shaded by deck umbrellas. Kayaking in Baird Cove, south of the marina, is a pleasurable pastime at high water.

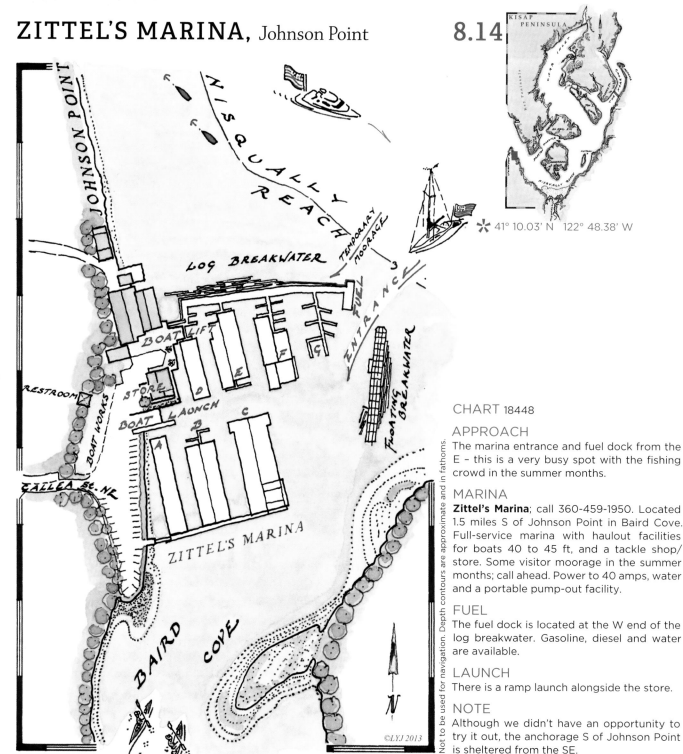

✳ 41° 10.03' N   122° 48.38' W

CHART 18448

APPROACH
The marina entrance and fuel dock from the E – this is a very busy spot with the fishing crowd in the summer months.

MARINA
Zittel's Marina; call 360-459-1950. Located 1.5 miles S of Johnson Point in Baird Cove. Full-service marina with haulout facilities for boats 40 to 45 ft, and a tackle shop/store. Some visitor moorage in the summer months; call ahead. Power to 40 amps, water and a portable pump-out facility.

FUEL
The fuel dock is located at the W end of the log breakwater. Gasoline, diesel and water are available.

LAUNCH
There is a ramp launch alongside the store.

NOTE
Although we didn't have an opportunity to try it out, the anchorage S of Johnson Point is sheltered from the SE.

Not to be used for navigation. Depth contours are approximate and in fathoms.

©LYJ 2013

The quiet of the early evening. Looking south to the capitol building from Olympia's Port Plaza.

Boston Harbor & Shelton to Allyn

The author surveys the view from Stretch Point State Park.

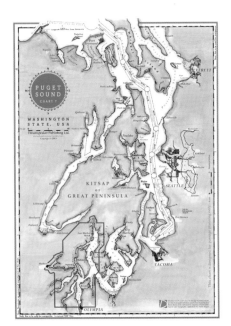

CAUTIONARY NOTE
Be aware of the shoal areas in Budd Inlet on the approach to Olympia. Stay within the marked channels when entering East Bay or West Bay.

Olympia, the capital of Washington State, is very enjoyable to visit by boat, with ample moorage just minutes from the vibrant heart of the city. Here you will find easy provisioning, a bustling, art-friendly boardwalk and preserved historic district, landscaped parks and a choice of fun eateries, shops, galleries and theaters.

Before making our way to the mill town of Shelton at the head of Hammersley Inlet, we stopped at Boston Harbor Marina to top up the tanks. The one-hour cruise up the inlet was quite lovely, and we returned from Shelton with apple pie cupcakes for afternoon tea. Anchoring off undeveloped Hope Island State Park, we rowed to the inviting pebble and shell beach before retiring for the night.

We began our exploration of Case Inlet's state parks with tiny McMicken Island. Anchoring in the cove, we rowed to shore and spent the warm afternoon strolling along the sand spit and wading in the warm water. Further north off Pickering Passage, popular Jarrell Cove State Park is a weekend haven for local boats. Hike the forested park trails or sip on a shaved ice treat from the marina store. Prior to indulging in a luxurious shower at Fair Harbor Marina, we spent a perfect beach day at Stretch Point State Park.

Sheltered Vaughn Bay, on the northeast shore of Case Inlet, is a very pleasant anchorage in which to spend the night. Choose a trip up to the friendly community of Allyn for lunch, or stay anchored and beachcomb along the sandy spit.

With two final parks on our list, we made an early start for small Joemma Beach State Park, a perfect midweek anchorage. Continuing on to Henderson Inlet, we anchored *Dreamspeaker* off peaceful Woodard Bay and took a gentle row to the shaded pocket beach.

TIDES
Tide Height Station: Olympia

CURRENTS
Tidal Current Station: Tacoma Narrows

WEATHER
NOAA Weather Radio WX4: Puget Sound
NOAA VHF Weather Channel 1 or 3
www.nws.noaa.gov/nwr

NOTE
It would be prudent to pre-plan your transiting of Hammersley Inlet to Oakland Bay and Shelton, as there are numerous shoal areas and up to 5-knot currents. If you study the tide and current tables, choosing a rising tide with a moderate current, and you stay alert, you will enjoy the scenic, one-hour trip.

HISTORIC FACTS
On May 26, 1792, Lt. Peter Puget and his party of 16 men, including Mr. Joseph Whidbey, arrived at the head of Budd Inlet, Olympia, the most southerly point reached on their inland expedition. It was here that the famous latitude of 47 degrees, 3 minutes north was recorded.

Olympia became the capital city of the Washington Territory in 1853. Edmund Sylvester, the city's founder, donated 12 acres of land on which to build the capitol, located on a hill overlooking what is now Capitol Lake. The Washington State Capitol is the home of the government of the state of Washington, and the campus includes buildings for the Supreme Court and the Governor's Mansion.

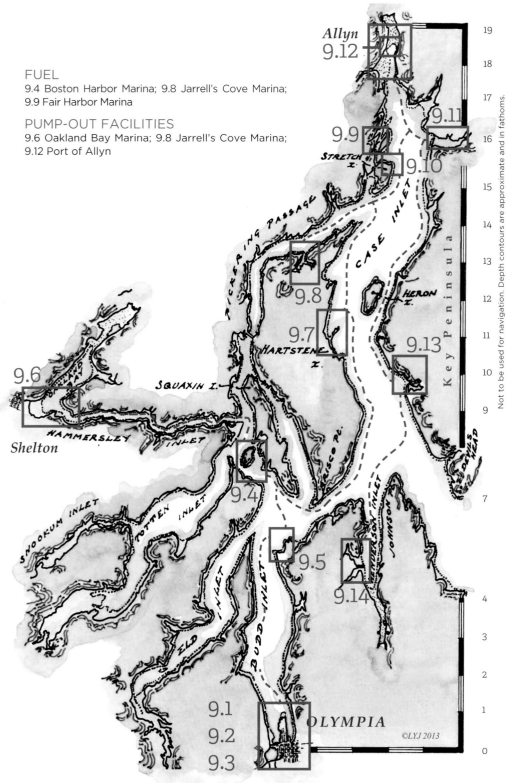

9 OLYMPIA & SOUTH SOUND "WEST"

FUEL
9.4 Boston Harbor Marina; 9.8 Jarrell's Cove Marina;
9.9 Fair Harbor Marina

PUMP-OUT FACILITIES
9.6 Oakland Bay Marina; 8.8 Jarrell's Cove Marina;
9.12 Port of Allyn

FEATURED DESTINATIONS

Percival Landing at high water.

The farmers' market – no shortage of fresh produce.

Lots of boats and boating in South Sound.

Leaving Boston Harbor, we turned south at Dofflemyer Point and navigated our way along the final stretch of Budd Inlet to the City of Olympia. The imposing dome of the Washington State Capitol dominated the skyline as we negotiated the shipping channel and passed the big ship commercial dock and Port Plaza. Tying up at the Percival Landing visitor dock, the tip of *Dreamspeaker's* keel settled gently into the soft mud. We had arrived at the southernmost limit of Puget Sound at one of the lowest tides of the year!

Olympia is one of the most pleasant cities to visit by boat and surprised us with its genuine friendliness. The ample visitor moorage is backed by a bustling, art-friendly boardwalk and a choice of eateries and coffee shops. It is also just minutes from the vibrant heart of the downtown core, with its preserved historic district, landscaped parks and man-made lake. The Olympia Farmers' Market is the second largest in the sound, with over 200 fresh produce, bakery and arts-and-crafts vendors to choose from (all local). Provisioning at this wonderful market, with its indoor and outdoor stalls and festive atmosphere, is a delightful experience for the whole family.

In need of a good hike, Laurence and I took the Capitol Lake Path through Heritage Park and up a trail to the Capitol Campus (the magnificent capitol building is well worth a visit, with tours daily). Alternatively, hop on and off the free Dash shuttle, which follows a circular route from the farmers' market to downtown and the campus. Days could be spent exploring the city and browsing through the unique mix of clothing, vintage and antique shops, art galleries and gift stores. The choice of West Coast and ethnic restaurants and cafes is excellent (most have a happy hour), as is the selection of theater productions, music gigs and eclectic films.

LOCAL FACTS
Intercity Transit's free Dash shuttle follows a circular route from the farmers' market to downtown and the Capitol Campus. Monday to Saturday (approx. every 15 minutes).

The Olympia Farmers' Market runs April to October. Thursday to Sunday, 10 a.m. to 3 p.m. No pets.

FUN FACTS
Sample a free yoga class at the Yoga Loft on Legion Way.

Enjoy an affordable haircut at the Fosbre Academy of Hair Design, located on 5th Avenue SW.

Taste the wines of South Sound at the Olympia Wine Tasting Bar on 5th Avenue SW.

Take a free Public Art Tour; call 360-709-2678.

Go on a self-guided Downtown Historic District Walking Tour; maps available at the visitor center.

Discover the amazing Olympia Supply Company on Columbia Street, which has stocked "serious hardware since 1906," and still do!

Seek out Canvas Works on Columbia Street SE for inspiring fabrics, yarns and notions.

FOOD FACTS
Try these favorites: Mercato Ristorante on Market Street for Fresh Italian fare. Acqua Via's Mediterranean-inspired menu on Capitol Way. Inspired West Coast cuisine at Waterstreet Cafe on Legion Way and Water Street.

THEATER FACTS
Capital Playhouse, a premier arts education and musical theater performance space, and Harlequin Productions, which produces quality, real-life theater, are both on 4th Avenue E.

EVENTS
Free Wednesday concerts in July and August at 7 p.m. in Sylvester Park, downtown Olympia.

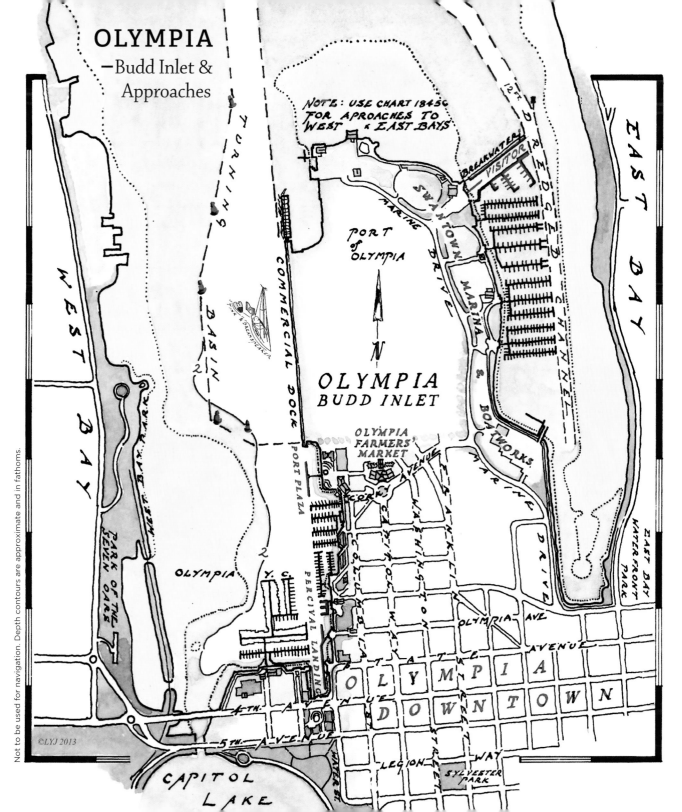

OLYMPIA
—Budd Inlet & Approaches

NOTE: USE CHART 18456 FOR APPROACHES TO WEST & EAST BAYS

Not to be used for navigation. Depth contours are approximate and in fathoms.

©LYJ 2013

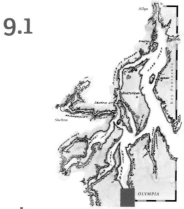

✳ 47° 04.00' N   122° 54.55' W

CHART 18456

APPROACH
The waypoint lies at the junction of the shipping channel into West Bay (9.2) and the dredged channel into East Bay (9.3). Stay within the marked channel for a clear run in.

ANCHOR
No designated anchorage, but temporary anchorage is possible N of Olympia Yacht Club in 6 - 12 ftm (36 - 72 ft). Good holding in mud, but open to the N.

MARINAS
West Bay: Percival Landing and Port Plaza (see 9.2 for details). East Bay: Swantown Marina and Boatworks (see 9.3 for details).

It took no time for us to ease into Olympia's welcoming and relaxed ambience, enjoying the convenience of a very walkable downtown, moorage in the heart of the city and handy provisioning at Bayview Thriftway. There is also a lively farmers' market, and a plethora of good restaurants, cafes and coffee shops to choose from. The variety of clothing, gift and antique stores complement this diverse mix.

Arriving at the start of the family-fun Sand in the City festival, we strolled through the shaded pavilions of Percival Landing, one of the city's three waterfront parks, and along the boardwalk to Port Plaza, which had become "a beach for the weekend," with artists creating elaborate sand sculptures from over 240 tons of sand. The entire plaza was in a beach party mood, as we climbed the steps of the observation tower for a view of the south harbor and the capital city's majestic dome.

✳ 47° 03.09' N   122° 54.40' W

CHART 18456

APPROACH
The water is deep and the run in is clear to the visitor moorage and marinas that line the east shoreline. No wake – dead-slow!

ANCHOR
No designated anchorage, but temporary anchorage is possible N of Olympia Yacht Club in 6 - 12 ftm (36 - 72 ft). Good holding in mud, but open to the N.

PUBLIC DOCKS
Port Plaza, operated by the Port of Olympia, has 500 ft of concrete, linear visitor moorage, primarily for day use. Complimentary 4 hours. If staying overnight, pay at the self-register kiosk at the top of the ramp. No power or water.

Percival Landing, operated by the City of Olympia, has 1,000 ft of linear moorage on a first-come basis. Complimentary 4 hours. Register on arrival at The Olympia Center, to the E of "E" Dock (Visa accepted). Showers and washrooms at Harbor House and Olympia Center. Pump-out facility on "F" Dock. No power or water.

Olympia Yacht Club offers reciprocal moorage at their visitor dock.

NOTE
Limited visitor moorage at Percival Landing during the Olympia Wooden Boat Festival (early May) and Olympia Harbor Days (early September).

Not to be used for navigation. Depth contours are approximate and in fathoms.

©LYJ 2013

With a boatload of laundry and in need of a good shower, we reserved a spot at Swantown Marina's visitor moorage. The splendid shower and laundry facilities are just a short walk up from the dock – a convenient picnic table and pocket park provide the perfect spot to read while the washing dries. The marina development includes a pleasant waterfront walkway, backed by landscaped lawns with shrubs and trees.

Bikes on board would be very handy, as the free Dash shuttle terminus, adjacent to the Olympia Farmers' Market (see 9.1), is a 20-minute walk from the marina. The shuttle follows a circular route from the farmers' market to downtown and the Capitol Campus. The area around the farmers' market is lively with cafes, restaurants and coffee shops, and the family-owned Olympia Seafood Company is open seven days a week.

✳ 47° 03.60' N 122° 53.81' W

CHART 18456

APPROACH
From the N, within the well-marked dredged channel. The run in is clear. Do not stray outside of the channel!

ANCHOR
No designated anchorage. The temporary anchorage was not tried out by the *Dreamspeaker* team.

MARINA
Swantown Marina. VHF Channel 16 & 65A; call 360-528-8049. Operated by the Port of Olympia; lines the W bank of East Bay. Visitor moorage (80+ slips) for boats up to 120 ft. Water, power to 50 amps and a pump-out facility. 24-hour security. Wi-Fi, showers, laundry facilities, garbage drop and waste oil dump. Haulout and boat repair on site at Swantown Boatworks; call 360-528-8059.

LAUNCH
A 2-lane public launch ramp is adjacent to the Rowing Center.

Not to be used for navigation. Depth contours are approximate and in fathoms.

The homestead at Hope Island State Park. The windmill pump is original, but the solar panels are a contemporary addition.

HOPE ISLAND STATE PARK, Squaxin Passage

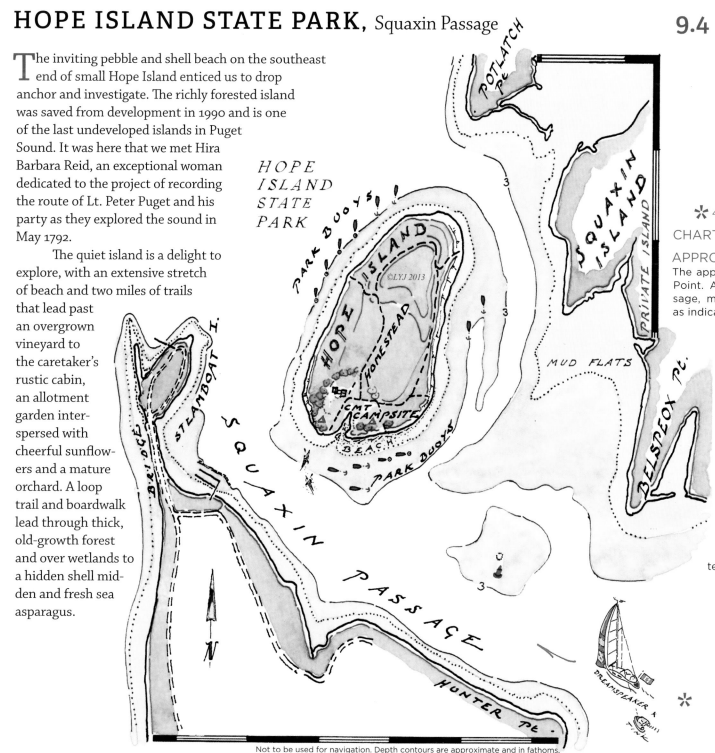

The inviting pebble and shell beach on the southeast end of small Hope Island enticed us to drop anchor and investigate. The richly forested island was saved from development in 1990 and is one of the last undeveloped islands in Puget Sound. It was here that we met Hira Barbara Reid, an exceptional woman dedicated to the project of recording the route of Lt. Peter Puget and his party as they explored the sound in May 1792.

The quiet island is a delight to explore, with an extensive stretch of beach and two miles of trails that lead past an overgrown vineyard to the caretaker's rustic cabin, an allotment garden interspersed with cheerful sunflowers and a mature orchard. A loop trail and boardwalk lead through thick, old-growth forest and over wetlands to a hidden shell midden and fresh sea asparagus.

✳ 47° 08.51' N   122° 54.01' W

CHARTS 18457, 18448

APPROACH
The approach waypoint lies NE off Hunter Point. A shoal patch lies in Squaxin Passage, marked by a starboard-hand buoy, as indicated.

ANCHOR
Pick up a park buoy, or anchor on the N or S side of the island in 5+ ftm (30+ ft) in sand and mud. Strong currents and stunning views of Mt. Rainier and the Olympic Mountains.

CAUTIONARY NOTE
The extensive mudflats between Potlatch Point and Belspeox Point are unmarked. The beaches and harbors of Squaxin Island are private and are only for the use of Squaxin Island tribal members.

NOTE
No dogs or fires, and no potable water on the island.

Not to be used for navigation. Depth contours are approximate and in fathoms.

BOSTON HARBOR, DOFFLEMYER POINT, Budd Inlet

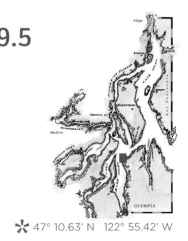

With a laid-back style all of its own, family-friendly Boston Harbor Marina is full of character and cheerful, local personalities who are more than happy to take your lines and fill you in on the town gossip. Famed for their Sunday breakfasts served on the shaded deck, the marina's neighborhood store also carries homemade soups, sandwiches and a sinful choice of soft ice cream flavors. The store is well stocked with a cross-section of provisions, including groceries, beer, wine, fresh seafood and locally smoked salmon. To add to the remarkable mix, you will also find some marine supplies and hardware, nautical charts, apparel and a selection of books, cards, gifts and interesting local artwork.

The sandy beach fronting the marina store has a picnic area, and you can enjoy your ice cream or beer on the store's outdoor patio, with a fine view to the Olympic Mountains.

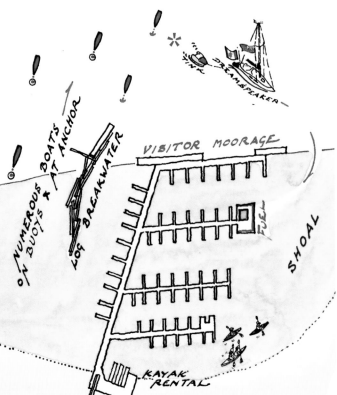

CHART 18456

APPROACH
From the NW, taking care to avoid the numerous boats on mooring buoys and at anchor. The run in to the fuel dock should be navigated with caution, as shoal water lies to the E.

ANCHOR
With numerous boats on buoys and at anchor to the N and W of the marina, anchoring is a challenge and not recommend in this busy harbor.

MARINA
Boston Harbor Marina. VHF Channel 16, switch to 68; call 360-357-5670. Visitor moorage on the end dock. Power to 20 amps and Wi-Fi (no showers). Bustling well-stocked store and outdoor patio. Open year-round.

FUEL
Gasoline, diesel and CNG tank exchange are available.

LAUNCH
A public boat launch lies to the W of the marina store and office.

CAUTIONARY NOTE
The wake from passing boats can be considerable, and caution should be exercised while docking at the visitor moorage.

Not to be used for navigation. Depth contours are approximate and in fathoms.

SHELTON – OAKLAND BAY, Hammersley Inlet

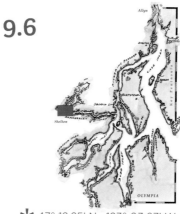

We really did go all the way to Shelton!

A small number of boaters take the time to venture into Hammersley Inlet and visit the mill town of Shelton. Curious to see what the westernmost city on Puget Sound had to offer, we planned our one-hour trip to coincide with a rising tide and snaked our way up the scenic inlet. We were warmly welcomed by a local boater as we tied up to the visitor dock.

A walk along the highway took us to Railway Avenue. The visitor center is housed in a historic caboose, and we were happy to discover Shelton's friendly community, offering a diverse selection of coffee shops and well-reputed restaurants; Xinh's (pronounced "Sin's") Clam and Oyster House, The Strip Steak House and Gianni's Cucina are three favorites. Visitors will also find excellent antique and vintage stores, an absorbing bookstore and museum and a small bakery that produces tasty apple pie cupcakes.

✳ 47° 12.25' N 123° 03.67' W

CHART 18457

APPROACH
Hammersley Inlet opens into Oakland Bay beyond Munson Point. The run in to the Oakland Bay Marina is clear.

ANCHOR
Convenient but noisy anchorage N of the marina. Peaceful anchorage in mud off Jacoby (Shorecrest) Park in 5+ ftm (30+ ft).

MARINA
Oakland Bay Marina; call 360-426-1425. Located at the Port of Shelton, and home of the Shelton Yacht Club. The marina provides a 120-ft visitor dock on a first-come basis. Moorage on the inside requires some tricky maneuvering. Power to 30 amps and a pump-out facility.

LAUNCH
At the marina.

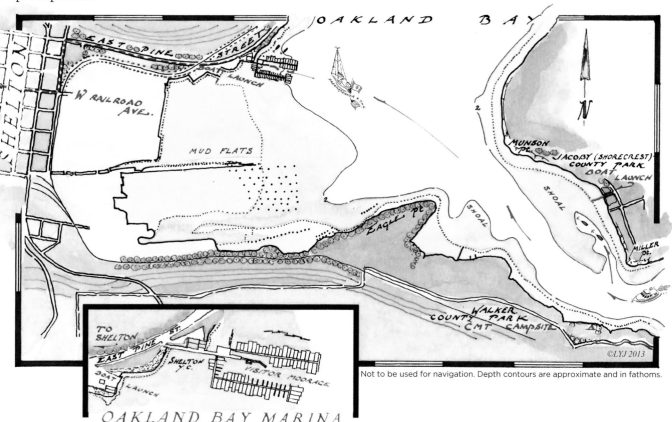

Not to be used for navigation. Depth contours are approximate and in fathoms.

©LYJ 2013

McMICKEN ISLAND STATE PARK, Case Inlet

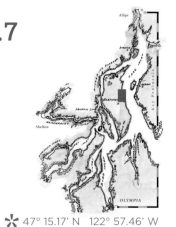

Legend has it that a Swedish sailor jumped ship and settled happily on lovely McMicken Island, and we were just as pleased to have this peaceful gem to ourselves. Arriving midweek, we anchored in the cove, packed a picnic lunch and rowed to shore, pulling *Tink* up on the shell and gravel beach. In the mood for a vigorous hike, we followed the shoreline trail that skirts the cliffs above the beach and crosses the island through thick second-growth forest.

Well exposed at low water and thick with sand dollars, the sand spit that connects McMicken Island to the Harstine Island shoreline creates a tranquil cove to play in. What a wonderful way to spend a sunny day – wading in the warm water, strolling along the beach looking for starfish and moon snails, and meeting up with good friends in the afternoon to exchange boating stories.

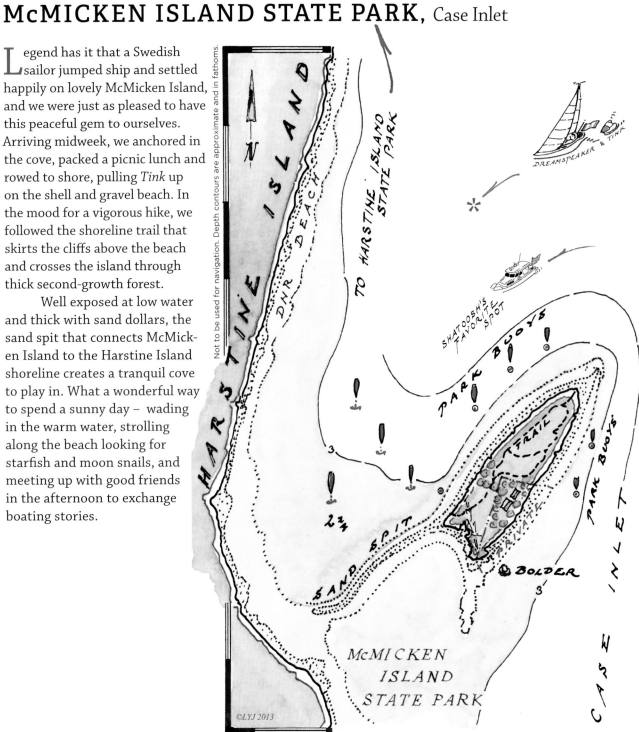

CHART 18456

APPROACH
From the E. The run in is clear.

ANCHOR
Pick up a park buoy or anchor in 3+ ftm (18+ ft), with good holding in sand and mud. Check depths under the keel on a minus tide when picking up a buoy on the N side of the island.

NOTE
Harstine Island State Park's unspoiled beach and forest trail lie approximately one mile north of McMicken Island and are best visited at low water.

The spit at McMicken Island State Park not only protects the anchorage but is convenient for a stroll at low water.

Two men and a dog go sailing in Jarrell Cove State Park.

JARRELL COVE STATE PARK & MARINA,
Pickering Passage

This enchanting park is named after Mrs. Philura Jarrel, the first pioneer woman to settle on Harstine Island. A plethora of park buoys and two park docks occupy the long finger of Jarrell Cove, a haven for local and visiting boaters. The docks will often host colorful club rendezvous, especially on holiday weekends, while the anchorage supports a diversity of boat designs and sizes. Rowing to the shady head of the cove or hiking the forested park trails provide a variety of birding opportunities. Species recorded in the park include great blue herons, pileated woodpeckers, nesting bald eagles and guillemot colonies, as well as scores of wintering seabirds.

The friendly marina store stocks some groceries and marine hardware, fishing tackle, ice, beer, wine and ice cream. They have a book exchange, and their Hawaiian shaved ice flavors are a treat.

✳ 47° 17.30' N 122° 53.10' W

CHART 18456

APPROACH
From Pickering Passage – the run in is clear.

ANCHOR
It is best to pick up a park buoy, as there is little room to anchor between them. If you find a suitable anchorage, the holding in mud is good, in 2+ ftm (12+ ft). Southerly winds funnel through the cove.

PUBLIC DOCKS
The N and S docks provide a total of 650 ft of visitor moorage. A pump-out facility is available on the N dock; call 360-902-8844.

MARINA
Jarrell's Cove Marina; call 360-426-8823. Open 7 days a week, Memorial Day to Labor Day. 5 visitor slips on a first-come basis. Water, power to 30 amps, showers, laundry facilities and a marina store. Slip assignment at the fuel dock.

FUEL
At the marina fuel dock. Gasoline, diesel, propane and a pump-out facility are available.

CAUTIONARY NOTE
When approaching the S park dock, be aware of a reef that extends off the N point. The inner portion of the dock has shallow depths.

Not to be used for navigation. Depth contours are approximate and in fathoms.

©LYJ 2013

9.9 FAIR HARBOR MARINA, Case Inlet

Nestled between Reach Island and the mainland, inviting Fair Harbor Marina offers secure moorage, beautifully landscaped gardens and spacious, well-appointed showers. The Pavilion at Fair Harbor, with its dramatic stone fireplace and twinkling chandeliers, is often used for weddings and is the ideal venue for a sociable club gathering. Their country-style store is filled with an eclectic array of very tempting, well-chosen gifts and housewares.

9.9

B ✳ 47° 20.01' N 122° 49.11' W

CHART 18456

APPROACH
Enter the harbor by rounding the S end of Reach Island.

MARINA
Fair Harbor Marina; call 360-426-4028. Open 7 days a week in the summer months. Can accommodate boats up to 120 ft, and has 350 ft of visitor moorage and a security gate. Water, power to 30 amps and shower facilities. The store stocks marine hardware, books, charts, fishing gear, ice, ice cream, wine, beer and gifts. Dog friendly. Popular with club rendezvous. Call ahead for reservations.

FUEL
The fuel dock has regular gasoline only – propane and kerosene are also available.

BOAT LAUNCH
At the marina.

9.10 STRETCH POINT STATE PARK, Case Inlet

The tip of Stretch Point is now a charming state park with a shell and pebble beach that invites visitors to laze on a beach blanket, swim in the clear water, build driftwood sculptures or investigate the small saltwater lagoon. A popular picnic stop for local boaters and kayakers, the park has no facilities and is for day use only – please pack out all garbage.

©LYJ 2013

9.10

A ✳ 47° 19.88' N 122° 48.96' W

CHART 18448

APPROACH
Accessible by boat only, the small state park is located on the NE tip of Stretch Island. Approach with caution, as the beach shelves rapidly.

ANCHOR
Pick up a park buoy or anchor in 3+ ftm (18+ ft). Good holding in mud and sand. This is a fun picnic/day stop, and on a calm evening, a good overnight spot (park is for day use only).

VAUGHN BAY, Case Inlet

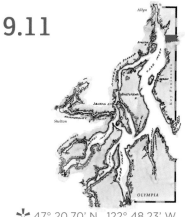

We were awoken by a chorus of barn swallows.

CHART 18456

APPROACH
The entrance lies along the N shore and is best navigated on a rising tide. Turn S after rounding the tip of the spit to avoid the sand bar that extends from the N shore.

ANCHOR
The bay provides good allround protection and holding in mud, in 1.5+ ftm (9+ ft).

LAUNCH
The boat launch is public and connects the bay to a community center and tennis courts.

NOTE
The sand spit is a public beach from the tip of the spit to the low tide line on its W side. All other beaches and tidelands are private.

✳ 47° 20.70' N   122° 48.23' W

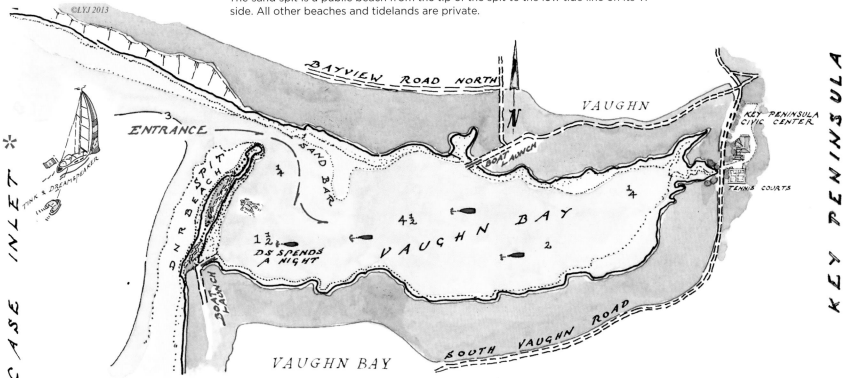

Not to be used for navigation. Depth contours are approximate and in fathoms.

Apart from the occasional disturbance from wakeboarders and jet ski-ers during the day, this is a quiet anchorage and the best in northern Case Inlet. We dropped anchor in nine feet of water and tucked in behind the spit to enjoy a glorious sunset behind the Olympic Mountain peaks.

We woke to a blue-sky day and the cheery chattering of barn swallows. Over 50 of these small birds had chosen to rest, clean and preen while perched on *Dreamspeaker's* spreaders and lifelines – what a joyful way to start any day! Then, without notice, they flew off to their next destination.

Although Vaughn Bay is lined with private homes and docks, it is a very pleasant bay to spend a few quiet hours rowing along the shore-line, beachcombing on the spit and digging your toes into the soft sand.

The small and friendly community of Allyn is the furthest north a boat can travel in Case Inlet. A long pier leads from the Port of Allyn dock to the Allyn Historic Church and waterfront park, with its green lawns, covered gazebo and welcoming stretch of beach.

Cross the road to Top of the Cork for a wine-tasting event, before visiting the intriguing Bear in a Box, a premier chainsaw sculpture studio. Provision at Allyn Market and Darby's Deli, or for those addicted to yarn, visit the charming Knit Shop. The Boat House serves tasty cod and chips, while a Big Bubba's burger and shake is a treat for the whole family. We indulged in a yummy, handmade Olympic Mountain Ice Cream, arguably the best in the Pacific Northwest, but perhaps not the geoduck flavor!

✳ 47° 22.23' N 122° 49.24' W

CHART 18456

APPROACH
Favoring the Key Peninsula shore, aim the bow for the center of the cable towers to avoid the shoal water to the W. Head to the Port of Allyn dock as indicated, where there is a least depth of 6 - 8 ft on a zero tide.

MARINA
The Port of Allyn provides generous visitor moorage with a pump-out facility. Call 360-275-2430. A 120-ft pier connects the dock to the Allyn Waterfront Park and beach.

LAUNCH
There is a public boat launch on the S side of the pier.

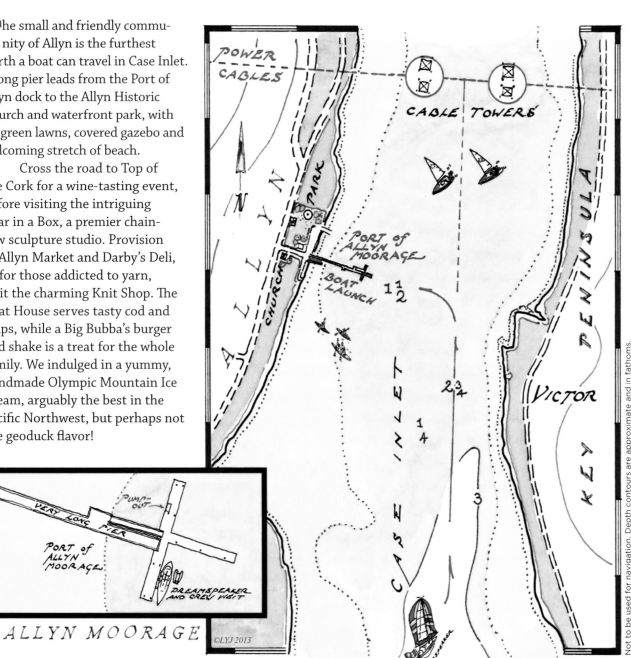

JOEMMA BEACH STATE PARK

TRAIL

JOEMMA BEACH STATE PARK

©LYJ 2013

CMT CAMPSITE

BAY PARK ROAD KP S

PARK BEACH

BOAT LAUNCH

PARK BUOYS

PARK DOCK

CASE INLET

SIGN PARK BOUNDARY PRIVATE

WHITEMAN COVE

KEY PENINSULA

N

Not to be used for navigation. Depth contours are approximate and in fathoms.

✳ 47° 13.17' N   122° 48.83' W

CHART 18456

APPROACH
The beach and park lie N of Whiteman Cove (now a lagoon) in a small bight. The park dock (absent in the winter months) is the most visible landmark.

ANCHOR
Pick up a park buoy or anchor in 3+ ftm (18+ ft). Fair holding in sand and mud – be aware of debris on the bottom when setting your anchor. Open to the SE.

PARK DOCK
The extensive park dock has 500 ft of moorage. The outer dock is a popular spot for crabbing and is used by water taxis on the weekends.

LAUNCH
A public boat launch lies N of the park dock.

Named for Joe and Emma Smith, who lived here from 1917 to 1932, Joemma Beach State Park is a perfect midweek anchorage, as it is a popular spot in the summer months with the weekend water sports crowd. We anchored a little too close to the park dock and pulled up a crab trap with our anchor. Lesson learned. We re-anchored west of the park buoys and enjoyed a peaceful evening.

The anchorage is backed by steep bluffs and a long stretch of pebble beach lined with sun-bleached driftwood. A section of the beach is shaded by twisted trees growing out of the sandstone cliffs, creating a perfect picnic spot. This is a low-key park that includes two maintained campsites and a basic Cascade Marine Trail (CMT) site. Stretch your legs on the short loop trail that ambles through shady forest.

Anchoring off Woodard Bay in Henderson Inlet, Laurence and I packed a picnic lunch and our Wellies, then we took a gentle row to the shaded, low-water pocket beach on Weyer Point. Seals and their pups were basking in the sunshine, while kayakers and paddle-boarders slipped quietly past us into the bay.

A Natural Resources Conservation Area, this peaceful 800-acre wildlife sanctuary includes five miles of undeveloped shoreline and provides a habitat for shorebirds and songbirds, river otters, bald eagles and one of the most significant heron rookeries in Washington State. There are three interpretive hiking trails to enjoy (rubber boots needed to get to shore at low water!), including a loop trail through mature second-growth forest.

If only seals could read.

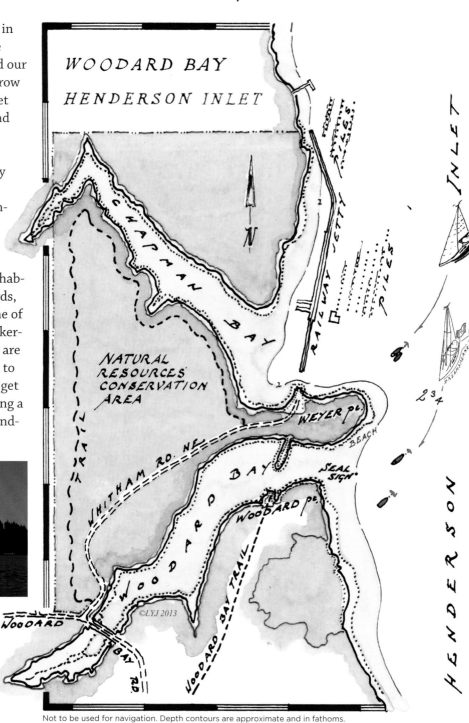

Not to be used for navigation. Depth contours are approximate and in fathoms.

✳ 47° 08.17' N 122° 50.14' W

CHARTS 18456, 18448

APPROACH
Woodard Bay lies S of Weyer Point in Henderson Inlet. The bay and its uplands are a Natural Resources Conservation Area. Chapman Bay is closed to boaters, and only non-motorized/human-powered craft are allowed in Woodard Bay. No dogs permitted.

ANCHOR
Anchorage is possible on either side of Weyer Point, with moderate protection from the SE. Holding is good in mud, in depths of 2+ ftm (12+ ft).

CAUTIONARY NOTE
Stay clear of the ruins off the pier and the many piles that litter the waters NW of Weyer Point.

NOTE
Do not approach seals or other wildlife, and stay 300 yds or more away.

Just beyond the Hood Canal's Great Bend is the Alderbrook Resort & Spa Visitor Dock. Anne steps ashore to dine at the resort.

Port Gamble & Pleasant Harbor to Union & Alderbrook

Peaceful Allyn Dock near the end of Hood Canal.

Excited to explore the deep waters and rocky beaches of Hood Canal, Laurence and I set off for the floating Hood Canal Bridge. We allowed ourselves a week to visit the canal's peaceful state parks and friendly communities before reaching the muddy tidal flats of Lynch Cove at its head.

On approaching the south fixed bridge span, we were met by a coast guard patrol boat from the U.S. Naval Submarine Base Bangor and were courteously informed that a submarine would be exiting the canal shortly and that we needed to divert to Port Gamble Bay. We took this unexpected opportunity to have a relaxed lunch in the charming town of Port Gamble before continuing on to Seabeck Bay.

During the shrimp season in late May, thousands of small boats flock to the canal, many of which launch near Seabeck, where the spotted shrimp festivities last for a few days. We stopped here to provision before making our way to Pleasant Harbor Marina for the night. Conveniently located in the north arm of Hood Canal, the marina has ample visitor moorage and an outdoor heated pool and hot tub to relax in.

Hoodsport offered a convenient spot to stock up on fresh produce and to enjoy happy hour refreshments before we dropped anchor off Potlach State Park for the night. The following morning we made our way around The Great Bend before heading on to Hood Canal Marina to top up on fuel, followed by the delightful Alderbrook Resort & Spa, with its convenient visitor dock and access to all of its first-rate amenities.

We completed our cruise with a side trip to Twanoh State Park, where we picked a bucket of fresh oysters before tying up at Allyn Dock, after which we rowed *Tink* to the beach at Belfair State Park for a warm-water swim.

TIDES
Tide Height Station: Pleasant Harbor

CURRENTS
Tidal Current Station: Bush Point

WEATHER
NOAA Weather Radio WX4: Puget Sound
NOAA VHF Weather Channel 1 or 3
www.nws.noaa.gov/nwr

NOTE
Currents in Hood Canal can exceed 2.5 knots, and winds will funnel between the steep hills surrounding the channel.

NATURAL HISTORY FACTS
Hood Canal is a long and narrow, glacier-carved fjord of salt water that winds through evergreen-covered hillsides for over 60 miles, separating the Kitsap Peninsula from the Olympic Peninsula. It is an area of great contrasts that includes 500 square miles of towering Olympic Mountains, quiet beaches, rivers, salt marshes, lush forests and an abundance of wildlife. Marine life flourishes in the warm waters of the Hood Canal watershed, including Dungeness crabs, spotted shrimp and the world's largest species of barnacles and octopus. It also hosts a variety of shellfish, such as Pacific oysters, manila and littleneck clams and geoducks.

HISTORIC FACTS
Captain George Vancouver was the first European to visit Puget Sound's westernmost body of water. In 1792, he named it "Hood's Channel," in honor of Admiral Lord Samuel Hood of the Royal Navy, although he mistakenly wrote "Hood's Canal" on his charts. While it is not a canal at all, it was nevertheless officially named "Hood Canal" in 1932. Today, only the Skokomish Tribal Nation calls Hood Canal home, although it was originally populated by the Twana people, who wintered here in communal long houses.

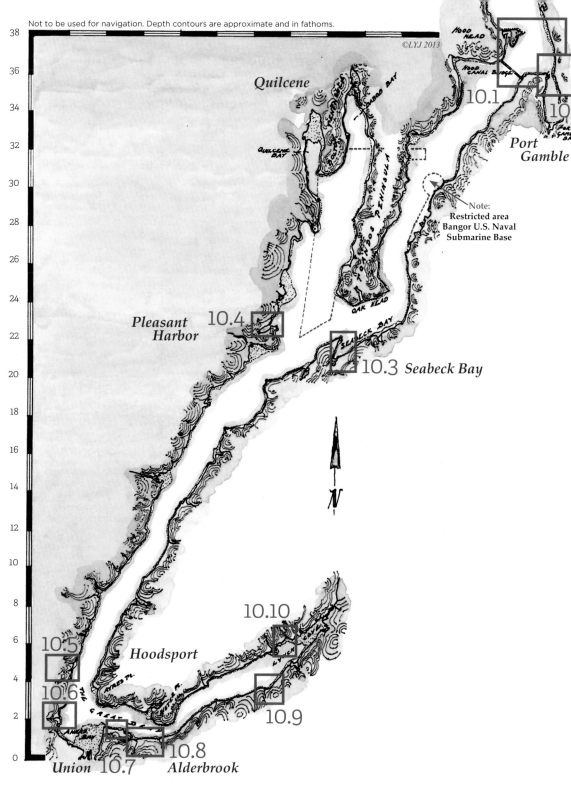

Not to be used for navigation. Depth contours are approximate and in fathoms.

©LYJ 2013

10 HOOD CANAL

FEATURED DESTINATIONS

FUEL
10.4 Pleasant Harbor Marina; 10.7 Hood Canal Marina

PUMP-OUT FACILITIES
10.4 Pleasant Harbor Marina; 10.5 Port of Hoodsport; 10.7 Hood Canal Marina; 10.8 Alderbrook Resort & Spa Visitor Dock; 10.10 Allyn Dock

CAUTIONARY NOTE
Stay well clear of the restricted area off the Bangor U.S. Naval Submarine Base. The area is constantly patrolled. Best to transit the restricted area via the west shore.

HOOD CANAL BRIDGE & Approaches

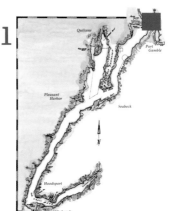

✳ 47° 53.36' N 122° 35.96' W

CHART 18477

APPROACH TO THE BRIDGE FROM PUGET SOUND

The Hood Canal Bridge is the longest floating bridge in the world and has fixed spans at either shore end. The N end has a minimum vertical clearance of 35 ft, and at the S end, it is 50 ft. If your mast exceeds these clearances, arrangements must be made to open the center span. To contact the bridge tower, call VHF Channel 13 (call sign WHP 721), or call 360-779-3233. Please give at least 1 hour of notice for the bridge crew to arrive.

APPROACH TO PORT GAMBLE

Via a marked, dredged entrance channel (see 10.2).

ANCHOR

If waiting for the bridge to open, temporary anchorage is possible in Bywater Bay. Protected anchorage can be found in Port Gamble Bay (see 10.2).

CAUTIONARY NOTE

The minimum clearance to both bridge spans is at all tidal levels. There is no difference in clearance between high or low water, because the spans of the bridge sit on floating pontoons. Anchor cables extending from the bridge pontoons to the canal bottom extend nearly 500 yds, both N and S of the bridge. Anchoring should not be attempted in this area.

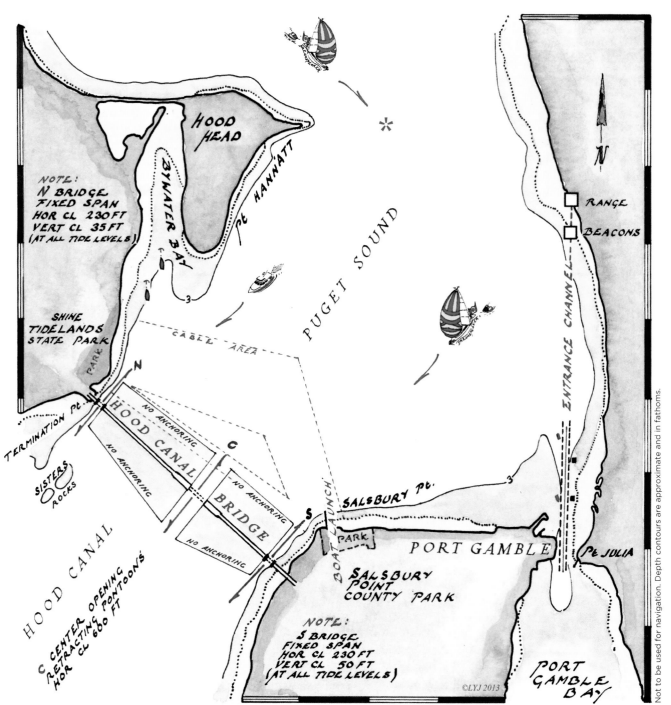

NOTE:
N BRIDGE
FIXED SPAN
HOR CL 230 FT
VERT CL 35 FT
(AT ALL TIDE LEVELS)

HOOD HEAD

BYWATER BAY

PT HANNATT

SHINE TIDELANDS STATE PARK

PUGET SOUND

CABLE AREA

RANGE BEACONS

ENTRANCE CHANNEL

N

TERMINATION PT.

HOOD CANAL BRIDGE

NO ANCHORING

C

S

SISTERS ROCKS

HOOD CANAL

C CENTER OPENING RETRACTING PONTOONS HOR CL 600 FT

BOAT LAUNCH

PARK

SALSBURY PT.

PORT GAMBLE

PT JULIA

SALSBURY POINT COUNTY PARK

NOTE:
S BRIDGE
FIXED SPAN
HOR CL 230 FT
VERT CL 50 FT
(AT ALL TIDE LEVELS)

PORT GAMBLE BAY

©LYJ 2013

Not to be used for navigation. Depth contours are approximate and in fathoms.

At the south fixed span of Hood Canal Bridge.

The Port Gamble General Store and Cafe – no provisions, but excellent sandwiches and specialty gifts.

PORT GAMBLE

Taking refuge in the entrance to Port Gamble Bay while a naval submarine was being escorted through the Hood Canal Bridge, Laurence and I set bow and stern anchors and rowed *Tink* to a small beach and kayak launch. With permission from the Olympic Outdoor Center, we secured our dinghy and walked up to the charming town of Port Gamble.

Rainier Avenue is lined with flowers and has fascinating shops, a bookstore, a tearoom and a restored Victorian theater. Port Gamble General Store and Cafe, which also houses a historical museum, is stocked with fanciful gifts, and they serve excellent sandwiches to eat in or enjoy outdoors.

The town and small sawmill were built in 1853, and the mill operated until 1995. Many of the historic Victorian homes and buildings have been preserved, and today, St. Paul's Episcopal Church is a popular venue for weddings.

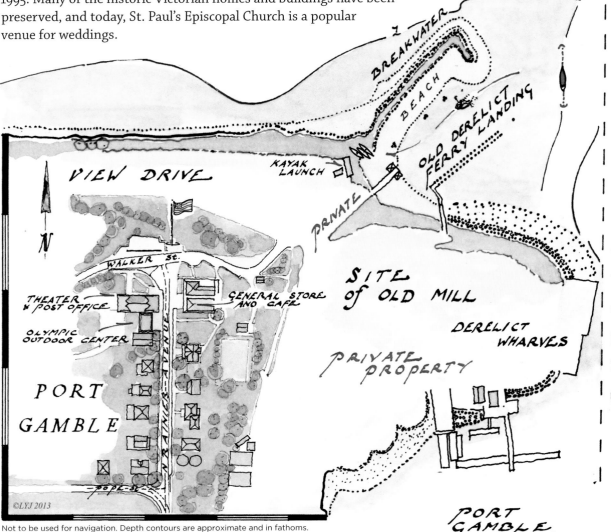

Not to be used for navigation. Depth contours are approximate and in fathoms.

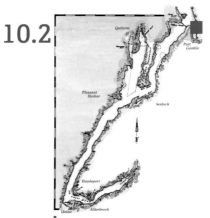

✱ 47° 52.12' N   122° 34.88' W

CHART 18477

APPROACH
Via the dredged entrance channel into Port Gamble Bay. The channel is well marked and has range beacons on the shore to the N to guide vessels in. Do not obstruct this channel, as it is used by large barges entering and exiting Port Gamble Bay.

ANCHOR
For protected anchorage in Port Gamble Bay, anchor N or S of the cable crossing area. It is reported as good holding in mud. Depths and bottom condition (and possible logging debris) unrecorded. Temporary anchorage is possible between the entrance channel and breakwater as indicated, in mud, in 2+ ftm (12+ ft). Set both bow and stern anchors to avoid swinging into the busy entrance channel.

NOTES
There is no designated public access to the town of Port Gamble from the water. Plans for visitor moorage are still in progress (2013).

SEABECK BAY

HOOD CANAL

ARTIFICIAL REEF

MISERY Pt.

BOAT LAUNCH

©LYJ 2013

SEABECK BAY

PROPOSED OLYMPIC VIEW MARINA

SHORE ACCESS EELGRASS

SEABECK LANDING GENERAL STORE

SEABECK

CONFERENCE CENTER

N

Not to be used for navigation. Depth contours are approximate and in fathoms.

47° 39.18' N   122° 49.26' W

Founded in 1856, the community of Seabeck was once larger than that of Seattle. Anchoring in Seabeck Bay, we rowed *Tink* to the small public beach opposite Seabeck Landing General Store. A popular community meeting place, the store is open seven days a week and is well stocked with provisioning supplies, some fresh produce, beer and wine, ice, ice cream and snacks.

Barbie's Seabeck Bay Cafe, located at the front of the store, offers homestyle cooking and outdoor seating with views over the water. Well frequented by locals, the cosy cafe is reputed for its generous crab-topped eggs Benedict, homemade fruit pies and yummy apple dumplings. Adjacent to the general store is an espresso shack, gift shop and Seabeck Pizza, which has several locations and is famous throughout Hood Canal for its hearty toppings.

CHARTS 18458, 18476

APPROACH
The approach waypoint lies E, off Misery Point. The run in is clear.

ANCHOR
As indicated, in mud, in 3+ ftm (18+ ft). Good protection from the S. Fairly protected in a summer northerly wind by Tonandos Peninsula.

MARINA
Plans for the Olympic View Marina are still in the works (2013).

LAUNCH
The public Marina Beach Launch is approximately 2 miles away.

FUN FACT
Misery Point Reef, near Seabeck Bay, was created when the Washington Department of Fish and Wildlife sank debris in order to produce both a fish habitat and a fishing reef. It is comprised of huge gray concrete slabs and steel I-beams, which are remnants from the old Hood Canal Bridge.

10.4 PLEASANT HARBOR

CHARTS 18458, 18476

APPROACH
The approach waypoint lies NE, off Black Point. Stay in the center of the entrance channel. The run in is clear.

ANCHOR
As indicated, in mud, in 3+ ftm (18+ ft). Good all-round protection.

PARK DOCK
Pleasant Harbor State Park has a 100-ft dock with good depths. No facilities.

MARINA
Pleasant Harbor Marina. VHF Channel 9 and 16; call 360-796-4611. Visitor moorage up to 175 ft (new docks and pilings). Water and power to 50 amps on the docks. On-site security. Shower, laundry, Wi-Fi and pump-out facility on visitor dock. Groceries, beer, wine, ice and gifts at the store. Reciprocal club moorage. Reservations available and groups welcome; call ahead.

FUEL
Fuel dock and check-in at the end of "D" dock. Call 360-796-4611. Gasoline, diesel and propane are available.

✳ 47° 40.04' N 122° 54.19' W

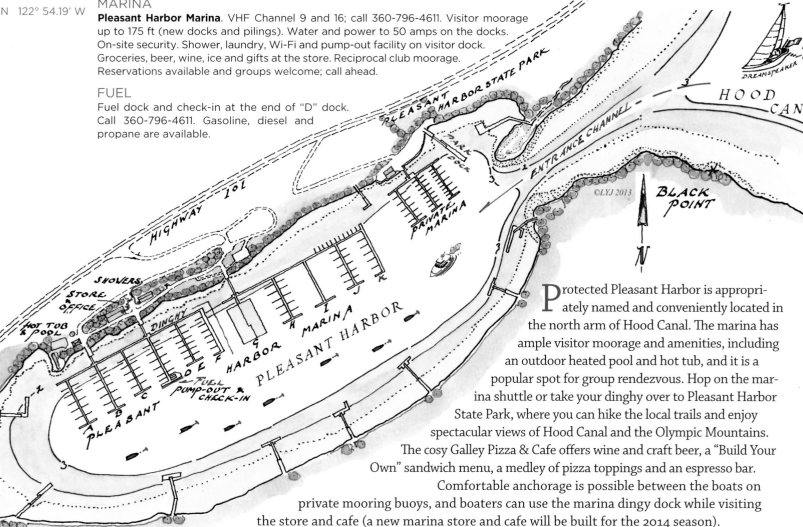

Protected Pleasant Harbor is appropriately named and conveniently located in the north arm of Hood Canal. The marina has ample visitor moorage and amenities, including an outdoor heated pool and hot tub, and it is a popular spot for group rendezvous. Hop on the marina shuttle or take your dinghy over to Pleasant Harbor State Park, where you can hike the local trails and enjoy spectacular views of Hood Canal and the Olympic Mountains. The cosy Galley Pizza & Cafe offers wine and craft beer, a "Build Your Own" sandwich menu, a medley of pizza toppings and an espresso bar. Comfortable anchorage is possible between the boats on private mooring buoys, and boaters can use the marina dingy dock while visiting the store and cafe (a new marina store and cafe will be built for the 2014 season).

Not to be used for navigation. Depth contours are approximate and in fathoms.

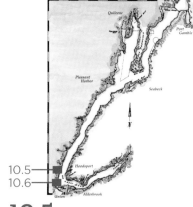

10.5 HOODSPORT

Low on boat provisions, Laurence and I were happy to discover the Hoodsport IGA, a well-stocked supermarket that is easily accessible from the Port of Hoodsport public dock. Gas and diesel are available at the Shell station. Public access to the town is also possible from the beach fronting the small park, and El Puerto de Angeles IV has a visitor dock. This local Mexican restaurant is known for its great views of Hood Canal, good food and strong drinks!

10.5

✳ 47° 24.21' N   123° 08.19' W

CHART 18476

APPROACH
The approach waypoint lies due W, off the public moorage. The run in is clear.

ANCHOR
As indicated, on the narrow shelf. Temporary anchorage in mud, in 2+ ftm (12+ ft). Open to weather and wake.

MARINA
The Port of Hoodsport public dock has visitor moorage on a first-come basis. There are 6 fingers for 16-ft boats and an end dock of 40 ft. Overnight moorage for a fee. This is a popular weekend spot for locals. Open to weather and wake.

10.6

✳ 47° 21.96' N   123° 08.90' W

CHART 18476

APPROACH
From the N, approaching with caution, as the drop-off to the shelf off the park is rapid.

ANCHOR
Pick up a park buoy or anchor as indicated, in mud, in 2+ ftm (12+ ft). This is a good anchorage in settled summer weather, as there is little protection from the N and S.

10.6 POTLATCH STATE PARK

Named for the many potlatch ceremonies held here by the Skokomish, the park features a wooded campground, a short loop trail and a grassy picnic area overlooking the swimming beach and frolicking seals in Annas Bay. A variety of activities are also offered, from interpretive programs for kids to shellfish harvesting. We dropped anchor for the night and held well in a strong southerly wind that came out of the flats in south Annas Bay.

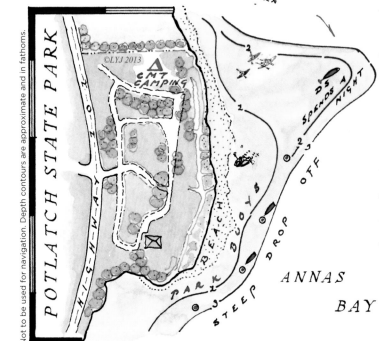

UNION, HOOD CANAL MARINA

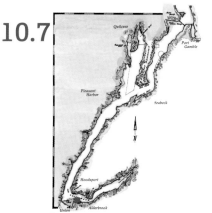

www.hood-canal-marina.com

The well-maintained Hood Canal Marina has partnered with Alderbrook Resort & Spa, two miles to the west, to offer complete marina services. Across Highway 106, the eclectic Union Country Store (open Memorial Day to Labor Day) is a welcome find. Stock up with a selection of treats, including fresh-from-the-oven French bread and pastries, espresso, smoked salmon, a choice of cheeses and specialty wines and gifts, and a variety of yummy Olympic Mountain Ice cream flavors.

We enjoyed a delicious meal of authentic, affordably-priced Mexican dishes on the outdoor patio of 2 Margaritas. Be sure to try their excellent choice of salsas (the mushroom salsa was our favorite) and unique margarita combinations.

To preserve the 1890 Victorian mansion opposite the marina, community members have formed the McReavy House Museum of Hood Canal Foundation, which also operates an arts and cultural center.

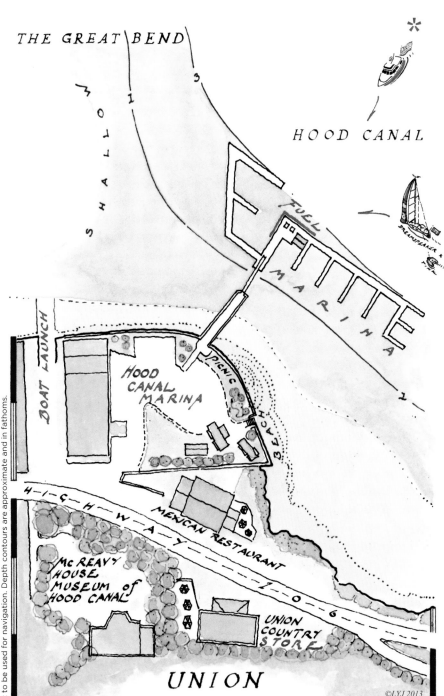

Not to be used for navigation. Depth contours are approximate and in fathoms.

CHART 18476

APPROACH
The waypoint lies NE, off the marina. The run in is clear.

MARINA
Hood Canal Marina. Call 360-898-2252. Visitor moorage up to 40 ft. Water, power to 30 amps and pump-out facility on the docks. Restrooms available, but no showers or laundry facilities. Reservations recommended.

FUEL
The fuel dock at the marina is open 8 a.m. to 5 p.m. Gasoline and diesel are available. Maximum boat length 50 ft; larger vessels with advance notice. Mobile marine technician on call.

LAUNCH
There is a county boat ramp adjacent to the marina.

It's worth going beyond The Great Bend to the Dock at Alderbrook Resort. Jeff Caven - Alderbrook Resort photo.

ALDERBROOK RESORT & SPA

ALDERBROOK
RESORT & SPA

www.alderbrookresort.com

Alderbrook Resort & Spa, with its convenient visitor dock, access to all resort amenities and spectacular sunset views, comes as a welcome surprise to boaters who have never ventured beyond The Great Bend in Hood Canal.

Designed and landscaped in the traditional West Coast grand-resort style, Alderbrook also offers family cottages, green lawns for picnicking or a game of badminton, a large outdoor fire pit (with real logs) and an indoor heated pool and hot tub. We were delighted by the takeout picnic boxes available from the elegant resort restaurant. Rather than dining back on board, we sunk into a comfy sofa, warmed by the outdoor fire pit, and dug into a stack of grilled Hood Canal oysters.

The energetic can take in a round of golf, hike the scenic resort trails or rent a paddleboard. For those who enjoy a little pampering, the restful day spa invites you in with its fragrant essential oils. The resort also offers a valet service for short trips to local attractions.

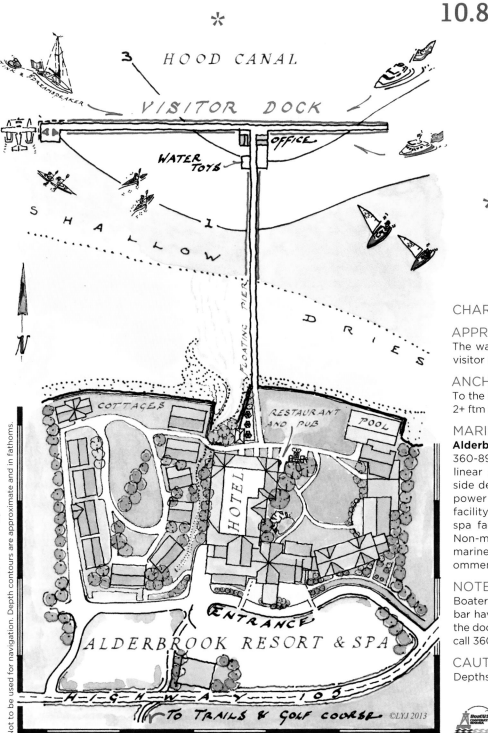

Not to be used for navigation. Depth contours are approximate and in fathoms.

✳ 47° 21.09' N   123° 03.94' W

CHART 18476

APPROACH
The waypoint lies NE, off the W end of the visitor dock. The run in is clear.

ANCHOR
To the N and W of the visitor dock, in mud, in 2+ ftm (12+ ft). Good protection from the S.

MARINA
Alderbrook Resort & Spa Visitor Dock. Call 360-898-2252. Approximately 1,500 ft of linear moorage for visitors. Average outside depth at mean low tide is 15 ft. Water, power to 50 amps, Wi-Fi and pump-out facility on the dock. Shower, laundry and spa facilities. Designated floatplane dock. Non-motorized watercraft rental. Mobile marine technician on call. Reservations recommended. Groups welcome.

NOTE
Boaters visiting the resort, spa, restaurant or bar have complimentary day/evening use of the dock. For restaurant and spa reservations, call 360-898-2200.

CAUTIONARY NOTE
Depths shallow to the W of the dock.

10.9 TWANOH STATE PARK

With warm water, a beautiful beach with a roped-off swimming area and a tidal wading pool backed by picnic lawns, Twanoh State Park is a delightful, family-friendly destination. The park's wooded hillsides offer a shaded, one-and-a-half-mile loop trail through hemlock and fir that snakes, in parts, alongside Twanoh Creek. Twanoh is also popular for shellfish harvesting, and oyster beds are seeded annually. Oyster season is open year-round. For clamming season dates, check with the Washington Department of Fish & Wildlife.

Not to be used for navigation. Depth contours are approximate and in fathoms.

©LYJ 2013

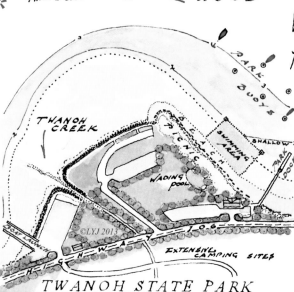

©LYJ 2013

Not to be used for navigation. Depth contours are approximate and in fathoms.

10.10 ALLYN DOCK,
Hood Canal

The well-maintained Allyn Dock and boat launch is a popular weekend spot for local boaters. From here, the waters of Hood Canal begin to reduce to shallow mudflats at its head. Timing our tides, we pulled on swimsuits and Wellies, then rowed *Tink* to the beach at Belfair State Park for a spot of warm-water wading. Further on, at the mouth of Big Mission Creek, we enjoyed a dip in even warmer water in a well-protected bathing hole formed by a saltwater lagoon.

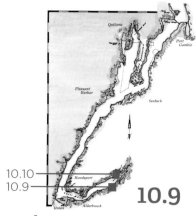

10.9

✳ 47° 22.92' N   122° 58.71' W

CHART 18476

APPROACH
The waypoint lies NW, off the extensive Twanoh Creek Delta, which dries. Stay well offshore to clear the shallows.

ANCHOR
N and E of the park buoys in mud, in 3+ ftm (18+ ft). Good protection from the S.

PARK DOCK
In shallow water. The 40-ft dock is for small runabouts and dinghy tie-up.

LAUNCH
A public boat launch and small-boat pump-out facility are W of the park dock and buoys.

10.10

✳ 47° 24.86' N   122° 53.98' W

CHART 18476

APPROACH
After rounding the spit, the run in is clear to a bight, where the Allyn Dock is visible.

ANCHOR
As indicated, in mud, in 2 - 3 ftm (12 - 18 ft). Moderate to good protection from all winds.

MARINA
Allyn Dock, operated by the Port of Allyn, has 350 ft of visitor moorage. The minimum depth at MLLW is 5 ft. Water, power to 50 amps and a pump-out facility on the dock.

LAUNCH
There is a public 1-lane launch ramp.

Selected Reading

Buerge, David. *Chief Seattle*. Seattle: Sasquatch Books, 1992.
Mount Rainier. Seattle: Sasquatch Books, 1992.

Bunzel, Mark. *Waggoner Cruising Guide*. Anacortes, WA: Burrows Bay Associates, 1994 to present. Updated and published annually.

Hilson, Stephen E. *Exploring Puget Sound and British Columbia*. Seattle: Evergreen Pacific Publishing, 1996.

Kutz, David. *The Burgee: Premier Marina Guidebook*. Kingston, WA: Pierside Publishing, 2007.

Miles, John C. *Koma Kulshan: The Story of Mount Baker*. Seattle: The Mountaineers Books, 1984.

Morgan, Murray Cromwell. *Puget's Sound: A Narrative of Early Tacoma and the Southern Sound*. Seattle: University of Washington Press, 1979.

Mueller, Marge & Ted. *Afoot & Afloat: North Puget Sound & the Strait of Juan de Fuca*. Seattle: The Mountaineers Books, 2006.
Afoot & Afloat: South Puget Sound & Hood Canal. Seattle: The Mountaineers Books, 2006

Northwest Boat Travel. Woodinville, WA: Vernon Publications, LLC, 1978 to present. Updated and published annually.

Scherer, Migael. *A Cruising Guide to Puget Sound and the San Juan Islands: Olympia to Port Angeles*. Blacklick, OH: McGraw-Hill, 2005.

Sept, J. Duane. *The Beachcomber's Guide to Seashore Life in the Pacific Northwest*. Madeira Park, BC: Harbour Publishing, 2009.

Warren, James R. *Where Mountains Meet the Sea: An Illustrated History of Puget Sound*. Northridge, CA: Windsor Publications, 1986.

Yates, Stephen M. *Marine Wildlife: From Puget Sound Through the Inside Passage*. Seattle: Sasquatch Books, 1998.

Notes

Notes

INDEX TO DESTINATIONS

OTHER WORKS by the Authors

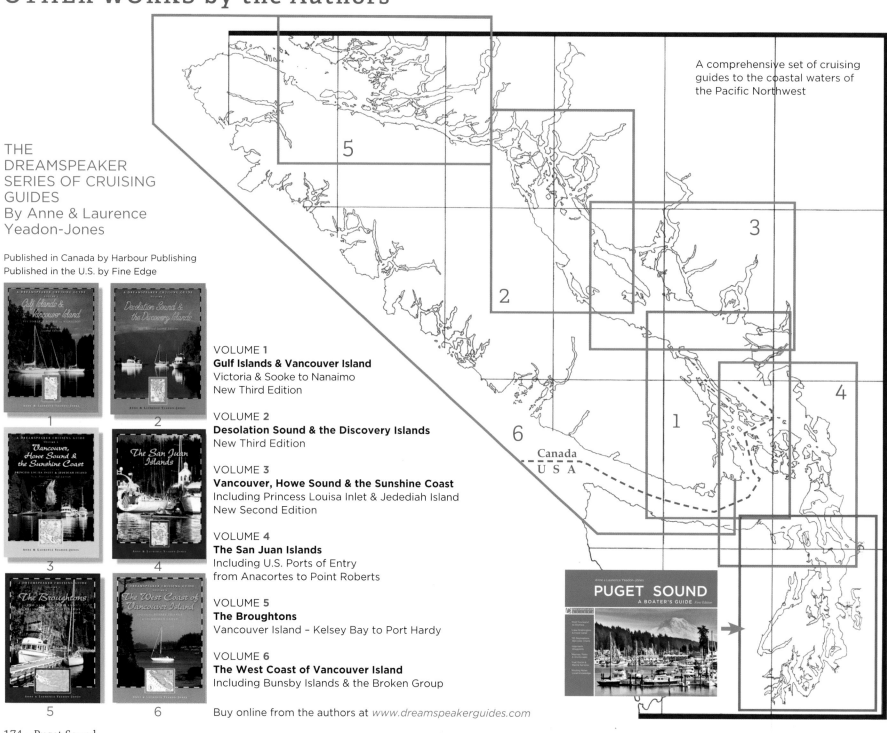

THE
DREAMSPEAKER
SERIES OF CRUISING
GUIDES
By Anne & Laurence
Yeadon-Jones

Published in Canada by Harbour Publishing
Published in the U.S. by Fine Edge

A comprehensive set of cruising guides to the coastal waters of the Pacific Northwest

VOLUME **1**
Gulf Islands & Vancouver Island
Victoria & Sooke to Nanaimo
New Third Edition

VOLUME **2**
Desolation Sound & the Discovery Islands
New Third Edition

VOLUME **3**
Vancouver, Howe Sound & the Sunshine Coast
Including Princess Louisa Inlet & Jedediah Island
New Second Edition

VOLUME **4**
The San Juan Islands
Including U.S. Ports of Entry
from Anacortes to Point Roberts

VOLUME **5**
The Broughtons
Vancouver Island – Kelsey Bay to Port Hardy

VOLUME **6**
The West Coast of Vancouver Island
Including Bunsby Islands & the Broken Group

Buy online from the authors at *www.dreamspeakerguides.com*

OTHER WORKS by Dreamspeaker Guides

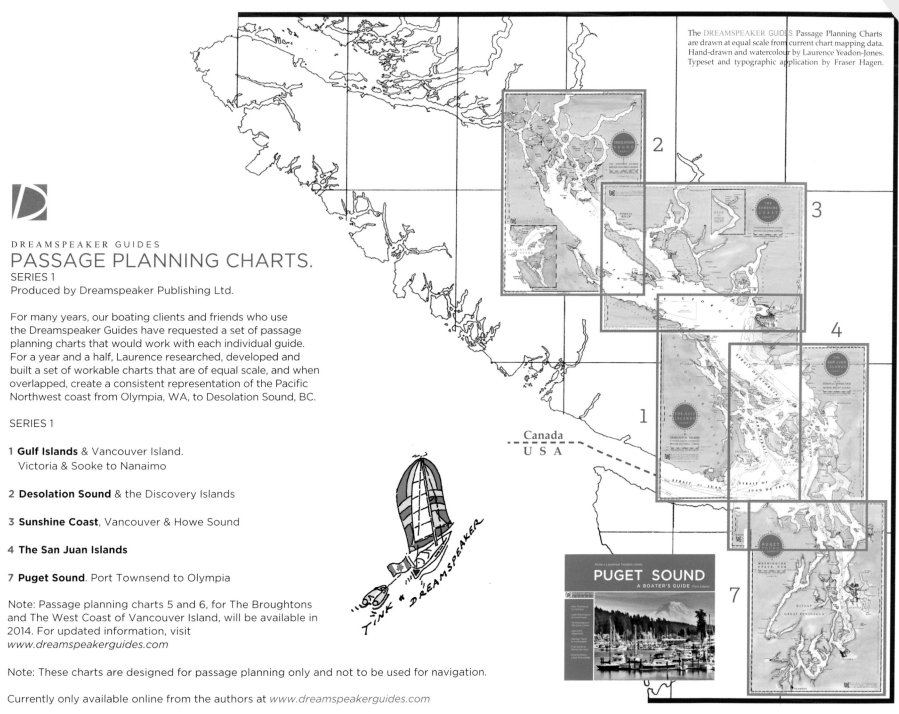

The DREAMSPEAKER GUIDES Passage Planning Charts are drawn at equal scale from current chart mapping data. Hand-drawn and watercolour by Laurence Yeadon-Jones. Typeset and typographic application by Fraser Hagen.

DREAMSPEAKER GUIDES
PASSAGE PLANNING CHARTS.
SERIES 1
Produced by Dreamspeaker Publishing Ltd.

For many years, our boating clients and friends who use the Dreamspeaker Guides have requested a set of passage planning charts that would work with each individual guide. For a year and a half, Laurence researched, developed and built a set of workable charts that are of equal scale, and when overlapped, create a consistent representation of the Pacific Northwest coast from Olympia, WA, to Desolation Sound, BC.

SERIES 1

1 Gulf Islands & Vancouver Island.
   Victoria & Sooke to Nanaimo

2 Desolation Sound & the Discovery Islands

3 Sunshine Coast, Vancouver & Howe Sound

4 The San Juan Islands

7 Puget Sound. Port Townsend to Olympia

Note: Passage planning charts 5 and 6, for The Broughtons and The West Coast of Vancouver Island, will be available in 2014. For updated information, visit *www.dreamspeakerguides.com*

Note: These charts are designed for passage planning only and not to be used for navigation.

Currently only available online from the authors at *www.dreamspeakerguides.com*

PUGET SOUND

Even in the gentlest breeze, this cat-rigged sailboat enters Eagle Harbor.